BECOMING A LAWYER

Discovering and Defining Your Professional Persona

Toni Jaeger-Fine

Assistant Dean
Fordham University
School of Law

WEST ACADEMIC PUBLISHING

© 2019 LEG, Inc. d/b/a West Academic
    444 Cedar Street, Suite 700
    St. Paul, MN 55101
    1-877-888-1330

West, West Academic Publishing, and West Academic are trademarks of West Publishing Corporation, used under license.

Printed in the United States of America

ISBN: 978-1-64020-199-6

In loving memory of my parents

Wilma and Seymour Fine

ACKNOWLEDGMENTS

I am grateful to so many people who have influenced and informed the development of my own professional persona and this project. I cannot possibly thank them all here, but there are some individuals that must be recognized.

My idea for this book was nascent until I met Tessa Boury, formerly of West Academic Publishing, who encouraged me to put form to this idea and submit a proposal. Her encouragement is the reason that this book came to be. After Tessa left West, Bonnie Karlen seamlessly assumed the role of acquisition editor. I am grateful to them and to the entire West Academic team for their confidence in this project.

I have benefitted greatly from discussions about this project with many colleagues, some of whom also have read drafts, others who have permitted me to quote their views about how to be a great legal professional. Special thanks to Andrew Bonzani (Interpublic Group), Tessa Boury (Mitchell Hamline School of Law), Oliver Brahmst (White & Case), John M. Caccia (Skadden, Arps, Slate, Meagher & Flom), Nestor Davidson (Fordham Law School), Matthew Diller (Fordham Law School), Eric F. Grossman (Morgan Stanley), Grant Hanessian (Baker & McKenzie), Javier El-Hage (Human Rights Foundation), Alex Jorge (Campos Mello Advogados), Brian D. King (Freshfields Bruckhaus Deringer), Francesca L. Odell (Clearly Gottlieb Steen & Hamilton), Russell Pearce (Fordham Law School), The Honorable Loretta A. Preska (United States District Court for the Southern District of New York), Amadeu Ribeiro (Mattos Filho, Veiga Filho, Marrey Jr. e Quiroga Advogados), P. Anthony Sammi (Skadden, Arps, Slate, Meagher & Flom), Ken Schwartz (Skadden, Arps, Slate, Meagher & Flom), Linda Sugin (Fordham Law School), and William Michael Treanor (Georgetown University Law Center). Bernard Daraz provided outstanding assistance as a reader (and in many other ways) and Mohamed Sweify is behind much of the research and many of the citations. Both have been invaluable partners in this endeavor and wonderful to work with.

I thank my students over my more than 25 years of teaching. They have challenged me at every step to be both a better teacher and a better student. I have learned more from my students than I ever could hope to teach them.

I thank my bosses, current and former, at Fordham Law School: Associate Dean Nestor Davidson, Dean Matthew Diller, Vice Dean Sheila Foster, Professor Thomas H. Lee, Dean Michael M. Martin, Associate Dean Linda Sugin, and Dean William Michael Treanor. Each has been a mentor, a friend, and a model of the kind of person and professional I strive to be.

I am also thankful for the support and friendship of members of the Fordham University leadership: Father Joseph M. McShane, S.J., Fordham University President; the late Dr. Stephen Freedman, formerly Fordham University Provost; and Dr. Ellen Fahey-Smith, Assistant Vice President and Chief of Staff of Fordham University's Office of the Provost. Dr. Freedman passed away suddenly while I was in the final stages of writing this book. His relentless pursuit of excellence, his passion, and his persistent faith in the potential of every human being are attributes I will try to emulate and gifts I will forever treasure.

Nothing I do would be possible without my team in the Office of International and Non-J.D. Programs at Fordham Law School: Anthony Agolia, Bernard Daraz, Jane Holmes, Marty Slavens, and Megan Smiley. They always do so much so well with so little. Each has carried extra burdens to give me the time to complete this project. They also have been unwitting subjects in my often-clumsy efforts to learn the art of management, and they have been gentle but forthcoming with insights and advice. I adore each of them.

Above all, I thank Desiree, my wife, best friend, steady partner in all, creative inspiration, confidant, and editor. Her influence can be found on every page. She inspires me, encourages me, and helps to make me a better person, every single day.

ABOUT THE AUTHOR

Toni Jaeger-Fine is an Assistant Dean at Fordham Law School. She has taught or lectured domestically and in Argentina, Brazil, China, Colombia, Croatia, Czech Republic, Dominican Republic, Egypt, Germany, Hungary, Italy, Japan, Kazakhstan, Mexico, the Netherlands, Nigeria, Peru, Romania, Spain, Switzerland, Taiwan, and Vietnam. Dean Jaeger-Fine is the author of numerous articles on a wide range of topics published in the United States and abroad, as well as several books: *American Legal Systems: A Resource and Reference Guide*; *An Introduction to the Anglo-American Legal System* (which has been translated into Italian, Korean, and Portuguese), *The U.S. LL.M.: From Whether to When, What, Where, and How*; and *Mastering the U.S. Legal System*. She is a regular speaker to delegations hosted by the U.S. Department of State, Senior Counselor to the International Section of the Federal Bar Association, and an application reader for the Schwarzman Scholars program.

Previously, Dean Jaeger-Fine served as associate director of the global law program at NYU School of Law. She was twice a Fulbright Senior Specialist Program grant recipient, and is past chair of the sections on Post-Graduate Legal Education, International Legal Exchange, and Legal Education for Foreign Lawyers of the Association of American Law Schools. Dean Jaeger-Fine was associated with the law firm of Crowell & Moring in Washington, D.C., where her practice focused on commercial, appellate, and administrative litigation. She is a *cum laude* graduate of Duke Law School and received her B.A. from Harpur College, where she was elected to *Phi Beta Kappa*.

TABLE OF CONTENTS

PART IV. CONCLUSION

BECOMING A LAWYER

Discovering and Defining Your Professional Persona

PART I

LEGAL PROFESSIONAL PERSONA FUNDAMENTALS

CHAPTER 1

THE LEGAL PROFESSIONAL PERSONA REVEALED

I have followed literally hundreds of attorneys throughout their careers, and time and again I am struck by the reality that those who succeed are not necessarily those with the greatest academic prowess. Instead, those who thrive in the practice possess certain additional qualities that lead them to success.[1] It is these characteristics that I unpack and discuss in this book. Through my students and other contacts within the legal community in New York City, throughout the country, and around the world, I have seen that—despite differences in law and culture across geography and over time—there is an underlying similarity in the attitudes and behaviors that make for an effective and successful legal professional: Qualities that are at the heart of the legal professional persona.

A. WHAT IS THE LEGAL PROFESSIONAL PERSONA?

"I know it when I see it."[2]

I have come to appreciate that while there are certain essential elements that make up one's legal professional persona, there is no singular definition. One's professional persona will be unique to each individual, it will evolve over time, and its specific characteristics will be highly contextual.

This book helps lawyers and law students navigate this phenomenon by identifying and discussing the attitudes and behaviors that are at the core of a strong professional persona. It does not include substantive knowledge, technical skills, or ethical prescriptions or guidelines; these are taught in law school and assumed for every legal professional. Law schools, however, do a notoriously poor job of helping students develop their initial

---

[1] One of the lawyers quoted later in this book was a first-year law student I taught many years ago, and I still recall how that student, even at such a formative stage, was exceptionally gifted across a range of competencies.

[2] *Jacobellis v. Ohio*, 378 U.S. 184, 197 (1964) (Stewart, J., concurring).

3

professional personae. This book will help fill that gap, and can be transformative for anyone entering the practice, questioning their role in the practice, or hoping to improve the way in which they practice (or assume an array of other positions).

B. DEVELOPING A PROFESSIONAL PERSONA WITH INTENTIONALITY

This book is a practical and utilitarian guide to ways in which we can embrace attitudes and behaviors that are respected, admired, and appreciated by others; that allow us to be the best legal professionals we can be; and that distinguish us from others who lack a robust professional persona. The elements of the professional persona championed here are within the reach of all of us—each feature is eminently achievable with the right amount of effort and intentionality. Indeed, what distinguishes those who are exceptional at what they do reflects deliberate and sustained effort, not innate ability.[3]

What's more, our professional persona is something—one of the relatively few things—over which each of us has complete control. If you want a strong professional persona, start acting like you do,[4] and so it will be. Once you begin to cultivate your professional persona, treat it like the valuable and precious asset that it is, nurturing and protecting it at all costs.

Some of what follows may seem obvious, but an important goal of this book is to encourage readers to be more deliberate about their actions and behaviors so that each of us can become the very best professional possible. There is a difference between knowing the right thing to do when asked and knowing and doing that thing at the appropriate time without being prompted.

An example is instructive: Each semester I teach a seminar associated with externship placements. At the start of that

---

[3] The differences between expert performers and normal adults "reflect a life-long period of deliberate effort to improve performance." K. Anders Ericsson, Ralf Th. Krampe, & Clemens Tesch-Römer, The Role of Deliberate Practice in the Acquisition of Expert Performance, 100 Pscychol. R. 363, 400 (1993), available at http://projects.ict.usc.edu/itw/gel/EricssonDeliberatePracticePR93.pdf.

[4] This is a take on a quote presented in Chapter 7.C.2., infra ("If you want a mentor, start acting like you do.").

seminar, I distribute a questionnaire that deals with a number of topics addressed in this book. One question is the following: "You are a law student and have accepted an invitation to a small dinner party to be hosted by your instructor. What do you do after the dinner?" When presented directly with this question, most students appreciate that they should thank the instructor. And yet, when I host a series of small dinner parties for students at the start of each semester, precious few follow up with an email or note of gratitude. This suggests some disconnect between what we know we should do when guided and what we do in the real world without the benefit of Socratic questioning or reminders. Being more intentional about our actions and behaviors allows us always to reach the right result, even in the absence of prompts.

C. THE INEXTRICABLE LINK BETWEEN PROFESSIONAL PERSONA AND PERSONAL IDENTITY AND GOALS

Earlier I noted that the professional persona that each of us develops is unique. This is because each of us embraces a professional persona that by necessity is informed and driven by our personal identity and agenda. One cannot successfully navigate the challenges of developing the former without being deeply in touch with the latter. The concept of a legal professional persona also implicates authenticity, a concept discussed later in this book.[5] Authenticity instructs that each of us follow the dictates of his or her own personality, spirit, values, and character. A professional persona based on an inauthentic concept of self simply is not durable.

Many of us—and this may be particularly true of lawyers— significantly under-invest in self-awareness. This in turn compromises our ability to develop a strong professional persona, which requires that we be supremely aware of our personal identity and agenda—the things that motivate us, the things we care about, the things that make us happy, and the things we want out of our lives; and, yes, the things that frustrate, anger, and destabilize us. We should achieve a consonance between the personal and the professional, because

---

[5]   See Chapter 4.C.6., infra.

ultimately the personal drives—and must drive—the professional.

D. MY JOURNEY IN DEVELOPING A LEGAL PROFESSIONAL PERSONA

This book is based heavily on my own professional trajectory and many years building and refining my own professional persona.

My professional path has given me varied experiences, first in private practice at the Washington, D.C.-based law firm Crowell & Moring LLP, where I was a summer associate and then an associate for almost 6 years; and then in academia, first at The George Washington Law School (2 years, as an adjunct professor), followed by New York University School of Law (7 years), Cardozo School of Law (6 years), and finally Fordham University School of Law (12 years and counting).

I credit my time at Crowell & Moring as a period of immense professional transformation. I entered as an utterly naive law student with no meaningful appreciation for what it meant to be a professional. My years there exposed me to outstanding attorneys, lawyers graced by a supreme sense of professionalism infused with a joyous approach to life. Their influence has served as the foundation for my own professional persona.

Throughout my career, I have had to learn how to be supervised, gracefully, by a range of bosses with very different styles, many of which were compatible with my own and some of which were not. I have had relationships with clients, opposing parties, co-counsel, and many others, some of which needed to be navigated delicately. I have had to learn how to collaborate with colleagues, at times with ease and at other times with effort. I also have reached a stage in my career where I am privileged to supervise a staff, giving me insights into the pressures on the other side of the table and the need to manage individuals in a way that builds their strengths and advances their individual goals while serving larger institutional objectives.

In my more than 25 years in academia, I have additionally been given the opportunity to teach, serve as academic advisor to, and guide thousands of law students (and mentor some of them), giving me insights into the behaviors and attitudes of newer professionals from younger generations and from around the world. Some of these students have fairly refined professional personae, but many others lack a meaningful appreciation for what this means.

In solidifying my own understanding of what the legal professional persona entails, I have had conversations with many legal luminaries working across a range of contexts about what they believe characterizes success in our profession. Their insights confirm that success is a product of far more than cognitive ability and substantive knowledge. Some of the most compelling insights are recounted throughout this book—quotes from partners from Baker & McKenzie, Clearly Gottlieb Steen & Hamilton, Freshfields Bruckhaus Deringer, Skadden, Arps, Spate, Meagher & Flom, and White & Case; the chief legal officers of The Human Rights Foundation, The Interpublic Group, and Morgan Stanley; a judge on the United States District Court for the Southern District of New York; and the Deans of Fordham Law School.

Writing this book and reflecting intentionally on my many years working in different settings with a range of people has had the unintended but splendid consequence of helping me better understand my motivations, my strengths, and my weaknesses, and of making me re-think elements of my own professional persona, reinforcing the fluid nature of the journey on which each of us embarks in our professional development.

E. ROADMAP

This book is in four parts: This first part is foundational, introducing the concept of the Legal Professional Persona (Chapter 1), The Business of Law: The Changing Landscape of Legal Practice (Chapter 2), and Legal Professional Persona Building Blocks (Chapter 3). Part II deals with professionalism from the inside—self-management concepts such as Mindset and Dispositions (Chapter 4), Time Management and Organization (Chapter 5), and Wellbeing and Sustainability (Chapter 6). Part III is about professionalism with the outside— Working with Others (Chapter 7), Talent Management (Chapter

8), Effective Communication (Chapter 9), and Your Public Professional Persona (Chapter 10). Questions will follow most chapters. Part IV briefly summarizes the major points in this book and offers practice tips for ready reference (Chapter 11).

The habits of mind and personal characteristics explored in Part II have their external counterparts in the discussion in Part III dealing with how lawyers relate to the world. Many of the elements in Parts II and III mirror each other and are intimately intertwined. For this reason, although one's legal professional persona is a confluence of many different features forged into an integrated whole, there inevitably is some overlap among the various elements discussed in the chapters that follow. Some features of the legal professional persona are in fact different sides of the same coin.

CHAPTER 2

THE BUSINESS OF LAW: THE CHANGING LANDSCAPE OF LEGAL PRACTICE

A. LEGAL PRACTICE TODAY

1. Back in the Day. . . .

When I was a first-year associate in the mid-1980s, a rite of passage was a lecture delivered in the early weeks of each intake by the head of the firm's management committee explaining the basics of law firm economics, including the costs borne by the firm—everything from our fancy office space on Pennsylvania Avenue to client development to light bulbs and toilet paper. Between such costs and the fact that the firm could not realize all our billable hours, we were somberly told that we would not generate net revenue in our first or second years. We were an investment in the firm's future.

This was very much the traditional approach to law practice, especially in mid-sized and large law firms. Such firms hired entry-level associates expecting them to be bright, teachable, and hard working, but not expecting much else. The firm would train and mentor associates and shape them for what was expected to be a longstanding association with the firm.

Times have changed. While law remains a noble profession, a craft, and for many a calling, the practice of law has become more of a business—a business that has become increasingly commoditized and commercialized.[1] Many of the underlying norms that traditionally governed the profession are in a state of flux.

---

[1] Commentators have described the "migration of law practice from a professional culture to a commercial culture." Randy D. Gordon & Nancy B. Rapoport, Virtuous Billing, 15 Nev. L.J. 698, 705 (2015), available at https://scholars.law.unlv.edu/cgi/viewcontent.cgi?article=1594&context=nlj.

2. Where Do Law Graduates Go?

It is useful at the outset to take a snapshot of where law school graduates initially are employed. The most recent NALP data show that a majority of law graduates go into private practice (52.9%), followed by business (15.6%), government (10.5% as judicial clerks and 11.0% in other government jobs), and public interest (6.9%).[2]

Because one's professional persona is heavily contextual, each of us should try to understand the environment in which we work. It is critically important that we adapt our persona to the particular milieu in which we find ourselves, in both large and small ways.

Private Practice

The majority of law graduates end up in private practice in law firms, including large, medium, and small law firms, as well as solo practice. This figure also includes the new models of law firms discussed below.[3]

Smaller- to mid-sized law firms often provide associates with more varied work, more client contact, more hands-on experience, more flexible schedules, a more relaxed environment, a shorter track to partnership, and greater input into firm management processes. Salaries, benefits, and support staff and other resources are likely to be more modest than at larger law firms. There are of course exceptions, such as highly prestigious boutique firms which offer many of the tangible benefits associated with BigLaw.

Large law firms offer more complex matters, a spectrum of sophisticated clients, and outstanding salaries, benefits, and support, but often provide less direct client interface and more repetitive, behind-the-scenes work. Most large firms take on significant pro bono representation, often handled largely by associates. Of course, BigLaw also demands long hours and billable hour requirements, can be extremely competitive, and

---

[2] See National Association for Law Placement, Jobs & JDs, Employment for the Class of 2016—Selected Findings, available at https://www.nalp.org/uploads/SelectedFindingsClassof2016.pdf.

[3] See Section A.3., infra.

has a long and tenuous track to partnership. Such firms are typically more formal in atmosphere.

There is also a range of new models of law firms that have begun to appear.[4] Details vary but generally these new models offer attorneys greater flexibility in working arrangements.

Business

Many lawyers work for non-law firm businesses, which include in-house jobs, law clerk, temporary, and other non-traditional attorney and non-attorney positions in companies. Some of these jobs provide exceptional opportunities for those with an entrepreneurial spirit and, in particular, skills in technology. These employment settings range from traditional corporate establishments to new, highly innovative, informal environments. Salaries and benefits as well as resources will vary significantly among such positions.

Government

Government positions include judicial clerkships and other positions at all levels of state, federal, and municipal governments. Government positions will vary in terms of the level of responsibility, resources, the variety and sophistication of work, and salary and benefits. Judicial clerkships traditionally were for a year or two in duration, but now many courts have more permanent clerkships. Government jobs often offer some form of statutory tenure. Many government jobs are highly competitive, and some require significant practice experience.

Public Interest

Public interest lawyer positions range from working for impact organizations such as the ACLU and the NAACP, to those that deal with more discrete issues affecting individual clients. These jobs are highly competitive and look for candidates who have a demonstrated interest in the issues within their mission. Attorneys working in these settings often report high levels of job satisfaction because, among other things, they have significant client contact, their work makes a meaningful

---

[4] See id.

difference in the lives of others, and much of the work they do involves cutting-edge issues.

Public interest offices tend to be more informal than more traditional law firm or business positions, but this will vary. Attorneys in these offices tend to be under immense pressure due to the volume of work and limited resources. Salaries, of course, are usually more modest than in private practice or business.

3.   The Modern Law Firm

The modern law firm has changed and continues to change in a number of fundamental ways. Young lawyers and law students who pursue this kind of practice should be aware of the nature of private practice today.

Entry Level Attorneys Are a Greater Investment for Firms than Ever Before

As this chapter's opening anecdote suggests, entry-level associates are an investment that a firm makes in its future. More and more, clients are refusing to pay for that investment in terms of billable hours recorded by junior associates,[5] a trend that has become more pronounced.[6]

The refusal to pay for the time of junior associates destabilizes the leverage model on which mid-sized and large law firms are based. Under this paradigm, partner compensation reflects revenue that they themselves generate (through billings and origination fees) and revenues from hours

---

[5]   See, e.g., Clark D. Cunningham, Should American Law Schools Continue to Graduate Lawyers Whom Clients Consider Worthless?, 70 Md. L. Rev. 499, 499 (2011), available at http://digitalcommons.law.umaryland.edu/mlr/vol70/iss2/14.

[6]   Id. at 503. See also id. at note 28.

billed by associates.[7] The leverage model is broadly based on the following formula:[8]

Leverage = [Associate Hours × Hourly Billable Rate] – [Salary/Bonus + Benefits + Overhead]

As clients increasingly demand discounts off "rack" rates, flat fee, and other forms of alternative fee arrangements, the concept of profitability being tied to leverage is further altered.

Increased Lawyer Mobility

There was a time when lawyers remained at a single firm for their entire careers. In the last decades, lawyers have become increasingly mobile. A typical graduate can expect to have some five to eight legal jobs over the course of a career.[9] Careers have become "more like a collection of experiences (a portfolio) and a lot less linear"[10] than they had been. One survey shows that more than 72% of law firm leaders believe that increased lateral movement will continue into the future.[11] The new pattern of increased lawyer mobility has important and troubling implications for firms, including with respect to the hiring and training of junior associates.[12]

---

[7] Richard L. Abel, American Lawyers 192 (1989). See also id. at 193 (referring to leverage as "exploitation"); New York State Bar Association Report of the Task Force on the Future of the Legal Profession 14 (April 2, 2011), available at https://www.nysba.org/futurereport/ ("The current economic model for law firms evolved over the course of the twentieth century. This model was built upon a foundation of senior lawyers practicing alone or in partnership with the support of employed junior lawyers and nonlegal support staff to deliver legal services to clients. By leveraging the work of their employees, partners could increase their profits beyond what they stood to earn as individuals."); Patrick J. Schiltz, On Being A Happy, Healthy, and Ethical Member of an Unhappy, Unhealthy, and Unethical Profession, 52 Vand. L. Rev. 871, 902 (1999).

[8] See Robert L. Nelson, Partners With Power: The Social Transformation of the Large Law Firm 77 (1988).

[9] See Report of the Task Force on the Future of the Legal Profession, supra note 7, at 24, citing Gary A. Munneke & Ellen Wayne, The Legal Career Guide: From Law Student to Lawyer 23 (2008). See also Eli Wald & Russell G. Pearce, Being Good Lawyers: A Relational Approach to Law Practice, 29 Geo. J. Legal Ethics 601, 633 (2016) (internal citations omitted), available at https://ir.lawnet.fordham.edu/cgi/viewcontent.cgi?article=1709&context=faculty_scholarship.

[10] Terri Mottershead, Innovating Talent Management in Law Firms, ABA Law Practice Today (November 14, 2016), available at http://www.lawpracticetoday.org/article/innovating-talent-management-law-firms/.

[11] Thomas S. Clay & Eric A. Seeger, An Altman Weil Flash Survey, Law Firms in Transition 42 (2018), available at http://www.altmanweil.com/LFiT2018/.

[12] See Section C., infra.

Flat or Declining Demand

Overall demand for law firm services has been flat or declining.[13] As the most recent Altman Weil Flash Survey indicates, the overall demand for legal services has decreased and there is "a continuing downward trend."[14] The report starkly predicts that "[d]emand for law firm services will not return to pre-recession levels—ever."[15]

As a result of this diminished demand, there are too many lawyers in many law firms. Average billable hours have shrunk by hundreds of hours per attorney since before the recession and are unlikely to rebound.[16] Overcapacity is having a negative impact on profitability in 58% of all law firms.[17] Recent surveys report that more than 59% of non-equity partners, more than 50% of equity partners, more than 25% of associates, and more than 40% of other lawyers are insufficiently busy.[18]

Limited Access to Equity Partnership

Given the under-utilization of equity partners, more than 39% of firms surveyed have taken the drastic step of de-equitizing partners,[19] and more than 67% of firms believe that

---

[13] For large law firms, there is some good news, with growth seen in the ranks of the top New York City Law Firms. See Christine Simmons, Top Law Firms in New York Remain in Growth Mode, New York Law Journal (July 9, 2018), available at https://www.law.com/newyorklawjournal/2018/07/09/top-law-firms-in-new-york-remain-in-growth-mode/.

[14] Clay & Seeger, supra note 11 at iii. See also id. at 9; Georgetown Law Center for the Study of the Legal Profession, 2018 Report on the State of the Legal Market 4 (2018), available at http://www.legalexecutiveinstitute.com/wp-content/uploads/2018/01/2018-Report-on-the-State-of-the-Legal-Market.pdf (law firms are experiencing "very sluggish growth in demand for their services, continuing decline in productivity, relatively modest increases in rates, continuing downward pressure on realization, and some upward pressure on direct expenses."). See also id. ("Demand growth for law firm services . . . was essentially flat in 2017.").

[15] Clay & Seeger, supra note 11 at iii (2018).

[16] Id.

[17] Id. at vi.

[18] Id. at 25, 26

[19] Id. at 31.

the move toward fewer equity partners is a permanent trend.[20]
The road to partnership thus is more elusive than ever.[21]

New Models of Law Firms

New types of law firms have begun to appear.[22] These "new
law" models[23] offer reduced costs, more flexible fee patterns, and
increased efficiency for clients,[24] as well as innovation, value,
predictability, flexibility, relationship building, and the ability
to develop talent in a way that matches individual needs.[25]

A number of types of new law models have been identified:[26]

- Companies that offer legal and general business/
  project management advice.

- Accordion companies, which provide networks of
  trained, experienced attorneys to fill short-term
  law firm staffing needs.

- Virtual law practices and companies, in which
  attorneys work primarily remotely to save on
  overhead.

- Law firms and companies offering tailored,
  specialty services with unique fee arrangements or

---

[20] Id. at 35. See also Hildebrandt Consulting 2018 Client Advisory, The Legal
Market in 2017, available at https://www.privatebank.citibank.com/ivc/docs/2018
CitiHildebrandtClientAdvisory.pdf; 2018 Report on the State of the Legal Market, supra
note 14, at 13 ("most firms significantly slowed the growth in their equity partner
ranks."); Report of the Task Force on the Future of the Legal Profession, supra note 7, at
22–23.

[21] See, e.g., Jordan Furlong, Law is a Buyer's Market: Building A Client-First Law
Firm 168 (2017).

[22] There are a "wide variety of new business organizations that have arisen in
recent years to remedy the market's failure to deliver business organizations responsive
to the complaint of either lawyers or of clients." Joan C. Williams, Aaron Platt, & Jessica
Lee, Disruptive Innovation: New Models of Legal Practice, 67 Hastings L.J. 1, 2 (2015),
available at: http://repository.uchastings.edu/faculty_scholarship/1279. See also id. at 3
("Many lawyers have founded—and joined—businesses that organize legal practice in
novel ways. The variety is dazzling.").

[23] Id. at 22.

[24] Id.

[25] Deborah Epstein Henry, Suzie Scanlon Rabinowitz, & Garry A. Berger, Finding
Bliss: Innovative Legal Models for Happy Clients & Happy Lawyers (2015).

[26] Williams, Platt, & Lee, supra note 22, at 26–81. With regard to value, new law
models offer legal fees that are half or one-third those of big law. See id. at 8.

delivery models, including monthly subscription fees.

The success of these models is perhaps best demonstrated by Axiom, which is said to serve more than half of the Fortune 100 companies as clients.[27] *The New York Times* predicts that the future "may look a lot like Axiom Law."[28] Boasting more than 2,000 lawyers around the globe—some of whom work from home and others who work in one of Axiom's 18 offices in North America, Europe, and Asia-Pacific—Axiom is said to offer efficiency and quality for commoditized legal work and flexibility for its staff.[29]

These new models often engage experienced attorneys trained by large law firms and make effective use of cloud-based technology tools that offer seamless communication networks among attorneys who are widely dispersed. This allows new law models to save on overhead (particularly space) and to outsource administrative work and office management.[30] These alternative business models and the value-added propositions that they offer represent a potentially "game-changing business model."[31]

Alternative Law Firm Staffing

Law firm staffing has changed in a number of ways in recent years, giving lawyers more options than before and offering important roles for non-attorneys.

Non-Equity Partners, Permanent Staff Lawyers, and Contract Attorneys—Attorneys at law firms are no longer limited to the traditional categories of associate and equity partner. Lawyers today can assume the role of counsel, non-equity partner, or permanent staff attorney, to name a few common

---

[27] See https://www.axiomlaw.com/.

[28] Andrew Ross Sorkin, Big Law Steps Into Uncertain Times, The New York Times (September 24, 2012), available at https://dealbook.nytimes.com/2012/09/24/big-law-steps-into-uncertain-times/.

[29] See https://www.axiomlaw.com/.

[30] Williams, Platt, & Lee, supra note 22, at 9.

[31] Shannon L. Spangler, Disruptive Innovation in the Legal Services Market: Is real change coming to the business of law, or will the status quo reign? 8 (2014), available at https://www.americanbar.org/content/dam/aba/administrative/litigation/materials/2014_aba_annual/written-materials/disruptive_innovation.authcheckdam.pdf.

types of positions. These lawyers are salaried, permanent employees with no equity in the firm and often no expectation of equity partnership. Law firms also increasingly make use of contract attorneys, which allow firms to ramp up during periods of peak demand without committing to fulltime employees.[32] Indeed, a majority of law firms staff for average rather than peak demand, using part time and contract lawyers to fill the gap.[33]

C-Suite Executives—Law firm staff members now often include a range of executives performing non-lawyer functions. The range of new professions is dizzying in breadth and includes positions such as discovery specialist, trial preparation specialist, cybersecurity specialist, fee analyst and strategic pricing director, data analyst, legal knowledge engineer, legal technologist, legal process analyst, legal project manager, legal risk manager, and innovation manager.[34]

The presence of these types of positions at many law firms offers lawyers a range of career possibilities not previously available to them.

Competency-Based Development Models

Previously, associates advanced in lockstep fashion; promotions and salaries were based mainly on years of service. In recent years, law firms have moved toward competency models for advancing and compensating attorneys.[35] Some law

---

[32] See, e.g., The Emergence of Nontraditional-Track Lawyer Career Paths: A Resource Guide for Law Firms and Law Schools, available at https://www.nalp.org/uploads/2014NCMTFResourceGuide.pdf. Large firms that have adopted these practices include King & Spalding, Orrick, Ropes & Gray, Seyfarth Shaw, and Winston & Strawn.

[33] Clay & Seeger, supra note 11 at xii, 44; Report of the Task Force on the Future of the Legal Profession, supra note 7, at 22 ("[P]rojects requiring larger groups of supporting lawyers are increasingly likely to be staffed with contract lawyers, or even for the work to be contracted to entities that handle legal process outsourcing.").

[34] Report of the Task Force on the Future of the Legal Profession, supra note 7, at 22.

[35] See, e.g., Donald J. Polden, Leadership Matters: Lawyers' Leadership Skills and Competencies, 52 Santa Clara L. Rev. 899, 912 (2012), available at https://digital commons.law.scu.edu/cgi/viewcontent.cgi?article=2718&context=lawreview; Brendan Pierson, Associate Competency Models Here For The Long Haul, Law 360 (May 25, 2010) ("Major law firms are increasingly embracing competency models for their associates, both to speed their professional development and make them more marketable to clients, and experts say that trend shows no signs of slowing down any time soon."). One writer notes that "[c]ompetencies are here to stay. . . ." Ann Rainhart, The Evolving Practice of Law: Competency Development in Law Firm Combinations, 11 U. St. Thomas L. J 87, 88 (2013), available at https://ir.stthomas.edu/cgi/viewcontent.cgi?article=1342&context

firms have had competency models in place for some time, while others' are of more recent origin.[36] A 2009 NALP Foundation survey found that 74% of respondent firms had, were developing, or planned to develop core competencies,[37] and although estimates are hard to come by, it is likely that the number today would be significantly higher as interest in competency models grows.[38]

Competency models are based on an articulated set of core skills and behaviors that a firm believes are important to success in the organization. Firms generate performance criteria and benchmarks based on these factors, which are incorporated into associate evaluations. Decisions regarding compensation and promotion are based on an associate's performance with respect to those benchmarks.[39] Competency models go well beyond legal knowledge and basic lawyer skills and include significant behavioral components as well[40]—all elements of your legal professional persona.

=ustlj; Mottershead, supra note 10; Neil W. Hamilton, Law Firm Competency Models & Student Professional Success: Building on a Foundation of Professional Formation/Professionalism, 11 U. St. Thomas L.J. 6, 9 (2013) ("There is strong evidence that this trend of developing competency models is widespread."), available at https://ir.stthomas.edu/cgi/viewcontent.cgi?article=1339&context=ustlj.

[36] See Pierson, supra note 35.

[37] The NALP Foundation for Law Career Research and Education, Survey of Law Firm Use of Core Competencies and Benchmarking in Associate Compensation and Advancement Structures (July 2009), available at https://www.nalpfoundation.org/surveyoflawfirmuseofcorecompetenciesandbenchmarks.

[38] See Blane R. Prescott, Larry Richard, & Michael Short, Hildebrandt White Paper, Merit-Based Compensation and Promotion for Associates: The Challenges of Designing and Implementing a New Approach 1 (September 2009), available at http://lawyerbrain.com/sites/default/files/merit_compensation_article_-_brp_-_lrr_-_mds.pdf.

[39] See Hamilton, supra note 35, at 6 ("many law firms are moving toward "competency models" that define the characteristics of the most effective and successful lawyers in the firm and are then using those characteristics in the assessment and development (and, in some cases, the hiring), of junior lawyers). See also Prescott, Richard, & Short, supra note 38, at 1.

[40] For example, the Altman Weil Sample Associate Evaluation form includes elements such as thoroughness (including level of preparedness, efficiency, ability to work independently, professional development, client relations, business development, judgment/maturity, initiative, responsiveness, commitment, dedication to firm, and office relations. See http://www.altmanweil.com/dir_docs/resource/c723f030-ccd1-4b3b-854c-022105d04016_document.pdf.

B. EXTERNAL INFLUENCES ON
THE PRACTICE OF LAW

Today's legal services climate is client-centric and technology driven; the market for legal services is more transparent than ever before; and the monopoly over the provision of legal services that lawyers and law firms once enjoyed has disappeared as competition comes from numerous sources. All told, there are significant pressures on the traditional model of legal practice.

1. The Buyer's Market: Increased Competition and Pressure from Clients

The market for legal services, whose terms once were dictated largely by law firms, is now a buyer's marker. Clients want better and more legal services for less money, and they are now spending more internally and on a smaller panel of firms. Increased transparency in pricing and value arms clients with better information about the services they purchase.

The More-for-Less Movement

In today's buyer's market for legal services, clients have become increasingly sensitive to price and value.[41] Corporate clients need to do more with smaller or flat budgets, which in turn leads to a demand for legal services that are delivered more efficiently, often outside the traditional billable hour method.[42] This trend, which began during the 2007 recession, has continued even after the effects of the recession have moderated,[43] and most law firm leaders believe that client

---

[41] See, e.g., Report of the Task Force on the Future of the Legal Profession, supra note 7, at 20–21.

[42] See, e.g., Sue Reisinger, The "More For Less" Challenge in Legal Departments (October 2, 2017), available at https://www.law.com/corpcounsel/sites/corpcounsel/2017/10/02/the-more-for-less-challenge-in-legal-departments/?slreturn=20180806162102; Williams, Platt, & Lee, supra note 22, at 8; Report of the Task Force on the Future of the Legal Profession, supra note 7, at 74.

[43] "[C]lients' increased attention to legal spending did not fade as economic indicators improved." Lizzy McLellan, Millennials Won't Destroy Your Law Firm. Can They Save It?, The American Lawyer (October 23, 2017), available at https://www.law.com/americanlawyer/sites/americanlawyer/2017/10/23/millennials-wont-destroy-your-law-firm-can-they-save-it/.

sensitivity to price is a part of the new normal.[44] In response, law firms are starting to add pricing directors to their ranks.[45]

Various alternative fee arrangements are now common.[46] One 2016 survey reveals that 100% of large law firms and 88% of medium-sized law firms employ alternative fee arrangements[47] in response to clients' "regular[ ] demand" for such fees.[48] Alternative billing strategies include fixed pricing for discrete services, flat fees, portfolio pricing for multiple matters, contingency fees and other fee arrangements tied to outcome, and other fee variations.[49] In addition to alternative fee arrangements, firms have offered legal advice hotlines, access to work product from other client matters, associate secondments to clients, and other perks designed to retain or increase client business.[50]

Convergence

A number of corporate clients who once used many outside counsel find that their needs can best be met through reducing the number of firms they employ.[51] This form of consolidation, once common for lawyers serving a few industries like pharmaceutical and insurance, has expanded to all kinds of corporate clients[52] and promises to be the " 'wave of the

---

[44] The 2017 Altman Weil survey reports that more than 95% of respondents expect greater price competition. Clay & Seeger, supra note 11 at 1.

[45] Id. at 5.

[46] Report of the Task Force on the Future of the Legal Profession, supra note 7, at 12.

[47] American Bar Association Commission on the Future of Legal Services, Report on the Future of Legal Services in the United States 26 (August 2016), available at https://www.americanbar.org/content/dam/aba/images/abanews/2016FLSReport_FNL_WEB.pdf.

[48] Id.

[49] Id.

[50] See, e.g., Miriam Rozen, No Pain, No Gain for Law Firms as Client Demands Get More Extreme, The American Lawyer (November 14, 2017), available at https://www.law.com/americanlawyer/sites/americanlawyer/2017/11/14/no-pain-no-gain-for-law-firms-as-client-demands-get-more-extreme/.

[51] "Some large clients have employed convergence initiatives to reduce the number of firms they use, eliminating firms that do not provide value for the fees charged." Report of the Task Force on the Future of the Legal Profession, supra note 7, at 19. See also id. at 21.

[52] Dan Packel, "The Wave of the Future": Law Firm Panels are Creating a New In-Crowd, The American Lawyer (July 29, 2018), available at https://www.law.com/americanlawyer/2018/07/29/the-wave-of-the-future-law-firm-panels-are-creating-a-new-in-crowd/.

future.' "[53] The practice seeks pricing efficiencies, but also looks for firms that provide other benefits, such as information sharing, strong legal management processes, effective use of technology, and risk sharing; and that offer diversity within their ranks.[54] Another major benefit associated with preferred networks rather than having a sprawling list of active law firms is the potential for genuine relationship building.[55]

The Build Rather than Buy Trend

Faced with stagnant budgets and more legal work, companies often find that legal insourcing is the most effective and efficient approach.[56] Reportedly 73% of legal work today is insourced.[57] Two-thirds of law firms report losing business to corporate law department insourcing,[58] and most predict that the trend will continue or accelerate.[59] In-house legal departments have developed to accommodate not only more work, but progressively more *sophisticated* work.[60] It has been said that clients are becoming law firms' biggest competitor.[61]

Increased Transparency

There is ever-greater transparency in the legal profession, further shifting the balance of power between lawyers and clients. Legal services have been "demystified," and consumers are "more knowledgeable, sophisticated and connected than ever

---

[53] Id.

[54] Id.

[55] Id.

[56] See Dan Clark, Legal Ops On the Rise As In-House Budgets Get Tighter, Survey Says, Corporate Counsel (June 26, 2018), available at https://www.law.com/corpcounsel/2018/06/26/legal-ops-on-the-rise-as-in-house-budgets-get-tighter-survey-says/.

[57] ALM Intelligence and Morrison Foerster, General Counsel Up-At-Night Report 14, available at https://media2.mofo.com/documents/170622-gc-up-at-night-report.pdf.

[58] Clay & Seeger, supra note 11 at ix.

[59] Id. at 1, 12 (2018); Hugh A. Simons & Gina Passarella, The Rise (and Fall?) of In-House Counsel, The American Lawyer (February 25, 2018), available at https://www.law.com/americanlawyer/2018/02/25/the-rise-and-fall-of-in-house-counsel/.

[60] Simons & Passarella, supra note 59. See also Dan Packel, Will Law Firms Be Ready When the Next Recession Hits?, The American Lawyer (May 22, 2018) (quoting Hugh Simons), available at https://www.law.com/americanlawyer/2018/05/22/will-law-firms-be-ready-when-the-next-recession-hits/.

[61] Jordan Furlong, Who's your biggest competitor?, Law21 (August 7, 2014), available at https://www.law21.ca/2014/08/whos-biggest-competitor/.

before."[62] The beginning of transparency for law firms can be traced to the creation of corporate general counsel and the Am Law 100 rankings,[63] aided by what Richard Susskind calls the "electronic legal marketplace"[64]—lawyer raters such as Avvo, Martindale-Hubbell Peer Review Ratings, Best Lawyers, Law Dragon, Chambers, and Super Lawyers, all of which are readily available to consumers. The Association of Corporate Counsel (ACC) has announced a "value index" which allows ACC members to share evaluations of the law firms they engage[65] and 25 general counsel from major companies have formed a GC Thought Leaders Experiment, which uses and shares data to allow general counsel to compare the quality and efficiency of legal services offered by pedigreed global law firms.[66] This is true also at the level of individual consumers, who have access to online lawyer reviews as well as court help centers,[67] smartphone apps, and do-it-yourself legal services.[68]

2. Technology, Innovation and the Unbundling of Legal Services

Additional and significant pressures on the traditional law firm model come from technology, other forms of innovation, and the unbundling of legal services. All of these developments (along with the growth of in-house legal departments, as discussed above), contribute to the loss of monopoly status once enjoyed by law firms over the provision of legal services.

---

[62] Spangler, supra note 31, at 3 (internal citation omitted).

[63] See International Bar Association, Legal Policy and Research Unit, "Times are a-changin": disruptive innovation and the legal profession 12 (May 2016), available at https://www.ibanet.org/LPRU/Disruptive-Innovation.aspx.

[64] Richard Susskind, Tomorrow's Lawyers: An Introduction to Your Future 47, 91 (2d ed. 2017).

[65] See ACC Value Challenge, available at https://www.acc.com/valuechallenge/getinvolved/lawfirms.cfm.

[66] See GC Thought Leaders Experiment, available at https://www.advancelaw.com/thought-leaders-experiment/; An Open Letter From 25 General Counsel, Corporate Counsel (July 11, 2017) ("Through a large data set, across our companies, we are moving beyond the anecdotal to measure what really works."), available at https://www.law.com/corpcounsel/almID/1202792672000/An-Open-Letter-From-25-General-Counsel/.

[67] See, e.g., https://www.americanbar.org/groups/delivery_legal_services/resources/pro_se_unbundling_resource_center/self_service_centers.html.

[68] See, e.g., Sarah Kellogg, The Uncertain Future: Turbulence and Change in the Legal Profession, Washington Lawyer (April 2016), version available at https://www.dcbar.org/bar-resources/publications/washington-lawyer/articles/april-2016-uncertain-future.cfm.

Technology

"There is little reason to doubt that, if given enough time and resources, innovators in the fields of artificial intelligence, robotics, or other technological fields could discover ways to make machines that can perform all of the core functions that lawyers now perform." Brian Sheppard[69]

The recent pace of technological change in the legal industry has been astonishing and includes a vast range of products and services, such as discovery (including a product that can draft an initial round of discovery requests[70]); legal research; document generation; prediction of case outcomes; contract management; due diligence; practice, project, and workflow management; online dispute resolution; online legal guidance; legal open sourcing; big data; artificial intelligence predictors and problem solving; and mass document search are fundamentally altering the way law is practiced.[71] Software algorithms and stronger interconnectedness between human and artificial intelligence suggest that technological advances will continue to evolve.[72] More than 85% of attorneys surveyed believe that technology will replace human resources in the provision of legal services.[73]

---

[69] Brian Sheppard, Incomplete Innovation and the Premature Disruption of Legal Services, 2015 Mich. St. L. Rev. 1797, 1808, available at https://digitalcommons.law.msu.edu/cgi/viewcontent.cgi?article=1150&context=lr.

[70] See Stephanie Forshee, The AI Tech That's Saving Walmart's In-House Lawyers Time, Corporate Counsel (May 7, 2018), available at https://www.law.com/corpcounsel/2018/05/07/the-ai-tech-thats-saving-walmarts-in-house-lawyers-time/.

[71] See, e.g., John O. McGinnis & Russell G. Pearce, The Great Disruption: How Machine Intelligence Will Transform the Role of Lawyers in the Delivery of Legal Services, 82 Fordham L. Rev. 3041 (2014), available at https://ir.lawnet.fordham.edu/cgi/viewcontent.cgi?article=5007&context=flr.

[72] See id. at 3045 (2014); Susskind, supra note 64, at 13.

[73] Id. at 61. See also Chris Johnson, Artificial Intelligence Beats Big Law Partners in Legal Matchup, The American Lawyer (October 31, 2017), available at https://www.law.com/americanlawyer/sites/americanlawyer/2017/10/31/artificial-intelligence-beats-big-law-partners-in-legal-matchup/ ("Lawyers from DLA Piper, Allen & Overy and other firms were soundly beaten in a first-of-its-kind challenge against software developed by Cambridge University law students."); Marques Winick, I, Lawyer: Is Artificial Intelligence the Attorney of the Future?, Michigan Business & Entrepreneurial Law Review (January 12, 2018), available at http://mbelr.org/i-lawyer-is-artificial-intelligence-the-attorney-of-the-future/; Hugh Son, JPMorgan Software Does in Seconds What Took Lawyers 360,000 Hours, Bloomberg (February 27, 2017), available at https://www.bloomberg.com/news/articles/2017-02-28/jpmorgan-marshals-an-army-of-developers-to-automate-high-finance (contract intelligence software "reviews documents in seconds, is less error-prone and never asks for vacation"); Stephen Rynkiewicz,

One two-month long contract review test found that LawGeex Artificial Intelligence achieved an average accuracy rate of 94% compared with an average lawyer accuracy rate of 85%.[74] Even more striking, what took lawyers an average of 92 minutes took the machine 26 seconds.[75] The experiment may actually understate the gains from AI:

> The lawyers who reviewed these documents were duly focused on the task: it didn't sink to the bottom of a to-do list, it didn't get rushed through while waiting for a plane or with one eye on the clock to get out the door to a meeting or to pick up the kids. The margin of efficiency may be even greater than the results presented here.[76]

In a 2016 report, Deloitte estimates that 114,000 legal jobs will be automated in the next 20 years, and that an additional 39% of jobs are at "high risk" of becoming redundant over the next two decades.[77]

Other Innovations

Legal industry innovations go beyond the high-tech solutions described above. These include the large accounting

---

Paralegal robot reviews patent documents, ABA Journal (July 17, 2017), available at http://www.abajournal.com/news/article/patent_document_robot_legal_review ("patent drafting software... automates paralegal work, bringing more rigor to the task of researching prior art and potentially saving thousands of dollars on a filing."); Xavier Beauchamp-Tremblay, How Far Are Lawyers From Drafting Smart Contracts?, Slaw (August 3, 2017), available at http://www.slaw.ca/2017/08/03/how-far-are-lawyers-from-drafting-smart-contracts/; Ian Lopez, This Australian AI Aims to Be a "Law Firm Without Lawyers," Legaltech news (November 17, 2017), available at https://www.law.com/legaltechnews/sites/legaltechnews/2017/11/17/this-australian-ai-aims-to-be-a-law-firm-without-lawyers/; Elizabeth Dwoskin, This Silicon Valley start-up wants to replace lawyers with robots, The Washington Post (September 14, 2017), available at https://www.washingtonpost.com/news/innovations/wp/2017/09/14/this-silicon-valley-startup-wants-to-replace-lawyers-with-robots/?noredirect=on&utm_term=.b3cd70ef73f9; LawGeex, Comparing the Performance of Artificial Intelligence to Human Lawyers in the Review of Standard Business Contracts (February 2018), available at https://www.lawgeex.com/AIvsLawyer/.

[74] LawGeex, supra note 73, at 14.

[75] Id.

[76] Id. at 20.

[77] See Jane Croft, More than 100,000 legal roles to become automated, Financial Times (March 15, 2016), available at https://www.ft.com/content/c8ef3f62-ea9c-11e5-888e-2eadd5fbc4a4.

firms, other alternative service providers, and the unbundling of legal services.

The Big Four Accounting Firms—The Big Four accounting firms recently have accelerated their entry into the market for legal services, "quietly expanding their legal arms."[78] They offer services such as automated contracts, outsourcing legal departments, building proprietary technology to perform legal tasks, and assisting U.S. clients with international legal matters.[79] The Big Four efforts to penetrate the legal industry are a significant threat to traditional law firms because of their combined market size, name recognition, profitability, lack of fragmentation, overlap in clients with law firms, and overlap in services provided by traditional legal services providers.[80]

Alternative Service Providers and the Unbundling of Legal Services—The traditional law firm monopoly over the provision of legal services is further compromised by a range of alternative legal service providers. If law firms do not provide reliably high-quality services at predictable and reasonable prices, it is said, "there are other providers that will."[81] Such service providers offer litigation support services, operations management, foreign outsourcing services, document generating services and discovery services, to name a few. Aided by the standardization or commoditization of much legal work, these businesses are thriving.

---

[78] Nicholas Bruch, David B. Wilkins, & Maria J. Esteban Ferrer, Taking on the World: The Big Four in the Global Legal Market, The American Lawyer (October 18, 2017), available at https://www.law.com/americanlawyer/sites/americanlawyer/2017/10/18/taking-on-the-world-the-big-four-in-the-global-legal-market/.

[79] Id.; Dan Packel, Deloitte Will Acquire Part of US Law Firm in New Legal Venture, The American Lawyer (June 6, 2018), available at https://www.law.com/americanlawyer/2018/06/06/deloitte-will-acquire-part-of-us-law-firm-in-new-legal-venture/; Roy Strom, As Law Firms Stall, Who Will Overtake Them in the Innovation Race?, The American Lawyer (January 30, 2018), available at https://www.law.com/americanlawyer/sites/americanlawyer/2018/01/30/as-law-firms-stall-who-will-overtake-them-in-the-innovation-race/; Chris Johnson, PwC to Launch US Law Firm, Law.com (September 20, 2017), available at https://www.law.com/sites/almstaff/2017/09/20/pwc-to-launch-us-law-firm/.

[80] See ALM Intelligence, Elephants in the Room, Part I: The Big Four's Expansion in the Legal Services Market 7, 8, available at https://www.alm.com/intelligence/solutions-we-provide/business-of-law-solutions/analyst-reports/elephants-in-the-room-the-big-4s-expansion-in-the-legal-services-market/.

[81] Clay & Seeger, supra note 11, at iii.

The threat to traditional law practice from these services is real—and is perceived as real: More than 50% of law firm leaders believe that outsourcing legal work will continue,[82] and more than 80% of lawyers surveyed believe that commoditized legal work and competition from non-legal service providers will be a permanent trend.[83]

The technology revolution has a significant upside: As technology continues to perform much of the work formerly performed by junior associates, such lawyers will have the chance to work on more sophisticated bespoke services earlier in their careers. It also gives technologically savvy, entrepreneurial lawyers outstanding opportunities to work in this growing field.

C. WHAT DOES THIS ALL MEAN FOR YOUR LEGAL PROFESSIONAL PERSONA?

The discussion above all comes back to the need to develop a robust legal professional persona.

The current state of legal practice is in itself a reason why lawyers and law students should be attuned to developing their legal professional personae. As one commentator noted, "[t]he issue of professional identity formation has taken on greater urgency during the economic crisis."[84] Thriving in today's legal world means being much more than a good lawyer; knowledge of substantive law and procedure and technical skills are no longer the panacea for success that they may have been in simpler times. Today's legal landscape calls for capable attorneys who differentiate themselves through behaviors and attitudes reflective of a strong professional persona.

Elements of the legal professional persona are prominent in competency-based development models that are becoming a standard for determining compensation and advancement in many law firms and companies. Underperformance at law firms is tied closely to weak business development skills and efforts.[85]

---

[82] Id. at 52.

[83] Id. at 11.

[84] Charlotte S. Alexander, Learning to be Lawyers: Professional Identity and the Law School Curriculum, 70 Md. L. Rev. 465, 466 (2011), available at http://digitalcommons.law.umaryland.edu/cgi/viewcontent.cgi?article=3451&context=mlr.

[85] Id. at 36.

A majority of firms now consider as "major factors" in equity partnership decisions demonstrated business development skills, excellence in client relationship management, and demonstrated leadership and management skills,[86] all essential aspects of the legal professional persona. Those who can utilize their professional persona to successfully navigate business development and manage relationships well are poised for success.

Finally, the decline of mentorship and training in many law firms and other contexts reinforces the need for each of us to be more intentional about developing a professional persona. Effective mentoring and training often become casualties of the current law practice environment due to a number of the factors discussed above—in particular, the refusal of many clients to pay for the work of entry-level associates and an increase in lawyer mobility (meaning smaller returns on investment in associate training and mentoring). The confluence of increasing price-sensitivity of clients[87] and associate attrition creates a perfect storm under which many firms are reluctant to invest heavily in the hiring, training, and mentoring of new talent.[88] This presents yet another reason why each of us needs to take active measures to develop and sustain an effective professional persona.

---

[86]   Clay & Seeger, supra note 11, at 34.

[87]   See Section B.1., supra.

[88]   See id. See also Patrick J. Schiltz, Legal Ethics in Decline: The Elite Law Firm, The Elite Law School, and the Moral Formation of the Novice Attorney, 82 Minn. L. Rev. 705, 740 (1998) ("The extraordinary pressure to bill hours is almost single-handedly responsible for the death of mentoring. Time that a lawyer spends either mentoring or being mentored is, for the most part, nonbillable. Thus, pressure to bill hours . . . is necessarily pressure not to mentor. There is no stronger pressure experienced by lawyers in private practice today."), available at http://coloradomentoring.org/wp-content/uploads/2013/09/Schiltz-P-Legal-Ethics-in-Decline-The-Elite-Law-Firm-The-Elite-Law-School-and-the-Moral-Formation-of-the-Novice-Attorney-82-Minn.-L.-Rev.-705-February-19981.pdf.

CHAPTER 3

LEGAL PROFESSIONAL PERSONA BUILDING BLOCKS

This chapter discusses some of the fundamental building blocks of a professional persona: The process by which humans achieve competence, which involves questioning, reflection, observation, and being coached; the importance of habit formation, which saves us time and mental energy for less routine and more important decisions; elements of intelligence that every lawyer should have; and leadership.

This chapter is somewhat more theoretical than the chapters that follow, as the topics discussed here are essential foundations that underlie many of the more specific behaviors and attitudes discussed in Parts II and III.

A. (UN)CONSCIOUS (IN)COMPETENCE

Learning is a lifelong process, and it is more complicated than we may recognize. Our ability to achieve competence in particular areas is destabilized by various cognitive biases that render us resistant to development. To overcome those challenges, we need to persistently engage in questioning, reflection, and observation and imitation, and open ourselves to coaching by those whose judgment we trust.

1. The Competence Problem

The Competence Model: From Unconscious Incompetence to Unconscious Competence

In the 1970s, an employee of Gordon Training International named Noel Burch devised a matrix to describe the way we become proficient at things, known variously as the stages of competence, the learning matrix, or the competence model.[1] This model is often presented as a matrix with competence running

---

[1] See Marie Bryson, The Four Stages of Learning: They're a Circle, Not a Straight Line (July 7, 2016) available at http://www.gordontraining.com/leadership/four-stages-learning-theyre-circle-not-straight-line/.

along the horizontal axis and consciousness along the vertical axis or as a ladder on which an individual moves along four rungs: The lowest step is unconscious incompetence, the next is conscious incompetence, followed by conscious competence, and finally unconscious competence.

Step 1: Unconscious Incompetence—The stage of unconscious incompetence is where an individual does not know something and is unaware of his limitations or of the importance of what he does not know. At this stage, the person lacks any real appreciation for what he must learn, its value, or the disadvantages he faces without that knowledge or skill. He is blissfully ignorant, entirely comfortable with a deficiency that he does not even realize he possesses.

Step 2: Conscious Incompetence—At the stage of conscious incompetence, the individual does not know how to do something but is aware of his limitations and the value of what he does not know. This stage lacks the comfort of unconscious incompetence because the individual recognizes his shortcomings but has yet to overcome them.

An article written by a CrossFit athlete who also ran a marathon demonstrates through a sports analogy the unconscious/conscious competence binary.[2] The author notes that the reason that people are more impressed with those who run a marathon than they are with those who compete in CrossFit competitions is that we all have experience running, at least as children, and thus some basic appreciation for what it means to run. Those of us who are not runners have a *conscious* level of incompetence. But CrossFit is completely foreign to most of us; we have absolutely no conception of what CrossFit activity is or what it entails, so we lack even a basic level of appreciation for what a CrossFit athlete does. As to CrossFit, we are *unconsciously* incompetent. This sports analogy illustrates the difference between the first two stages of Burch's matrix, and gives us a convenient platform from which to understand how the model works in practice.

---

[2] Michael Lanwehr, Can CrossFit Prepare You for a Marathon? One Coach Decides to Run The NYC Marathon Without Training, Part 2 (December 14, 2015), available at https://www.puori.com/blog/marathon-crossfit-part-2.

Step 3: Conscious Competence—At the stage of conscious competence, the individual has learned a skill but execution of that skill still requires deliberate effort. The person must consciously focus on the skill and its various components to accomplish it.

Step 4: Unconscious Competence—The last step on the learning ladder, unconscious competence, is what we should strive to achieve. When we reach the stage of unconscious competence, we have achieved mastery over a skill and can perform it with little effort—the skill has become automatic, something of second nature.[3] We are entirely comfortable in performing this activity and do so without conscious effort.

The two levels of competence—conscious and unconscious—can be understood with another sports analogy. Perhaps you have seen someone riding a skateboard and thought to yourself, "That doesn't look too difficult!" When you have that reaction, the skateboarder you are watching probably has reached the stage of unconscious competence. It is at this stage that she makes skateboarding look easy. She exerts no apparent effort in skateboarding, although she performs with a high level of proficiency. But watch someone who has just learned how to skateboard attempt her new hobby and our reaction is very different: "That looks really hard!" As observers, we can almost see the very deliberate effort that the new skateboarder must exert. The obvious exertion undertaken by the novice skateboard enthusiast reflects her still conscious level of competence.

Managing Our Cognitive Biases

Our ability to achieve competence over particular tasks is complicated by principles of cognitive bias, which to an extent hard-wire us to deflect or disregard signs of incompetence.

Cognitive bias is "a mistake in reasoning, evaluating, remembering, or other cognitive process, often occurring as a result of holding onto one's preferences and beliefs regardless of contrary information."[4] Cognitive biases, referred to as human

---

[3] The stage of unconscious competence has much in common with habitual behavior, as discussed in Section B., infra.

[4] Chegg Study, Cognitive Bias, available at https://www.chegg.com/homework-help/definitions/cognitive-bias-13.

"design flaws,"[5] are adaptive behaviors that allow us to make sense of a world full of contradiction.

Cognitive dissonance and the Dunning-Kruger effect, discussed below, are specific cognitive biases that demonstrate how as humans we are constitutionally disposed toward thoughts and behaviors that resist learning and achieving competence over new things.

Cognitive Dissonance and Confirmation Bias—Cognitive dissonance occurs when we are confronted with conflicting beliefs, attitudes, or actions. This conflict creates discomfort, which we try to alleviate by changing a belief, attitude, or action to eliminate or minimize the dissonance in an attempt to achieve cognitive consistency.[6] Cognitive dissonance is "the idea that if a person knows various things that are not psychologically consistent with one another he will, in a variety of ways, try to make them more consistent."[7]

Leon Festinger, the father of theories of cognitive dissonance, conducted numerous studies to demonstrate cognitive dissonance and our efforts to eliminate the psychological distress it produces, the most famous of which is reported in his classic work, *When Prophesy Fails: A Social and Psychological Study of a Modern Group That Predicted the Destruction of the World* (1956). In this work, Festinger and his co-authors examine the Seekers, a small UFO religious cult in Chicago. The Seekers predicted that an apocalyptic flood would destroy the earth before dawn on December 21, 1954, and that the faithful would be saved by visitors from outer space who would escort them to a spacecraft that would bring them to safety. Needless to say, neither event occurred.

One might have expected the Seekers to admit error and resume their normal lives. Instead, the most faithful of the Seekers doubled-down their belief system, claiming that the earth was saved from cataclysm precisely because of their

---

[5]   Martie G. Haselton, Daniel Nettle, & Damian R. Murray, Chapter 41: The Evolution of Cognitive Bias, in David M. Buss, Handbook of Evolutionary Psychology 968 (2016).

[6]   Leon Festinger, A Theory of Cognitive Dissonance 2–3 (1962).

[7]   Leon Festinger, Cognitive Dissonance, 207 Scientific American 93, 93 (October 1962), available at https://www.jstor.org/stable/pdf/24936719.pdf?refreqid=excelsior%3Acb6696c2a342e8a969a81965b4e3ccaf.

devotion. This is because of cognitive dissonance. The Seekers, having sunk enormous costs into their belief that the end of the world was imminent (quitting jobs, relocating, breaking from friends and family members, enduring ridicule, among other things) could not admit error. Instead, to minimize the dissonance, they reaffirmed rather than question or disavow their beliefs.

Closely related to cognitive dissonance theories is the notion of confirmation bias, under which we tend to actively seek information that confirms our pre-existing beliefs and disregard information that contradicts them.[8]

Dissonance and confirmation bias compromise our ability to learn and adapt to new ways of doing things, because these biases have the effect of defending the choices we have made, even in the face of valid contradictory information.

The Dunning-Kruger Effect: "We Are All Confident Idiots"[9]— Another powerful form of cognitive bias that affects our ability to learn is espoused by social psychologists David Dunning and Justin Kruger. Under the Dunning-Kruger effect, people tend to misperceive their own competence, leading to significant errors in self-evaluation. Those with low levels of ability in a particular field often assess their knowledge or skill as much higher than it actually is because they suffer from what Dunning and Kruger refer to as a sense of "illusory superiority."[10] This inability to accurately self-assess occurs because the "[t]he knowledge and intelligence that are required to be good at a task are often the same qualities needed to recognize that one is not good at that task—and if one lacks such knowledge and intelligence, one remains ignorant that one is not good at that

---

[8] See, e.g., Raymond S. Nickerson, Confirmation Bias: A Ubiquitous Phenomenon in Many Guises, 2 Review of General Psychology 175 (1998), available at http://psy2.ucsd.edu/~mckenzie/nickersonConfirmationBias.pdf.

[9] David Dunning, We Are All Confident Idiots, Pacific Standard (October 27, 2014), available at https://psmag.com/social-justice/confident-idiots-92793.

[10] Justin Kruger & David Dunning, Unskilled and Unaware of It: How Difficulties in Recognizing One's Own Incompetence Lead to Inflated Self-Assessments, 77 J. Personality & Soc. Psychol. 1121, 1122 (1999), available at https://www.avaresearch.com/files/UnskilledAndUnawareOfIt.pdf. See also David Dunning, Chapter Five—The Dunning-Kruger Effect: On Being Ignorant of One's Own Ignorance, 44 ScienceDirect 247 (2011), available at https://www.sciencedirect.com/science/article/pii/B97801238552 20000056.

task."[11] Lacking self-awareness, low-ability people experience a "miscalibration" in self-assessment.[12]

The Dunning-Kruger phenomenon raises challenges for us as we seek to move from unconscious incompetence to conscious incompetence and finally to the stages of competence. When we lack skill, we experience an inflated sense of confidence about our abilities. Surely each of us has known someone who is boastful and arrogant while actually quite ignorant or inept. Paradoxically, people in this state of unconscious incompetence have great difficulty improving because they lack the metacognition—the ability to think contemplatively about what they know, to demonstrate genuine awareness—to accurately assess their abilities.[13] More humble and modest people can enjoy profound insights and levels of self-assessment.

The Dunning-Kruger effect has been validated across a range of settings involving skills as varied as logical reasoning, grammar, emotional intelligence, financial literacy, numeracy, firearm care and safety, debating skill, college coursework, chess playing, medical lab work, medical studies, performing CPR,[14] and teaching ability. One classic study at the University of Nebraska asked faculty members how they rated themselves for teaching ability; a full 68% rated themselves in the top 25% for teaching ability, and more than 90% rated themselves above average.[15]

The *Lie Witness News* segment of Jimmy Kimmel Live! is an amusing and revealing manifestation of the Dunning-Kruger

---

[11] David Dunning, The Psychological Quirk That Explains Why You Love Donald Trump, Politico Magazine (May 25, 2016), available at https://www.politico.com/magazine/story/2016/05/donald-trump-supporters-dunning-kruger-effect-213904.

[12] Kruger & Dunning, note 10.

[13] As Dunning noted, "[l]ogic itself almost demands . . . lack of self-insight: For poor performers to recognize their ineptitude would require them to possess the very expertise they lack . . . Poor performers—and we are all poor performers at some things—fail to see the flaws in their thinking or the answers they lack." Dunning, supra note 9. See also Dunning, supra note 11 (noting that people in general "have little insight about the cracks and holes in their expertise. . . . [T]he knowledge and intelligence that are required to be good at a task are often the same qualities needed to recognize that one is not good at that task—and if one lacks such knowledge and intelligence, one remains ignorant that one is not good at that task.").

[14] See Dunning, supra note 11.

[15] K. Patricia Cross, Not can, but *will* college teaching be improved?, 17 New Directions for Higher Education 1 (Spring 1977), available at https://onlinelibrary.wiley.com/doi/pdf/10.1002/he.36919771703.

effect. This segment features questions containing demonstrably false facts posted to random people. The results are often hilarious. Dunning and his colleagues conducted research along the same lines in which they found that some 90 percent claimed knowledge about at least one of the nine fictitious concepts they were asked about. In fact, "the more well versed respondents considered themselves in a general topic, the more familiarity they claimed with the meaningless terms associated with it in the survey."[16]

Although the Dunning-Kruger effect was so named in the late 1990s, its essential characteristics have been recognized for centuries, by thinkers as profound and diverse as Confucius ("Real knowledge is to know the extent of one's ignorance"[17]), Socrates ("The only true wisdom is in knowing you know nothing"[18]), Shakespeare ("The fool doth think he is wise, but the wise man knows himself to be a fool"[19]), Charles Darwin ("Ignorance more frequently begets confidence than does knowledge"[20]), Bertrand Russell ("[T]hose who feel certainty are stupid, and those with any imagination and understanding are filled with doubt and indecision"[21] and "The trouble with the world is that the stupid are cocksure and the intelligent are full of doubt"[22]), Alexander Pope ("A little learning is a dang'rous thing"[23]), Albert Einstein ("The more I learn, the more I realize how much I don't know"[24]), Arnold Glasow ("The trouble with

---

[16] Dunning, supra note 9.

[17] Original source unknown. See https://www.brainyquote.com/quotes/confucius_ 101037. Throughout this book there are quotations whose original sources have been difficult to confirm. Regardless of who said them, when, and where, they offer useful insights.

[18] Original source unknown. See https://www.brainyquote.com/quotes/socrates_ 101212.

[19] William Shakespeare, As You Like It, Act V, Scene 1, available at https://www. opensourceshakespeare.org/views/plays/play_view.php?WorkID=asyoulikeit&Act=5&Sc ene=1&Scope=scene.

[20] Charles Darwin, The Descent of Man, Volume 1, at 3, available at http://darwin-online.org.uk/content/frameset?pageseq=1&itemID=F937.1&viewtype=text.

[21] See https://www.goodreads.com/quotes/355363-one-of-the-painful-things-about-our-time-is-that.

[22] Original source unknown. See https://www.brainyquote.com/quotes/bertrand_ russell_101364.

[23] Alexander Pope, An Essay on Criticism, available at https://www. poetryfoundation.org/articles/69379/an-essay-on-criticism.

[24] Original source unknown. See https://www.goodreads.com/quotes/620163-the-more-i-learn-the-more-i-realize-how-much.

ignorance is that it picks up confidence as it goes along"[25]), and Bill Murray ("It's hard to win an argument with a smart person, but it's damn near impossible to win an argument with a stupid person"[26]).

Perniciously, the Dunning-Kruger effect impacts each of us at some point; none of us is immune.[27] Education alone does not save us; in fact, education "can produce illusory confidence."[28] The Dunning-Kruger phenomenon thus complicates our ability to learn; if we feel competent even when we are not, our interest in and incentives to acquire true learning are diminished.

2.   Tools for Achieving Unconscious Competence

"By three methods we may learn wisdom: First, by reflection, which is noblest; Second, by imitation, which is easiest; and third, by experience, which is the bitterest." Confucius[29]

Each of us should strive to achieve unconscious competence with respect to the skills and behaviors we need to be an accomplished legal professional. In climbing the ladder of competence, it is important that each of us takes ownership over the process of becoming an unconsciously competent professional. What follows is a discussion of tools required to move from unconscious incompetence to unconscious competence: Questioning, reflection, observation and imitation, and coachability.

Questioning

How do we manage our cognitive biases and achieve genuine Socratic appreciation for the unknown? Socrates, having acknowledged the universal state of man as ignorant, used questioning to fill gaps in knowledge. As is known by many

---

[25]   Original source unknown. See https://izquotes.com/quote/328568.

[26]   Original   source   unknown.   See   https://twitter.com/biiimurray/status/603262580119842816?lang=en.

[27]   Dunning, supra note 11 ("The key lesson of the Dunning-Kruger framework is that it applies to all of us, sooner or later. Each of us at some point reaches the limits of our expertise and knowledge. Those limits make our judgments that lie beyond those boundaries undetectable to us.").

[28]   Dunning, supra note 9.

[29]   See https://www.brainyquote.com/quotes/confucius_131984.

readers in the form of the Socratic method of teaching in law schools, Socrates believed that wisdom and learning are achieved by using questions to probe the validity of an assumption. Such questioning allows learners to analyze the logic of an argument and explore the unknown.

The first step to competence thus is to acknowledge our relative ignorance. Just as it is a common mantra within self-help circles that a first step in improvement is to recognize that you have a problem, a critical step in developing your professional persona is to evaluate as objectively as possible your weaknesses and identify the areas in which you would like to improve. It is important that we question our own competence rather than falling into the well-established pattern of exaggerating our skills and abilities.[30]

Reflection

Reflection is a process by which one intentionally evaluates and internalizes thoughts about her own work,[31] and as such is a form of proactive, self-guided learning. The process of reflection has been described as a "bedrock of professional identity."[32] Done with sincerity and commitment,[33] reflection is a tool that enables each of us to take an active role in and responsibility for our professional growth and development. Reflection can be thought of as a mechanism by which we perform a self-audit, a "self-improvement algorithm,"[34] a way to be "[ ]our own devil's advocate."[35] If done properly, it allows us to build new ways of understanding our actions and our motivations, evaluating our behavior, and adjusting what we do,

---

[30] David Dunning himself recognizes the value of the Socratic method of teaching. "In the classroom, some of [the] best techniques for disarming misconceptions are essentially variations on the Socratic method." Dunning, supra note 9.

[31] "Reflective practice is the integration of intentional thought and specific action within a professional context." Timothy Casey, Reflective Practice in Legal Education: The Stages of Reflection, 20 Clinical L. Rev. 317, 322 (internal citation omitted) (2014), version available at http://www.law.nyu.edu/sites/default/files/upload_documents/Timothy%20Casey%20-%20Stages%20of%20Reflection.pdf.

[32] Linda Finlay, Reflecting on "Reflective Practice," Practice-Based Professional Learning Centre, The Open University 2 (January 2008), available at http://www.open.ac.uk/opencetl/sites/www.open.ac.uk.opencetl/files/files/ecms/web-content/Finlay-(2008)-Reflecting-on-reflective-practice-PBPL-paper-52.pdf.

[33] See Section D., infra.

[34] Casey, supra note 31, at 321.

[35] Dunning, supra note 9.

all with an eye toward improving our decision-making processes for the future.

There is science to back up the value proposition of reflective practice. The brain's default mode, critical for the development of cognitive abilities, is activated by internal reflection.[36] Researchers have found that reflective practice can be a catalyst for growth that leads to better performance because "more deliberate cognitive processes" allow for the "articulation and codification of" knowledge[37] and gives us the ability to assess causal relationships between actions and outcomes, self-efficacy, judgment, and collaboration.

Reflective practice produces a number of specific benefits:

- *Self-Awareness*—Reflection leads to greater self-awareness because it lets us deliberate on the cause and effect of various potential actions and gives us insight into strengths and weaknesses. Reflecting on failures permits us to consider how they might have been avoided. Learning from our experiences allows us to adjust our behavior in the future, when necessary, and provides affirmation when we do something well. Reflective practice gives us insights into patterns of behavior—those of ourselves and of others. Such self-awareness also enables us to question assumptions that may underscore our decision-making processes and other behaviors.

- *Cause and Effect*—Reflection also reduces causal ambiguity.[38] A better understanding of the results of what we have done allows us to better connect our actions to outcomes.

- *Self-Efficacy*—Self-efficacy, a person's belief in her ability to succeed, is enhanced by reflective

---

[36] Giada Di Stefano, Francesca Gino, Gary P. Pisano, & Bradley R. Staats, Making Experience Count: The Role of Reflection in Individual Learning 5 (citations omitted) (2014), available at https://papers.ssrn.com/sol3/papers.cfm?abstract_id=2414478.

[37] Maurizio Zollo & Sidney G. Winter, Deliberate Learning and the Evolution of Dynamic Capabilities, 13 Organization Science 339, 340 (2002), available at https://pubsonline.informs.org/doi/pdf/10.1287/orsc.13.3.339.2780.

[38] Di Stefano, Gino, Pisano, & Staats, supra note 36, at 10 (citations omitted).

practice. Self-efficacy offers enormous benefits to professionals and is correlated with greater motivation to learn and ultimately succeed.[39] Although self-efficacy is derived from numerous sources, the "main and most reliable source is one's own prior experience with the tasks in question."[40]

- *Judgment*—Reflective practices enhance one's professional judgment. Reflective practice gives inexperienced lawyers the tools with which to develop greater intuition-based judgment.[41]

- *Collaboration*—Reflective practitioners more often seek a "real connection to the client"[42] and thus may well have better collaborative relationships with their clients.

Each of us needs to develop a process of habitual reflection that works for us. Because reflection is context driven and individualized, each person will approach his own reflective

---

[39] Id. at 8–9.

[40] Id. at 9. See also Filippa Marullo Anzalone, It All Begins with You: Improving Law School Learning Through Professional Self-Awareness and Critical Reflection, 24 Hamline L. Rev. 324, 340 ("Self-awareness allows an individual to experience or change his or her feelings. It can help an individual to develop a sense of self-efficacy, a readiness to learn, that will have a profound effect on his or her ability to learn") (internal citation omitted) (2001), available at https://papers.ssrn.com/sol3/papers.cfm?abstract_id= 718101.

[41] "Experts draw upon experience to distinguish relevant information from irrelevant, to assess the risks of different courses of actions . . . [T]he expert will choose a particular course of action [from among other possible courses of action] by using professional judgment." Casey, supra note 31, at 318. See also id. at 318–19 (citations omitted) ("Professional experience informs the expert's intuition, and shapes the exercise of judgment. . . . [T]he expert might also rely on 'gut,' or intuition, in the exercise of professional judgment. Professional experience allows the expert to analyze instantaneously the factors that could affect the professional performance or the outcome."); id. at 319 (citations omitted) ("Deliberate reflection provides the new professional with a process to develop professional judgment. New professionals lack experience—the very thing that allows a professional to exercise professional judgment. This deliberate process of reflection is necessary because new professionals cannot rely on intuition or 'gut' in the same manner as an expert. While the seasoned professional integrates seamlessly thought and action, the new professional must de-couple the action from the thinking about the action; the new professional must consciously activate a process to guide the rendering of professional judgment. This is not meant to imply that experienced professionals have no need for reflective practice. Rather, they are more likely to integrate reflection in their practice," a notion known as reflective practice.).

[42] Donald A. Schön, The Reflective Practitioner: How Professionals Think In Action 300 (1983).

practice in a different way, which is likely to change over time and be different across a range of situations.

Our individual reflective process must be genuine; "bland, mechanical, unthinking"[43] reflection is not effective. In approaching self-reflection, we need to confront and manage our weaknesses, mistakes, and failures. While any process of reflection should allow us space to acknowledge what we have done well, we should avoid rationalizing our actions, which serves only to reinforce behaviors that, upon proper reflection, could be improved.

The reflective cycle embraces intentional contemplation at three points in time relative to a specific action:[44] First, there must be reflection *before* taking an action. This includes carefully thinking through the possible approaches and the implications of each potential approach. Second, there must be assessment *during* an action as we seek to complete the relevant task. Donald Schön uses the term "reflection in action," which has the power to "reshape[ ] what we are doing while we are doing it."[45] Finally, there must be contemplation *following* completion of an action, which provides an opportunity to examine the efforts we have undertaken and the manner in which the task was completed.

To be meaningful, reflection must be systematic, rigorous, and continuous. Create a habit of reflection by building moments of reflection into your regular routine. These do not need to be large chunks of time but each of us should have a pattern of thoughtful analysis before and after decisions are made. Some professionals use journals for pre- and post-activity reflection. Many value having such a concrete activity as a ready-made framework within which to reflect.

Reflection, important as it is to professional development, has its limits; it cannot and should not account fully for our efforts to learn and achieve competence. The Dunning-Kruger

---

[43] Finlay, supra note 32. See also Casey, supra note 31, at 322 ("Reflective practice is not the same as occasional review or reflection about a past professional experience, rather, it is the ingrained habit of constant reflection.").

[44] Schön, supra note 42, at 309–10.

[45] Donald A. Schön, Educating the Reflective Practitioner: Toward a New Design for Teaching and Learning in the Professions 26 (1987).

effect weakens our ability to engage in genuine reflection. In one study, subjects took a test on reflectivity and were then asked to evaluate their own reflective skills. Consistent with Dunning and Kruger's hypotheses, most of those who were unreflective mistakenly believed that they did well.[46]

Another impediment to learning through reflection is that people who are highly rational and goal-oriented—as many lawyers are—may be less adept at developing and reflecting on multiple options.[47] Significantly, given the strong emphasis across professions on substantive knowledge, we are often distracted from the processes associated with effective problem solving.[48] Indeed, legal education may contribute to this shortcoming. Typical doctrinal classes relentlessly seek "the answer." This, coupled with legal education's evaluation of students based principally on external metrics, may in fact deter any disposition toward genuine contemplation. Lawyers thus need to overcome our natural and learned disinclination toward meaningful reflection.

Observation and Imitation

"Watch and listen to your seniors. Think about what factors go into their decisions. When you aren't sure about why they made a specific decision, ask them." Honorable Loretta A. Preska, United States District Court for the Southern District of New York[49]

Observation and imitation (also known as observational learning and vicarious learning) are important behaviors to adopt as we develop our professional persona. It is important that each of us has role models that we admire, and that we observe and imitate a range of professionals in various settings.[50]

---

[46] Gordon Pennycook, Robert M. Ross, Derek J. Koehler, & Jonathan A. Fugelsang, Dunning-Kruger effects in reasoning: Theoretical implications of the failure to recognize incompetence, 24 Psychol. Bull. Rev. 1774 (2017), available at https://link.springer.com/article/10.3758%2Fs13423-017-1242-7.

[47] Donald A. Schön & Chris Argyris, Theory in Practice: Increasing Professional Effectiveness 63–95 (1974, 2002).

[48] Donald A. Schön, supra note 42, at 21–49.

[49] Email from Judge Preska to the author (July 15, 2018), on file with the author.

[50] See the discussion of mentors and sponsors in Chapter 7.C.2., infra.

Studies confirm that behaviors are strengthened, weakened, or maintained by the modeling behavior of others.[51] Inappropriate or appropriate behavior can be modeled, and positive and negative reinforcements play a role in how we imitate the behavior of others.[52]

When imitating, we should choose diverse role models and adopt those features that fit our own personal style. Rather than imitating others "wholesale," it is more effective to "borrow[ ] selectively from various people to create your own collage, which you then modify and improve."[53] When observing the behavior of others, we must determine which behaviors we admire and fit our conception of our own professional persona and which do not.[54] Modeling thus necessitates the exercise of discretion and thoughtful reflection.

When observing behavior, it is also important that we try to understand the reasons behind the actions of others. Observing and imitating are of great benefit, but if we truly comprehend the decision-making processes motivating specific actions and behaviors, we can more readily adapt our own behavior to new situations.

Observing and modeling are particularly important considering the constraints imposed by our natural cognitive biases. By observing others, we can better assess our own relative strengths and weaknesses. It has been found that "research subjects were willing to criticize their own previous poor skills once they were trained up and could see the difference between their previous poor performance and their new improved performance."[55] Behavior modeling is based on the

---

[51] See Albert Bandura, Influence of Models' Reinforcement Contingencies on the Acquisition of Imitative Responses, 1 J. of Personality & Soc. Psychol. 589 (1965) (explaining the bobo doll experiment, in which children observing adults play with bobo dolls mirrored the activity they observed, whether it was aggressive or non-aggressive), available at http://citeseerx.ist.psu.edu/viewdoc/download?doi=10.1.1.461.6634&rep=rep1&type=pdf.

[52] Id. at 594.

[53] Herminia Ibarra, The Authenticity Paradox, Harvard Business Review (January–February 2015), available at https://hbr.org/2015/01/the-authenticity-paradox.

[54] See the discussion of authenticity in Chapter 4.C.6., infra.

[55] Mark Murphy, The Dunning-Kruger Effect Shows Why Some People Think They're Great Even When Their Work is Terrible, Forbes (January 24, 2017), available at https://www.forbes.com/sites/markmurphy/2017/01/24/the-dunning-kruger-effect-

notion that people will inevitably learn when they see things done in a specific way, and will learn things more quickly than they would without the benefit of observation.[56] Observation and imitation thus are crucial elements of the path to competence.

Coachability

Coachability refers to our capacity to solicit, receive, and integrate feedback. Coachability inherently invokes self-awareness and its essence is humility. Those who are coachable appreciate that there are other ways to approach situations and that there are things that we can learn from others. Being coachable is not a sign of weakness or vulnerability; it is, to the contrary, a sign of fortitude.

We all know people who lack the ability to be coached. These people believe that they are always right and would rather remain convinced of their correctness than improve what they do. They are arrogant; they refuse to take personal responsibility for their actions; they resist feedback by being defensive or making excuses; they blame others for their shortcomings; they lack general interest in self-assessment or self-improvement; they are not receptive to change or to learning new things or new approaches; they exude a sense of negativity and pessimism; and they are not team players. These individuals get stuck in the stage of unconscious incompetence and tend to plateau early in their careers.

Those who are coachable possess endless potential. They embrace a commitment to learning and improving; they accept responsibility for their behavior and do not look to place blame or responsibility on others; they demonstrate a strong sense of self-awareness by recognizing their own weaknesses; they demonstrate tolerance for a high degree of candor by soliciting, actively listening to, synthesizing, and integrating constructive feedback. Coachable individuals are willing to learn new things and ways of doing things, to go outside their comfort zone, and to engage in discussions that might be uncomfortable; and they collaborate and work well in teams and appreciate the

---

shows-why-some-people-think-theyre-great-even-when-their-work-is-terrible/ (reporting on a discussion with Professor Dunning).

[56] See Albert Bandura, Social Learning Theory 22 (1977).

perspectives of others, which they view as opportunities to learn and grow.[57]

Have you ever had a conversation with someone who was seeking advice or assistance, and who had a "but" response or counterargument to every suggestion you offered? These people are not easily coachable. These people are not truly looking for advice or solutions, they are looking for validation, and when they do not receive it they become defensive. Others who are not coachable are those who always have excuses and explanations for missteps. These people typically lack the insight and self-awareness to be truly coachable.

Being coachable requires that we accept that there are things that we do not know. This goes contrary to our natural tendencies and cognitive biases, which render us largely incapable of accurately assessing our own weaknesses. Consequently, there must be people whose judgment we come to trust so deeply and inherently that we accept their guidance even when we are unable to appreciate its wisdom. Have confidence in those whose judgment you value.

B. THE IMPORTANCE OF
INTERNALIZATION AND
HABIT FORMATION

"It makes no small difference . . . whether we form habits of one kind or of another . . . ; it makes a very great difference, or rather all the difference." Aristotle[58]

"Habit is . . . the enormous fly-wheel of society, its most precious conservative agent." William James[59]

---

[57] An article in Forbes sets forth the following aspects of coachability: Humility, action bias, purity of purpose, willingness to surrender control, and faith. August Turak, Are You Coachable? The Five Steps to Coachability, Forbes (September 30, 2011), available at https://www.forbes.com/sites/augustturak/2011/09/30/are-you-coachable-the -five-steps-to-coachability/.

[58] Aristotle, Nicomachean Ethics, Book II (translated by W.D. Ross), available at http://classics.mit.edu/Aristotle/nicomachaen.2.ii.html.

[59] William James, The Laws of Habit, 30 Popular Science Monthly 433, 446 (February 1887), available at https://en.wikisource.org/wiki/Popular_Science_Monthly/ Volume_30/February_1887/The_Laws_of_Habit.

"The chains of habit are too weak to be felt until they are too strong to be broken." Samuel Johnson[60]

"Habit is a cable; we weave a thread of it each day, and at last we cannot break it." Horace Mann[61]

Habits can be powerful tools that define us. Poor habits can undermine our growth while positive habits can advance our professional development. Habits serve us well because once we internalize behavior we save time and energy associated with decision-making and can react appropriately, even when under stress. The formation of constructive habits is hard work, but achievable with the right motivation and commitment.

1. The Nature of Habit

Habit has been defined as "a settled tendency or usual manner of behavior," "a behavior pattern acquired by frequent repetition or physiologic exposure that shows itself in regularity or increased facility of performance," and "an acquired mode of behavior that has become nearly or completely involuntary."[62] Habits are distinguishable from other behaviors because "[o]nly minimal, sporadic thought is required to initiate, implement, and terminate actions that in the past have been repeated in stable contexts. . . . [H]abit performance reflects the routine repetition of past acts that is cued by stable features of the environment."[63]

When building a professional persona, it is important to develop robust habits. Elements of our professional persona must take on a genuine pattern of regularity and become so routinized that they are essentially automatic and subconscious.

The lawyer's toolkit already provides a ready source of insight into the meaning and importance of habit. Rules of evidence at both the state and federal levels admit evidence of *habit* but not evidence of less predictable traits of character to

---

[60] See https://quoteinvestigator.com/2013/07/13/chains-of-habit/.

[61] See https://www.goodreads.com/quotes/1007349-habit-is-a-cable-we-weave-a-thread-of-it.

[62] See https://www.merriam-webster.com/dictionary/habit.

[63] Wendy Wood, Deborah A. Kashy, & Jeffrey M. Quinn, Habits in Everyday Life: Thought, Emotion, and Action, 83 J. Personality & Soc. Psychol. 1281, 1281 (2002), available at https://pdfs.semanticscholar.org/dac6/ddda7bc9e733d5bf4df12dd1d4d6c625 1faa.pdf.

prove conduct on a particular occasion.[64] For instance Rule 406 of the Federal Rules of Evidence recognizes that the force of habit is so strong and so deeply internalized that evidence of such behavior is admissible *even when not substantiated.* Compare this with character evidence, which generally is not admissible to show that a person behaved in a manner consistent with that character.[65]

The Advisory Committee notes for Rule 406 differentiate proof of character from habit evidence, describing habit "as more specific [than character evidence]. It describes *one's regular response to a repeated specific situation . . .* such as the habit of going down a particular stairway two stairs at a time, or of giving the hand-signal for a left turn."[66] Character, on the other hand, is a "generalized description of one's disposition, or of one's disposition in respect to a general trait, such as honesty, temperance, or peacefulness."[67] In order to be considered a habit, courts have found that the conduct or behavior in question must be reflexive or semi-automatic; frequently, consistently, and regularly engaged in; and specific or particular.[68]

The probative value of evidence of habit is a reflection of its stability, automatic nature, and reliability—the kind of stability, automatic nature, and reliability we should strive for in developing various elements of our own professional persona.

---

[64] Compare, e.g., Rule 404(a) and Rule 406 of the Federal Rules of Evidence.

[65] Federal Rule of Evidence 404.

[66] Federal Rule of Evidence 406, Notes of Advisory Committee on Proposed Rules (emphasis added), available at http://uscode.house.gov/view.xhtml?req=federal+Rule+of+evidence+406&f=treesort&fq=true&num=70&hl=true&edition=prelim&granuleId=USC-prelim-title28a-node218-article4-rule406.

[67] Id.

[68] See, e.g., *Simplex, Inc. v. Diversified Energy Sys., Inc.*, 847 F.2d 1290, 1293 (7th Cir. 1988) ("before a court may admit evidence of habit, the offering party must establish the degree of specificity and frequency of uniform response that ensures more than a mere 'tendency' to act in a given manner, but rather, conduct that is 'semi-automatic' in nature"); *Peshlakai v. Ruiz*, 39 F. Supp. 3d 1264, 1275 (D.N.M. 2014) (habit describes one's regular response to a repeated specific situation); *Nelson v. City of Chicago*, 810 F.3d 1061, 1073 (7th Cir. 2016) (offering party must establish degree of specificity and frequency of uniform response that ensures that conduct is semi-automatic in nature); *Batoh v. McNeil-PPC, Inc.*, 167 F. Supp. 3d 296 (D. Conn. 2016) (same); *Zubulake v. UBS Warburg LLC*, 382 F. Supp. 2d 536, 542 (S.D. N.Y. 2005) (habit is situation-specific and particularized such that it is capable of nearly identical repetition).

2. Why Habits Are Important

"Deep substantive knowledge and critical thinking skills are less than half the equation—attorneys need to develop good habits, reinforced by repetition." Andrew Bonzani, Senior Vice President, General Counsel & Secretary, The Interpublic Group[69]

Developing habits is important to our professional persona for a number of reasons: We rely on habits for many of the tasks that we undertake on a daily basis; habits help us save time and preserve energy for more important decisions; habits make us happier; and having good habits leads to developing other good habits.

We Rely on Habits for Much of Our Daily Routine

Habits have been viewed as thoroughly integral to organisms, both human and otherwise. Noted psychologist and philosopher William James found that "habit covers a very large part of life. . . . The laws of Nature are nothing but . . . immutable habits. . . ."[70] Researchers at Duke University have found that as much as 45% of our daily behaviors are the product of habit rather than decisions.[71] This is possible because of a process known as "chunking," whereby the brain converts a sequence of actions into a routine that happens automatically.[72] Chunking is the foundation of habit formation, and we rely on dozens or even hundreds of behavioral chunks each day.[73] If you are a Macintosh user, try switching to a PC, or *vice versa*, and see how difficult ordinary, automatic computer commands become. When you next visit the grocery store, buy products you have never tried before, and see how long these decisions take compared to simply grabbing the products you buy out of habit. Try putting your shoes on in a different order from what is your habit, or tying your shoelaces backwards. You will be surprised

---

[69] Email from Andrew Bonzani to the author (June 27, 2018), on file with the author.

[70] James, supra note 59, at 433.

[71] Wood, Kashy, & Quinn, supra note 63.

[72] Charles Duhigg, The Power of Habit: Why We Do What We Do in Life and Business 17 (2012).

[73] Id.

by how unsettling these simple activities can become in the absence of habit.

Habits Save Time and Energy

An essential characteristic of habits is that they make certain behaviors intuitive and automatic in nature. Once we have developed habits, they are repeated without effort and save time and energy. President Barack Obama understands the importance of developing habits that allow him to save time and energy for decisions that truly need his full attention:

> "You'll see I wear only gray or blue suits," [Obama] said. "I'm trying to pare down decisions. I don't want to make decisions about what I'm eating or wearing. Because I have too many other decisions to make. . . . You need to focus your decision-making energy. You need to routinize yourself. You can't be going through the day distracted by trivia."[74]

Biology confirms this common sense rationale for habit development: Having habits "simplifies the movements required to achieve a given result, makes them more accurate and diminishes fatigue."[75] Because of the human tendency "to do more things than [man] has ready-made arrangements for in his nerve-centers . . . our nervous system grows to the modes in which it has been exercised."[76]

Our brains in fact are disposed toward patterns precisely because following patterns conserves mental activity. The brain "is constantly looking for ways to save effort"[77] and "habits allow our minds to ramp down more often,"[78] saving the brain exertion and leaving more mental energy for more particularized thoughts and actions.[79] When a habit emerges, the brain "stops

---

[74] Michael Lewis, Obama's Way, Vanity Fair (October 2012), available at https://www.vanityfair.com/news/2012/10/michael-lewis-profile-barack-obama. See also Drake Baer, The Scientific Reason Why Barack Obama and Mark Zuckerberg Wear the Same Outfit Every Day, Business Insider (April 28, 2015), available at https://www.businessinsider.com/barack-obama-mark-zuckerberg-wear-the-same-outfit-2015-4.

[75] James, supra note 59, at 439.

[76] Id.

[77] Duhigg, supra note 72, at 17.

[78] Id. at 18.

[79] Id.

fully participating,"[80] thus preserving precious mental resources and allowing us to commit "our higher powers of mind... [to] their own proper work."[81] Studies bear this out: "As behaviours are repeated in consistent settings they then begin to proceed more efficiently and with less thought as control of the behaviour transfers to cues in the environment that activate an automatic response: a habit."[82]

Habits Allow Us to Work Better Under Pressure

Internalizing behavior allows us to work better under the pressure and strain lawyers experience on a daily basis, because it allows us to "internalize both the reflective and passionate traits of the true professional," which prevent us from acting on impulse, when angry, or without the necessary degree of reflection.[83] Habits, once developed, prepare us for the difficult situations that inevitably arise in the practice of law.[84]

Habits Make Us Happier

As if the professional case for internalization of behaviors were not enough, "the Jamesian conception of habit can be construed as one of the necessary and sufficient conditions to

---

[80] Id. at 20.

[81] James, supra note 59, at 447.

[82] Phillippa Lally, Cornelia H. M. van Jaarsveld, Henry W. W. Potts, & Jane Wardle, How are habits formed: Modelling habit formation in the real world, 40 European J. Soc. Psychol. 998, 998 (2010), available at https://centrespringmd.com/docs/How%20Habits%20are%20Formed.pdf.

[83] Jan L. Jacobowitz, Mindfulness and Professionalism, in Essential Qualities of the Professional Lawyer 203 (2013). See also Patrick J. Schiltz, On Being A Happy, Healthy, and Ethical Member of an Unhappy, Unhealthy, and Unethical Profession, 52 Vand. L. Rev. 871, 911–12 (1999) (noting that habits must be "deeply ingrained in you, so that you can't turn them on and off—so that acting honorably is not something you have to decide to do—so that when you are at work, making the thousands of phone calls you will make and writing the thousands of letters you will write and dealing with the thousands of people with whom you will deal, you will automatically apply the same values in the workplace that you apply outside of work, when you are with family and friends.").

[84] Daisy Hurst Floyd, The Authentic Lawyer: Merging the Personal and the Professional, in Essential Qualities of the Professional Lawyer 27–28 (2013) (Attorneys should "prepare for [challenging] situations by developing the right habits of thinking, doing, and being. These habits ... will guide conduct in a complex and demanding future.").

achieving happiness."[85] Because habits make us more efficient, we have more time to pursue non-work pleasures and interests.

Habits Beget Habits

As many of us have experienced in our own lives, the development of unhealthy habits can lead to a slippery slope. Start eating poorly for a few days or a week and you may notice that your eating habits continue to decline. Take time out from your exercise routine and it may take weeks to get back into a regular schedule. Allow your apartment to get a little untidy, and before you know it, the disorder spreads.

But there is good news: The converse is also true.

Paul O'Neill, Chairman of Alcoa, was able to convert what was described as "one of the largest, stodgiest, and most potentially dangerous companies" into a "profit machine and a bastion of safety."[86] It began with a single habit: Safety. O'Neill made safety a top priority and before long the company not only achieved an outstanding safety record, but in addition there was a ripple effect that led to other productive habits.[87] So-called "keystone habits" are those that become levers for other habits.[88] In the case of Alcoa, they completely transformed the identity of a major corporation.

Keystone habits also work with respect to individual habits. When people start exercising habitually they begin to eat better and smoke less, become more productive at work, use their credit cards less, and generally feel less stressed.[89] Making your bed in the morning has been tied to increased productivity, a greater sense of well-being, and stronger skills in sticking to a budget.[90] For reasons that are not entirely clear,[91] initial shifts in routine

---

[85] Philip T. L. Mack, In Praise of Habit: Making a Case for a Relation Between Happiness and William James's Conception of Habit, 11 William James Studies 96, 96, 99 (2015), available at http://williamjamesstudies.org/wp-content/uploads/2016/02/MACK.pdf.

[86] Duhigg, supra note 72, at 100.

[87] Id.

[88] Id.

[89] Id. at 101, citing James Prochaska.

[90] Id. at 109, citing James Prochaska.

[91] It may be that small habits give us a sense of pride and confidence and lead to positive feedback. See Colin Robertson, Keystone Habits: How One Habit Can Reshape

"start chain reactions" which develop into other good habits.[92] Even small habits can serve as keystone habits from which other habits emerge.[93]

By beginning with some minor professional habits, we gain confidence and feel proud of the professionalism they reflect. We may get positive feedback from others. Slowly, we are motivated to develop more and more significant habits that will come to define our professional persona.[94]

3.   How to Develop Good Habits

Developing good habits is not easy; it requires hard work, determination, and commitment. In order to succeed, we must make a conscious decision to develop new habits; commit and dedicate ourselves to that decision; visualize our new habits; devise a system to keep ourselves accountable; and reward ourselves for a job well done.

Commit to a Deliberate Decision

We must commit ourselves to a deliberate decision to adopt a particular habit. Understanding the importance of developing strong habits associated with our professional lives will give us a strong motivation to succeed.

The quickest way to develop habits is through a "significant emotional experience.[95] A significant emotional experience occurs, for instance, when a child touches a hot stove and burns her hand, causing pain and distress. The child will innately remember this negative experience and is unlikely to touch a hot stove again. Or imagine a man who has struggled with his weight for years and who could never quite commit himself to healthy eating and an exercise regime. The man suffers a life-threatening heart attack—a significant emotional experience—

Your Life (October 23, 2014), available at https://www.linkedin.com/pulse/201410231406 07-89207936-keystone-habits-how-one-habit-can-reshape-your-life/.

[92]   Duhigg, supra note 72, at 102–03.

[93]   Id.

[94]   Habit formation has also been tied to happiness due to the time and physical and mental energy conserved when we internalize behavior. See Mack, supra note 85, at 85.

[95]   Morris Massey, The People Puzzle 18–23 (1979).

and finally is frightened enough to commit himself to a healthy lifestyle.

In the context of law practice, a significant emotional experience of the type described above (burned hand, heart attack) would be unfortunate indeed: Missing a court deadline, inadvertently disclosing confidential client information, giving advice to a client that results in unanticipated tax consequences, to name a few. Engaging in this kind of behavior would be a significant emotional experience that would generate better professional habits, but the downside implications of such an action could be catastrophic.

I observed this in practice when I was a young lawyer: A colleague of mine gave the partner with whom she was working a case that appeared very favorable to a client. Only later—and after the partner had called the client with the good news—did she cite check the case, only to find that it had been overruled. This was for my colleague a significant emotional experience after which she developed the habit of meticulously cite-checking cases, but this was for her an unfortunate incident.

A far better and more proactive approach to developing habits is to set the mind to developing habits associated with a strong professional persona, based on the elements outlined throughout this book. To have the same pull as a negative significant emotional experience, the decision to create a strong professional persona must be one that is taken with intentionality and dedication. Because the speed with which we develop a new habit is largely determined by the intensity of the emotion that accompanies the decision to begin acting in a particular way, it is important to be fully committed to the formation of a new habit.

In order to feel the level of intensity required to develop positive habits, we should have a clear understanding of why we want to develop particular habits—to avoid negative significant emotional experiences, to be sure; but also to serve our clients and employer well; to feel the satisfaction of and personal pride in a job well done; to contribute to society; and for our own career advancement. A decision that is supported by factors that truly motivate us will be a decision that we pursue with a sense of purpose and consequence.

Re-Engineer Your Habit Loop

Most of us have habits that we would like to change. Charles Duhigg speaks of his own personal habit of getting up from his desk every afternoon at 3:00, going to the cafeteria, buying a chocolate chip cookie, and eating the cookie while chatting with colleagues. After his wife commented on his not-so-subtle weight gain, Duhigg decided that he needed to give up his daily cookie habit, and he describes exactly how he did that.[96]

Habits are formed in a three-step loop: (1) A cue or trigger that tells your brain (2) to perform a habitual action and (3) a reward, which helps the brain figure out if this loop is worth remembering for the future.[97] In the case of Duhigg's afternoon cookie, the time—3:00 p.m.—was the cue/trigger; the action was going to the cafeteria and eating a cookie while chatting with colleagues; and the reward was the nice feeling this ritual gave him.

In a habit loop, the cue and the reward become intertwined until the action is automatically repeated.[98] When we have habits that we want to change, we need to find a new routine that is triggered by the same cue and that offers a similar reward.

Duhigg found that he was able to re-engineer his afternoon cookie habit by testing out other behaviors to see which behavior would satisfy the craving and produce the same reward as the cookie. It turns out that it was not hunger or the need for a sugar rush that prompted Duhigg's cookie break—chatting with a colleague during a lull in the afternoon provided much the same reward. By testing different behaviors he was able to isolate that which provided the same reward, and then alter the behavior and cultivate a new, more favorable, craving to drive the loop.[99] So to change a habit, simply keep the old cue and reward, and "shift the routine and change the habit."[100] Try this approach to

---

[96] Duhigg, supra note 72, Appendix. See also https://charlesduhigg.com/how-habits-work/.

[97] Id. at 19.

[98] Id.

[99] Id. at 27.

[100] Id. at 62.

turn a habit of checking social media, for instance, into a habit that is more productive.

The habit loop works for creating new habits as well. Use as triggers things you do every day—your morning coffee, brushing your teeth, taking a shower, for instance. Insert a routine—organizing your desk, answering email, taking time to reflect, for example. Habits will emerge.

Practice, Practice, Practice

"How do you get to Carnegie Hall?" "Practice, practice, practice."[101]

Treat any new goal as a professional athlete or musician would approach her craft. Your decision to adopt new habits and all that this entails must be a commitment from which you do not waver and that allows for no exceptions. Do not make excuses and do not justify any deviations from your goal. In habit development, continuity is critical.[102]

One study on habit formation finds that "early repetition could be expected to result in larger increases as the association between situation and action is created."[103] Your resolve must remain strong even when your new habits are unpleasant or difficult to perform and even when you do not reap immediate benefits. Dr. James likens the restraint needed to develop habits with the rationale for holding insurance:

> The tax does [the policyholder] no good at the time, and possibly may never bring him in a return. But if the fire *does* come, his having paid it will be his salvation from ruin. So with the man who has daily inured himself to habits of concentrated attention, energetic volition, and self-denial in unnecessary things. He will stand like a tower when everything rocks around him, and when his

---

[101] Original source unknown. See https://www.carnegiehall.org/BlogPost.aspx?id=4295022505.

[102] "Never suffer an exception to occur till the new habit is securely rooted in your life. Each lapse is like the letting fall of a ball of string which one is carefully winding up; a single slip undoes more than a great many turns will wind again." James, supra note 59, at 450.

[103] Lally, van Jaarsveld, Potts, & Wardle, supra note 82, at 999.

softer fellow-mortals are winnowed like chaff in the blast.[104]

Like excellence in music or sports, a robust professional persona develops over time through hard work and the development of habit. Be patient as habit formation is a slow process; researchers say that the average time to reach peak automaticity is 66 days.[105] Perseverance is the key to solid and sustainable habit formation, despite the initial inertia that we may experience.

It simply does not work to act professionally only when you think someone important or influential is observing you. You must internalize these behaviors by engaging in them consistently. They will then become second nature and automatic—ensuring both that you will never fall short on your professional identity goals and that you save time and energy for more important, less routine decisions and actions.

Visualize Your New Habits

Some find it helpful to visualize a new habit by imagining themselves behaving in a particular manner in a particular situation. It has been found that "[t]he more often you visualize and imagine yourself acting as if you already had the new habit, the more rapidly this new behavior will be accepted by your subconscious mind and become automatic."[106] Imagine the professional you hope to become, and you will become it.

Keep Yourself Accountable

Keep yourself accountable to your commitment to positive habit formation. Tell a friend, family member, or colleague, who can help keep you responsible for your goals. This kind of external pressure gives many of us the incentive we may need. Others benefit from keeping a record or log of actions taken toward their goal. I keep a weekly diary that contains my to-do list. When I can turn the page with all items completed, it gives

---

[104] James, supra note 59, at 450.

[105] Lally, van Jaarsveld, Potts, & Wardle, supra note 82, at 1002.

[106] Brian Tracy International, 7 Steps To Developing A New Habit, available at https://www.briantracy.com/blog/personal-success/seven-steps-to-developing-a-new-habit/.

me enormous satisfaction; when I have to move unfinished tasks to the next week's page, I am frustrated with myself—frustrated enough that I try hard not to have to transfer items from one week to the next. One needs only to think of the popularity of Apple watches and other exercise trackers to know that many of us respond to this kind of stimulus. Although many people do respond to this kind of stimulus, surely it does not work for everyone; each person must find a method of motivation that drives him.

Reward Yourself

Congratulate yourself when you see elements of your professional persona improving; allow yourself some reward, even if your success is one small habit change. Simply acknowledging the moment, allowing yourself to enjoy it, and smiling can make a difference.[107]

4. You Can't Teach an Old Dog New Tricks. . . .

Conventional wisdom has it that habit formation is most easily achieved by the young.[108] While it may be best to cultivate habits while still young, habits can be developed at any age; well into my 50s I have been able to cultivate habits that have served me well. For instance, when surgery sidelined me from the gym for several months a few years ago, I decided to make the 2.8-mile walk from my home to my office each morning and back again each evening. The key, I discovered, in fact was to allow for no exceptions or excuses. If I had allowed myself to take public transportation whenever I was too busy or too tired, or when the weather was too cold, too hot, rainy, or snowy, I never would have been able to make this practice habitual. In writing

---

[107] Scientific evidence suggests that genuinely smiling can make you feel happier. See, e.g., Melinda Wenner, Smile! It Could Make you Happier, Scientific American (September 1, 2009) (quoting Charles Darwin as saying that "[t]he free expression by outward signs of an emotion intensifies it.), available at https://www.scientificamerican.com/article/smile-it-could-make-you-happier/.

[108] William Benjamin Carpenter, Principles of Mental Physiology, With Their Applications to the Training and Discipline of the Mind, and the Study of its Morbid Conditions 339 (1900) ("It is a matter of universal experience," it has been said "that every kind of training for special aptitudes, is both far more effective, and leaves a more permanent impress, when exerted on the growing organism, than when brought to bear on the adult."), version available at https://ia902607.us.archive.org/21/items/principles ofment00carprich/principlesofment00carprich.pdf.

this chapter, I gave myself a personal challenge: To change my habit of inserting two spaces after periods and colons (something that many of us who grew up using typewriters do, although the rationale for doing so has been long negated by word processing). It was difficult, and the first days were full of errors and frustration, but after a few weeks I managed to replace one habit for the other.

As of this writing, I am 57 years old—well beyond what traditionally has been viewed as the ideal age for habit development.[109] Whoever is reading this book, at whatever stage of life, should still strive resolutely to develop strong habits of practice.

C. THE INTELLIGENT LAWYER

Intelligence is a construct that is fraught with anxiety for many of us, but it need not be. While Intelligence Quotient (IQ), the traditional standard of intelligence, is generally believed to be immutable, it is far less important than many of us once believed. Emotional and social intelligence are the true drivers of success, and are readily learnable. And there are other forms of intelligence that lawyers can develop to enhance their legal professional personae.

1. Intelligence as Contextual and Multidimensional

"One's intelligence is the sum of one's habits of mind."
Lauren B. Resnick[110]

Intelligence is a complicated construct composed of various capabilities in different shapes and sizes. The notion of intelligence as multi-faceted has been described as "one of the most powerful, liberating forces ever to influence the restructuring of education, schools, and society."[111] Because intelligence grows incrementally through "a continuously

109 James suggests that 20–30 is the best age for developing habits. James, supra note 59, at 447.

110 Lauren B. Resnick, Making America Smarter, Education Week 38 (June 16, 1999), available at https://www.edweek.org/ew/articles/1999/06/16/40resnick.h18.html.

111 Arthur L. Costa & Bena Kallick, Changing Perspectives About Intelligence, in Learning and Leading with Habits of Mind: 16 Essential Characteristics for Success 5 (2008), available at http://www.ascd.org/publications/books/108008/chapters/Changing-Perspectives-About-Intelligence.aspx.

expandable repertoire of skills and ... through a person's efforts,"[112] we should devote constant efforts to self-improvement.

2. The Unspectacular Importance of Intelligence Quotient for Lawyers

One's IQ once was considered to be the sole or primary indicator of intelligence and success. There is no doubt that intelligence, in the classic sense, matters. IQ is a pretty good indicator of the extent of one's ability to engage in logic, abstract reasoning, learning ability, and working-memory capacity—how much information you can hold in your mind.[113]

But it is commonly believed that the results of such tests do not matter as much as once was believed. IQ scores fail to account for an array of other skills and behaviors that can be far more predictive of success. In other words, our IQ score is only a small part of the story of how far we go in life—academically and professionally (and personally). A high IQ alone is not an indicator of success.

Daniel Goleman, the most influential writer on emotional and social intelligence makes a compelling case that lawyers (and other professionals) should not care much about their IQ: Goleman finds that professionals need an IQ of 115[114] or higher to be able to handle the cognitive complexities of their work; beyond that, "intellect loses its power to determine who will emerge as a productive employee or an effective leader."[115] In other words, IQ scores above what you need to manage the rigors of law school and legal practice do not contribute in meaningful ways to our success. This is because analytical thinking is not enough to make us successful lawyers—our inter- and intra-

---

[112] Id. at 7.

[113] See, e.g., Yale School of Management, Center for Customer Insights, Why a high IQ doesn't mean you're smart, available at https://som.yale.edu/news/2009/11/why-high-iq-doesnt-mean-youre-smart.

[114] Only 15 percent of the population has an IQ of 115 or higher. See Mindware, Attain A 115 IQ—A High IQ (available at http://www.highiqpro.com/high-iq-115); IQ Basics, IQ Comparison Site, available at https://www.iqcomparisonsite.com/IQBasics.aspx.

[115] Daniel Goleman, They've Taken Emotional Intelligence Too Far, Time (November 1, 2011), available at http://ideas.time.com/2011/11/01/theyve-taken-emotional-intelligence-too-far/.

personal capacities are also deeply meaningful to our professional development.

Believing IQ to be a singular or even primary feature of intelligence gives rise to a form of intellectual laziness. Because most people consider one's IQ to be relatively fixed,[116] undue focus on IQ gives us very little incentive to develop other forms of intelligence.[117] Once we allow ourselves to recognize the value of cultivating other indicia of intelligence, we open ourselves to a world of possibilities.

The average IQ of lawyers appears to be well above the national average.[118] Lawyers' emotional and social intelligence, however, is below average.[119] Many of us thus fail to make full use of our potential by leaving our emotional and social intelligence underdeveloped. In addition, the non-lawyers that we work with on a daily basis, including many of our clients and staff members, enjoy levels of emotional and social intelligence that exceed ours, putting us at a notable disadvantage.

3.   The Primacy of Emotional and Social Intelligence

Our success is closely connected to how robustly we define our emotional and social intelligence.[120] The concepts of emotional and social intelligence are interrelated, but they have distinct features. Emotional intelligence focuses primarily on how we handle our own emotions, and "includes the ability to engage in sophisticated information processing about one's own and others' emotions and the ability to use this information as a

---

[116] But not everyone believes that IQ is fixed. See, e.g., Arthur Whimbey & Linda Shaw, Intelligence Can be Taught (1975). Others have demonstrated that intelligence is in part is a function of environment, including experience and mediation by parents, teachers, and caregivers. See Reuven Feurstein, Instrumental enrichment: An intervention program for cognitive modifiability (1980).

[117] See, e.g., Costa & Kallick, supra note 111, at 7.

[118] Gaston Kroub, Beyond Biglaw: Are You Smart Enough To Be A Good Lawyer?, Above the Law (November 18, 2014), available at https://abovethelaw.com/2014/11/beyond-biglaw-are-you-smart-enough-to-be-a-good-lawyer/.

[119] Id.

[120] The ability to see the world through the eyes of others is listed as one of the 26 effectiveness factors in the classical empirical study by Professors Marjorie M. Shultz and Sheldon Zedeck. See Marjorie M. Shultz & Sheldon Zedeck, Predicting Lawyer Effectiveness: Broadening the Basis for Law School Admission Decisions, 36 L. & Soc. Inquiry 620, 630 (summer 2011), available at http://citeseerx.ist.psu.edu/viewdoc/download?doi=10.1.1.418.7400&rep=rep1&type=pdf.

guide to thinking and behavior."[121] Social intelligence, on the other hand, is more about our ability to relate to others—how we bond with others, empathize with others, engage in social reasoning, and have concern for others. Social prowess, Goleman believes, is what led *homo sapiens* to their most remarkable evolutionary accomplishments.[122] Emotional intelligence thus focuses on "a crucial set of human capacities within an individual, the ability to manage our own emotions and our inner potential for positive relationships," whereas social intelligence goes "beyond a one-person psychology. . . to a two person psychology: what transpires as we connect."[123]

As indicated in the previous section, lawyers tend not to have strong emotional or social intelligence. This may in part be because as a group we are disproportionately "thinking" types rather than "feeling" types,[124] and as a result we "tend to be more logical, unemotional, rational, and objective in making decisions and perhaps less interpersonally oriented. . . ."[125]

Emotional and social intelligence are discussed in the sections below, and specific elements of these forms of intelligence are also discussed in subsequent chapters. At the outset, it bears noting the enormous impact these forms of intelligence can have on our professional development. One study concludes that the few attorneys who scored above average in emotional intelligence were "star performers" who "stood out from the rest."[126] Because so few attorneys demonstrate high levels, developing our emotional intelligence is a great

---

[121] David R. Caruso, John D. Mayer, & Peter Salovey, Emotional Intelligence: New Ability or Eclectic Traits?, 63 Am. Psychol. 503, 503 (2008), available at http://ei.yale. edu/wp-content/uploads/2013/11/pub172_MayerSaloveyCaruso.AmericanPsychologist. 2008.pdf.

[122] Daniel Goleman, Social Intelligence: The New Science of Human Relationships, Appendix C, 329 (2006).

[123] Id. at 5.

[124] Susan Daicoff, Lawyer Know Thyself: A Review of Empirical Research on Attorney Attributes Bearing on Professionalism, 46 Am. U.L. Rev. 1337, 1392–93 (1997) (referring to characteristics on the Myers-Briggs Type Indicator), available at http:// digitalcommons.wcl.american.edu/cgi/viewcontent.cgi?article=1406&context=aulr.

[125] Id. at 1394.

[126] See Steven J. Stein & Howard E. Book, The EQ Edge: Emotional Intelligence and Your Success 317 (2011). See also Goleman, supra note 115 ("In a high-IQ job pool, soft skills like discipline, drive and empathy mark those who will emerge as outstanding."). In addition, "[t]he emotional brain responds to an event more quickly than the thinking brain." http://www.shareguide.com/Goleman.html.

differentiator. We ignore emotions at our peril. The advantages of social intelligence likewise are several and fairly obvious: A robust level of social intelligence allows us to connect with others and build healthy and successful relationships based on trust and respect; enables us to read and understand people and situations; and gives us the tools to respond to people and situations in intelligent ways.

Emotional Intelligence

Different scholars view emotional intelligence differently but there is broad consensus that its fundamental essence relates to how we understand and process emotions in guiding our thinking and behavior. As Dr. Goleman writes, we may not be able to dictate the emotions we feel, but we do have choices in terms of how we express those emotions.[127] Learning to understand and control emotions is at the heart of emotional intelligence.

Psychologists Peter Salovey and John Mayer first coined the phrase "emotional intelligence,"[128] which they describe as "a set of conceptually related mental processes involving emotional information,"[129] which arms us with "the ability to monitor one's own and others' feelings and emotions, to discriminate among them, and to guide one's thinking and action."[130] They divide emotional intelligence into the following clusters:[131]

- Perceiving our own and others' emotions

- Understanding emotions

- Using emotions to facilitate thinking

- Managing emotions to achieve specific goals

Emotional intelligence in these ways enhances intellectual functioning and enables us to do our best work.

---

[127] Daniel Goleman, Emotional Intelligence: Why It Can Matter More than IQ 189–190, 119 (1995).

[128] See Yale Center for Emotional Intelligence, History, available at http://ei.yale.edu/who-we-are/history/.

[129] Peter Salovey, John D. Mayer, & Marc A. Brackett, Emotional Intelligence: Key Readings on the Mayer and Salovey Model 6 (2004).

[130] Id.

[131] Id. at 165.

In particular, emotional intelligence facilitates relationships and enables our interactions with clients, judges, colleagues, and others with whom we come into contact. Emotional intelligence also allows us to react in intelligent ways. Because emotions work faster than intellect,[132] when we react with our emotions rather than our thinking mind, emotional intelligence helps us respond more appropriately.

Employers take emotional intelligence into account as an important element of their hiring decisions and they seem to value emotional intelligence more than IQ.[133] An oft-cited survey finds that employees with emotional intelligence are preferred because they are more likely to stay calm under pressure; know how to resolve conflicts effectively; are empathetic to team members and react accordingly; lead by example; and make thoughtful business decisions.[134] Additional qualities admired in managers with high emotional intelligence include the ability to admit to and learn from mistakes; keep their emotions in check; have thoughtful discussions on difficult issues; listen as much as or more than they speak; take criticism well; and show grace under pressure.[135] Dr. Goleman's research confirms the importance of emotional intelligence in hiring, finding that more than two-thirds of major businesses look for elements of emotional intelligence in recruiting, advancement, and leadership development.[136]

Emotional intelligence can be developed throughout the course of one's life.[137] In fact, our emotional intelligence increases with age,[138] and emotional intelligence has been shown

---

[132] As Daniel Goleman notes, "[t]he emotional brain responds to an event more quickly than the thinking brain." Dennis Hughes, Interview with Daniel Goleman, Share Guide, available at http://www.shareguide.com/Goleman.html.

[133] CareerBuilder Survey, available at https://www.careerbuilder.com/share/about us/pressreleasesdetail.aspx?id=pr652&sd=8/18/2011&ed=08/18/2011.

[134] Id.

[135] Id.

[136] Cary Cherniss & Daniel Goleman, The Emotionally Intelligent Workplace: How to Select for, Measure, and Improve Emotional Intelligence in Individuals, Groups, and Organizations (2001).

[137] See, e.g., Daniel Goleman, available at http://www.danielgoleman.info/enhancing-emotional-intelligence/.

[138] Daniel Goleman, What Makes a Leader? In Organizational Influence Processes 240 (2d. ed. 2003) ("One thing is certain: emotional intelligence increases with age. Here is an old-fashioned word for the phenomenon: maturity.").

to increase after even a short period of training.[139] All of us—no matter how refined we think our emotional intelligence is[140]— should endeavor to enlarge it.

Social Intelligence

Social intelligence relates to how we get along with others, referred to colloquially as "people skills." Social intelligence can be thought of as "a combination of a basic understanding of people—a kind of strategic social awareness—and a set of skills for interacting successfully with them."[141]

Social intelligence thus reflects our ability to be socially aware and to manage our relationships intelligently. This includes the ability to pick up on the emotions of others and figure out what is really going on with them; to appreciate the perspective of others; to understand the impact of our communications on others; to cultivate relationships with a diverse array of people; to manage interactions effectively; and to engage with others toward a common goal.

Daniel Goleman in his book *Social Intelligence* divides the concept into two principal elements: Social awareness (primal empathy, atonement, empathic accuracy, and social cognition) and social facility (synchrony, self-presentation, influence, and concern).[142]

People with high levels of social intelligence typically have strong verbal fluency and conversational skills; understand social roles, rules, and scripts; exhibit strong listening skills; and have an understanding of "what makes other people tick." Such people know how to play different social roles to enable them to feel comfortable with different types of people; are socially self-confident; and have "social self-efficacy." They also have

---

[139] See, e.g., Delphine Nelis, Jordi Quoidbach, Moïra Mikolajczak, & Michel Hansenne, Increasing emotional intelligence: (How) is it possible?, 47 Personality and Individual Differences 36 (March 6, 2009), available at https://orbi.uliege.be//bitstream/ 2268/30253/1/Nelis%20PAID%202009.pdf.

[140] And remember the challenges to self-evaluation discussed in Section A.2., supra.

[141] See Karl Albrecht, Social Intelligence: The New Science of Success, available at http://karlalbrecht.com/articles/pages/socialintelligence.htm.

[142] Goleman, Social Intelligence, supra note 122, at 84.

"impression management skills," a blend between authenticity and managing and controlling our public image.[143]

As with emotional intelligence, social intelligence can be learned by developing attentiveness to others; learning to interpret cues we receive from others; and monitoring our own reactions in social situations.[144] Simply being more attentive to others and less self-absorbed—features that are achievable by all—enable us to expand our social intelligence.[145]

Wanting to be socially intelligent thus goes a long way toward developing such skills.

4.   Other Forms of Intelligence

Other forms of intelligence that lawyers would do well to develop include technological intelligence, law project management skills, and business literacy. There may well be other forms of intelligence that are important to specific practice areas and to serve particular clients.

Technological Intelligence

Technological advances have had enormous implications for the practice of law.[146] Law practice technology refers to the intersection of technology and the practice of law. It does not refer to being able to use the basic Microsoft suite of products that are commonly used by legal professionals and just about everyone else. Proficiency with using these tools is a given.[147]

Understanding the theoretical and practical underpinnings of current and emerging technologies and how they impact the practice of law, including the benefits and risks associated with each, can be an important differentiator for attorneys. This is true for those in any practice scenario—law firms, in-house,

---

[143] Ronald E. Riggio, What Is Social Intelligence? Why Does It Matter?, Psychology Today (July 1, 2014), available at https://www.psychologytoday.com/us/blog/cutting-edge-leadership/201407/what-is-social-intelligence-why-does-it-matter.   See   the discussion of authenticity, infra Chapter 4.C.6.

[144] See Nancy Snow, Virtue as Social Intelligence: An Empirically Grounded Theory 80 (2009).

[145] See Goleman, supra note 122, at 54.

[146] See Chapter 2.B.2., supra.

[147] Law students and law graduates who lack competence in these tools should learn them. Procertas offers a technology tool that allows legal professionals to assess and enhance their fluency in basic tools of the trade. See https://www.procertas.com/.

government, non-governmental organizations, etc. But the proliferation of law practice technology also has resulted in new career paths for lawyers—many firms now have C-suite executive positions that require law management expertise and there are a range of legal service provider positions that seek similar skill sets. This skill set is also valuable for entrepreneurs and others working in alternative legal services firms—a thriving area for development.[148]

Technological intelligence also allows us to comply with rules governing professional conduct requiring competence.[149] Such rules impose an obligation of maintaining competence, which includes "[keeping] abreast of changes in the law and its practice, including the benefits and risks associated with relevant technology. . . ."[150]

Law practice technology includes a range of practice systems and services: Client management, including conflict checks, document sharing, cloud storage, and billing; project management, including case management systems; data management, including technology assisted document drafting and review, eDiscovery, and cloud computing; knowledge and information management; artificial intelligence and predictive analytics; data and information security for law management; and courtroom and presentation technologies. Lawyers should also have basic familiarity with practice tools offered by the major legal information and technology vendors. All attorneys should work toward developing their competency with such tools and keeping appraised of this rapidly developing space.

Law Practice Management Skills

Law practice management, defined as "the art and science of creating and operating a sustainable law firm," embraces a range of skills that are extraordinarily important for

---

[148] See Chapter 2.B.2., supra.

[149] See, e.g., Rule 1.1 of the ABA Model Rules of Professional Conduct, available at https://www.americanbar.org/groups/professional_responsibility/publications/model_rul es_of_professional_conduct/rule_1_1_competence.html.

[150] Rule 1.1 of the ABA Model Rules of Professional Conduct, Comment 8, available at https://www.americanbar.org/groups/professional_responsibility/publications/model_ rules_of_professional_conduct/rule_1_1_competence/comment_on_rule_1_1.html.

attorneys.[151] These skills include project and operations management—things like billing, managing workload, staff management, financial management, office management, and marketing.

Once the province of managing partners or senior staff members, law practice management skills are critical for every attorney to possess. It is no longer sufficient just to be a good practitioner.

Legal project management has been described as "the newest trend in legal service delivery—promising effectiveness, efficiency, and lower cost."[152] Such techniques can help "identify best practices for scoping a matter, effectively communicating across the team, managing a budget, and monitoring progress."[153] Legal project management also involves working well with legal operations and procurement professionals.

Business Literacy

Understanding business basics is of critical importance for lawyers. Basic literacy in business matters provides two distinct advantages: It allows us to better understand both our clients and their needs[154] and law firms and other organizations for which we work. The fact that so many law firms and in-house legal departments offer "mini-MBA" programs for their attorneys suggests the importance of these skills for lawyers.[155]

Business concepts with which legal professionals should have a basic familiarity include financial literacy basics such as

---

[151] Richard S. Granat & Stephanie Kimbro, The Teaching of Law Practice Management and Technology in Law Schools: A New Paradigm, 88 Chi-Kent L. Rev. 757, 758 (2013), available at https://scholarship.kentlaw.iit.edu/cklawreview/vol88/iss3/6/.

[152] Sheri Palomaki & Felice Wagner, Legal Project Management from the Inside: 10 Things Law Firm Leaders Need to Know about Implementing Legal Project Management, Law Practice Today (August 2011), available at https://www.americanbar.org/content/dam/aba/publications/law_practice_today/legal_project_management_from_the_inside.authcheckdam.pdf.

[153] Id.

[154] See Chapter 7.D.1., infra.

[155] See Alina Dizik, Law Firms Embrace Business School 101, The Wall Street Journal (May 20, 2009), available at https://www.wsj.com/articles/SB124277243918636 539; Dan Packel, Law Firms Make a Push to Improve the Associate Experience, The American lawyer (June 28, 2018), available at https://www.law.com/americanlawyer/2018/06/28/law-firms-make-a-push-to-improve-the-associate-experience/.

financial statements, financial reporting, corporate finance, valuation, securities; alternative fee arrangements; human resources; and marketing. Attorneys who have an appreciation for these concepts are better prepared than others to fully appreciate the nature of their own businesses and those of their clients.

D. THE DEFINING NATURE OF LEADERSHIP

1. Leadership for Life

"[L]eadership is everyone's business."[156] Each of us is defined by the leadership qualities that we exhibit. Everything we do in every facet of our lives should be imbued with the outlook of a leader. Leadership does not depend on formal position, title, power, or authority;[157] it is a mindset, an approach, a professional orientation that reflects our view of ourselves with relation to others and our ability to inspire and unite. Everyone can—and should—exhibit leadership qualities.

2. Why Every Lawyer Needs to Be a Leader

It has only recently become fashionable to speak of leadership and lawyers in the same sentence. Once thought to be largely the province of those in business or politics, it is now widely recognized that lawyers need to inhabit traits of leadership to effectively compete and thrive in today's challenging marketplace.

Lawyers indeed hold many important positions of leadership. They hold a disproportionate percentage of positions in all levels of government, in business, and in non-profit organizations.[158] Of course they also occupy leadership roles in

---

[156] Donald J. Polden, Leadership Matters: Lawyers' Leadership Skills and Competencies, 52 Santa Clara L. Rev. 899, 903 (2012), available at https://digitalcommons.law.scu.edu/cgi/viewcontent.cgi?article=2718&context=lawreview.

[157] "Leadership is a process, not a position, a relationship, or a status." Deborah L. Rhode, Lawyers as Leaders 203 (2013). Leadership is distinctive from management. Management issues and approaches are discussed in Chapter 5, infra.

[158] Id. at 1; Neil W. Hamilton, Ethical Leadership in Professional Life, 6 U. St. Thomas L. J. 358, 378–79 (2009). See also Tom Bolt, From the Chair, Law Practice Today (December 14, 2015) ("The legal profession has provided a majority of American presidents and, more recently, almost half of the U.S. Congress. In the business world, lawyers constitute at least 10 percent of the S&P 500 companies' CEOs. In addition to

law firms, whether they are managing partners or members of the firm's governing board, or whether they are simply managing a team of junior lawyers in a particular practice area or group.[159]

But lawyers need to be leaders in more commonplace ways and in more routine settings. "Lawyers are called upon to lead every day."[160] The authors of a Harvard Law study confirm that "the concept of lawyer as leader. . . is not limited to those lawyers who find themselves in formal leadership positions."[161] All of us need the skills of a leader in our everyday work. Leadership, therefore, should be a goal for all of us, regardless of position or career path.[162]

Vision, interpersonal skills, self-awareness, the power to influence, and similar concepts discussed in this chapter, are critical across a range of contexts and are important attributes of a professional mindset at any level. Every attorney and aspiring attorney—including students and junior associates— are judged by whether they inhabit the traits and characteristics of a leader. Leadership skills for attorneys are particularly important because they offer "skills and abilities necessary for successful engagement in civic responsibilities, for meeting the requirements of client representation, and for managing the responsibilities within a law firm or law organization."[163]

---

serving in customary roles as judges, prosecutors, corporate counsel and law firm managing partners, members of the bar also serve in leadership roles as governors, state legislators, and leaders in government and nonprofit organizations. Every day, we see lawyers chairing community and charitable boards—lawyers leading in every aspect of our day to day life."), available at http://www.lawpracticetoday.org/article/from-the-chair-dec/.

[159] Rhode, supra note 157, at 1 ("Even when they do not occupy top positions in their workplaces, lawyers lead teams, committees, task forces, and charitable initiatives").

[160] Herb Rubenstein, Leadership for Lawyers 3 (2d ed. 2008). Lawyers "provide leadership in positions or roles that have formal directing authority (such as governmental appointments, service on boards of public and non-profit firms, and directing a law firm) and they demonstrate leadership through their influence and persuasion in relationships with clients. . . ." Polden, supra note 156, at 905.

[161] Ben W. Heineman, Jr., William F. Lee, & David B. Wilkins, Lawyers as Professionals and as Citizens: Key Roles and Responsibilities in the 21st Century, Harvard Law School Center on the Legal Profession 11, available at https://clp.law.harvard.edu/assets/Professionalism-Project-Essay_11.20.14.pdf.

[162] Polden, supra note 156, at 900, citing Gregory Williams, Teaching Leaders and Leadership, the Newsletter (AALS, Washington, D.C.), April 1999.

[163] Id. at 911.

Leadership for lawyers is particularly relevant today as
"[c]ontemporary leaders confront a landscape of increasing
competition, complexity, scale, pace, and diversity."[164] This
imperative is borne out by the fact that leadership has been
identified as a core competency in skills-based models of
review.[165]

3.   What Is a Leader?

Definition Is Elusive and Situational

No single definition of leadership will be appropriate across
the range of circumstances calling for leadership skills. There
are, however, traits that are highly predictive of leadership
talent. Among the competencies that have been identified as
central to leadership are decision-making, influence, fostering
innovation and managing change, conflict management,
communication;[166] maintaining strategic perspective, setting
and achieving priorities, increasing accountability;[167] and vision,
ethics, interpersonal skills, technical competence, and personal
capabilities such as self-awareness and self-control.[168] Others
have described leaders as those who model the way for others,
inspire a shared vision for change, challenge the process,
encourage others to act toward change, and encourage the
heart.[169] Motives, values, competence, and style are all part of
the leadership mindset.[170]

---

[164] Rhode, supra note 157, at 203. See also Deborah L. Rhode, 3 Lawyers and
Leadership, 20 The Prof. Law 1 (2010) ("Our profession's need for leaders with inspiring
vision and values has never been greater.").

[165] See Heather Bock & Lori Berman, Building and Using an Associate Competency
Model, Prof. Dev. Q. Aug. 2006, at 1–2. One firm defined leadership for this purpose as
"taking an active role in motivating, inspiring, and coaching people to enable team,
individual and organizational effectiveness." Id. See also Chapter 2.C., supra.

[166] Rhode, supra note 157, at 40–81.

[167] See information on Altman Weil Excellence in Law Firm Leadership Seminar,
June 7, 2017, Philadelphia, available at http://www.altmanweil.com/index.cfm/fa/se.
seminar_detail/oid/103b3292-2a0c-4b49-bc6b-d329e97cbcc8/seminars/Excellence_in_
Law_Firm_Leadership.cfm.

[168] Rhode, supra note 157, at 4.

[169] James M. Kouzes & Barry Z. Posner, The Leadership Challenge 11–20 (6th ed.
2017).

[170] David H. Maister, True Professionalism: The Courage to Care About Your
People, Your Clients, and Your Career 66 (2000). See also Tom Salonek, The 100 Building
Blocks for Business Leadership (2016); 101 Best Leadership Skills, Traits & Qualities—
The Complete List, available at http://briandownard.com/leadership-skills-list/.

In addition to being hard to define, the nature of leadership changes depending on the context.[171] There is no specific leadership strategy that works across the range of circumstances in which a professional may find herself. For this reason, one quality that all leaders share is adaptability. The ability to identify and implement the leadership style appropriate to a specific situation and to be agile and nimble, is critical to any aspiring leader.[172] Leaders, it has been said, need a "[r]epertoire of [s]tyles,"[173] "multiple approaches and an understanding of when each is the most appropriate."[174]

Given the disparate characterizations of essential leadership characteristics and the fact that leadership strategies are situation-based, understanding how to become a leader may seem like an insurmountable challenge. To the contrary, leadership competency is accessible to and achievable by a wide range of individuals with differing styles and levels of experience. Each of us can—and should—build a brand of leadership that is most comfortable for us, that makes use of our individual strengths, and that is adaptable to a broad range of circumstances.

Leaders Are Change Agents

Leaders must be able to foster change. Because leadership can be viewed as "the creation and fulfillment of worthwhile opportunities by honorable means,"[175] "a process by which an individual or a group influences others to achieve positive and ethical change,"[176] the ability to inspire and motivate others is a hallmark of a strong and effective leader.[177] A leader needs to

---

[171] Deborah L. Rhode, supra note 157, at 4 (2013).

[172] "Leaders need multiple approaches and an understanding of when each is most appropriate." Id. at 22.

[173] Id.

[174] Id. at 87.

[175] Rubenstein, supra note 160, at 13.

[176] Polden, supra note 156, at 903, citing Donald J. Polden, Educating Law Students for Leadership Roles and Responsibilities, 39 U. Tol. L. Rev. 353, 356 (2008).

[177] "Leadership is about producing change, while management focuses on producing predictability over processes." Roland B. Smith, The Struggles of Lawyer-Leaders and What They Need to Know, NYSBA Journal 38, 38 (March/April 2009), available at http://myccl.ccl.org/leadership/pdf/landing/NYSBAJournalMarApr09.pdf.

inspire others to share his vision and model the way toward that vision.[178]

Imagine an attorney on your team who has a spotty reputation for her work and loses clients on a regular basis, largely because she is said to be slow to respond to calls and emails, she sometimes goes to meetings unprepared, she fails to identify creative solutions to problems, and her judgment at times is questionable. Is this a person that could easily encourage others to follow her lead? Would anyone be induced to be influenced by her?

Now imagine an attorney who is known for his dedication to his clients, his thoughtful judgment, his outstanding counseling skills, his superb level of preparation, and his ability to make deals happen, in large part due to his effective negotiation prowess and his talent to think strategically and outside the box. This is the kind of person that can engage others to follow him.

Leaders Are Visionaries

To successfully promote change, leaders must be able to identify and pursue opportunities for impact.[179] Leaders thus are forward looking and innovative, have an entrepreneurial spirit,[180] and are able to imagine possibilities and find a common purpose.[181]

Leaders Have Impressive Technical Skills

The only way to begin to establish the credibility needed to lead is to demonstrate outstanding skill in what you do. Technical competence therefore is an essential pre-requisite to leadership.[182] If you want to be a lawyer who leads, you must first and foremost be an outstanding lawyer. Merely doing a good job is not enough to rise to the level of a leader. It is always necessary to take the extra step, to walk the extra mile. The

---

[178] Polden, supra note 156, at 904.

[179] Rhode, supra note 157, at 4, citing Maureen Broderick, Leading Gently, The American Lawyer, December 2010, 63–64.

[180] Rubenstein, supra note 160 at 13. Leaders also help motivate others. Id. at 25.

[181] Kouzes & Posner, supra note 169, at 97.

[182] Rhode, supra note 157, at 4 (referring to knowledge, preparation, and judgment), 9; Kouzes & Posner, supra note 169, at 34–35 (recognizing competence as an important characteristic associated with leaders); Maister, supra note 170, at 66.

credibility that comes with excellence is an essential element of leadership.[183] Just as leadership is an element of excellence, so too is excellence an important condition for leadership.

Leaders Have Strong Personal and Interpersonal Skills

The ability to lead requires a suite of personal and interpersonal skills, as discussed below.[184]

Leaders Have Strong Personal Skills—Leaders demonstrate an array of personal skills, including a strong ethical and moral core; self-awareness; an ability to self-regulate; commitment, motivation, enthusiasm, and energy; creativity; and decision-making skills.

Leaders have a strong moral compass. Because leaders need to motivate and inspire others, leaders must have a strong ethical and moral core and continuously display values that others admire and want to emulate. Integrity,[185] ethics,[186] trust, veracity, and credibility[187] have been found to be critical to development as a leader. Evidence of these goals and values must be found in prior behavior.[188] Building a solid core of values and morals as early as possible in our development helps pave the way for leadership.

Leaders are self-aware. Self-awareness is "the ability to recognize and understand your moods, emotions, and drives as well as their effect on others."[189] The best leaders, it has been said, are " 'exquisitely sensitive to the impact they are having on others,' and able to adjust their styles accordingly."[190] The

---

[183] Credibility needed to influence has been identified as an important element of leadership. See Polden, supra note 156, at 904. See also Robert Cullen, The Leading Lawyer: A Guide to Practicing Law and Leadership 9–12 (Thomson Reuters/West 2009).

[184] These skills overlap with the notion of emotional intelligence, discussed in more detail in Section C., supra.

[185] Rhode, supra note 157, at 4, citing Maureen Broderick, The Art of Managing Professional Services (2010).

[186] Id. at 10, citing Center for Creative Leadership, When it Comes to Leadership Talent (2009).

[187] Polden, supra note 156, at 903.

[188] Maister, supra note 170, at 67.

[189] Daniel Goleman, What Makes a Leader?, Harv. Bus. Rev. Nov.–Dec. 1998, reprinted at https://hbr.org/2004/01/what-makes-a-leader.

[190] Rhode, supra note 157, at 22, quoting Goleman, supra note 189.

importance of this particular skill has been widely recognized, with some scholars suggesting that "[s]elf-awareness may be the single most defining foundation for professional development."[191] It is important that we develop an ability to reflect thoughtfully on our own behaviors and how they impact others.

Leaders self-regulate. Self-regulation is about one's "ability to control or redirect impulses and moods" and "the propensity to suspend judgment—to think before acting."[192] Many of us have the tendency to communicate without thinking things through as carefully as we should. To reflect carefully on what we say, how we say it, and when we say it is an important attribute of maturity and emotional intelligence that is often overlooked, particularly in this age of instantaneous communication. Self-regulation also includes the ability to manage time, meet deadlines, and prioritize multiple commitments.[193]

Leaders exude personal energy, enthusiasm, motivation, and commitment. As Daniel Goleman defines it, motivation is "passion for one's work" and "a propensity to pursue goals with energy and persistence."[194] Commitment—genuine commitment—flows from this passion. And motivation and commitment have the power to evoke enthusiasm and energy— which are contagious.

Leaders are creative. Lawyers need to be creative with respect to problem solving when confronted with client matters. A lawyer with a creative bent and the inclination to think "outside the box" for solutions to legal problems is a lawyer who can be a true problem solver—something that clients genuinely value.

Lawyers also need to be creative on the business side. Those who develop "constructive new ideas on how to improve things"[195] rather than simply identifying problems are marked

---

[191] Rhode, supra note 157, at 10, citing Center for Creative Leadership, When it Comes to Leadership Talent (2009).

[192] Goleman, supra note 189.

[193] See Chapter 5.A., infra.

[194] Goleman, supra note 189.

[195] Maister, supra note 170, at 69.

for leadership. As discussed earlier,[196] the ability to promote innovation and manage market, legal, technological, and other changes is crucial, particularly in today's climate for lawyers.

Leaders are adept at decision-making. Decision-making is an essential leadership skill, and central to this is the "ability to make sound decisions and to develop decision-making processes that will enable subordinates to do the same."[197] Decision-making should have two primary attributes: Quality and acceptability.[198]

Leaders Have Strong Interpersonal Skills—Leaders are able to build strong relationships "built on trust, veracity and credibility."[199] Characteristics such as the ability to listen, inspire, and influence have been found to be central to leadership success.[200] Sensitivity to others has been identified as a particularly important feature of leadership.[201]

Leaders have empathy for others. Empathy speaks to "the ability to understand the emotional makeup of other people" and "skill in treating people according to their emotional reactions."[202] As with self-awareness, those who can put themselves in the position of other people and who can appreciate how others feel are well positioned to become leaders.

Leaders act collaboratively. Leaders are highly collaborative and inclusive in their approach. They engage others in decision-making processes and they listen to and take advice and suggestions from others.[203] They always seek input with ample

---

[196] See Chapter 2, supra.

[197] Rhode, supra note 157, at 40.

[198] Id.

[199] Polden, supra note 156, at 903.

[200] Rhode, supra note 157, at 4, citing Maureen Broderick, The Art of Managing Professional Services (2010).

[201] See, e.g., Justin Menkes, Heightened Sensitivity: why It's Such a Critical Leadership Component (June 27, 2011), available at https://www.tlnt.com/heightened-sensitivity-why-its-such-a-critical-leadership-component/.

[202] Goleman, supra note 189.

[203] Rubenstein, supra note 160, at 14 (a leader gets buy-in, is not dictatorial, and is collaborative).

time to reflect on advice received[204] and can explain, and are willing to explain, why they chose one path over another.

Leaders elicit and are responsive to feedback. Leaders elicit genuine feedback from all—those superior to them, those who report to them, and those at the same level. They create a safe and supportive environment in which others can offer critical suggestions, and make a genuine effort to act on thoughtful suggestions for improvement.

A sense of humility is important to leadership.[205] One must have some humility in order to meaningfully receive feedback and act on constructive criticism. Without humility, one is likely to believe that hers is the only legitimate approach. Those who have a healthy dose of humility are much more amenable to suggestions and to self-improvement.

Leaders have a genuine interest in and focus on maximizing the goals of the institution and others within the organization. A leader sublimates his self-interest to the larger goals of colleagues and the institution. "Enduring legacies are left by those who advance collective purposes and transcend personal needs in pursuit of common values."[206] In addition, a strong leader genuinely gets "satisfaction from the accomplishments of others."[207]

Once a leader has achieved a supervisory position, she must give feedback to others—as a way of ensuring both that the institution's interests are best served and that junior colleagues continuously develop themselves professionally. Guidance and criticism must be "supportive and nurturing," while on the other hand the leader needs to be "continually demanding, nagging [others] to stretch for [their] next achievement."[208] The best leader "is a friendly skeptic, a loving critic, a challenging

---

[204] A leader "engages in extensive prior consultation on major issues," id., and solicits views "in a timely fashion—early enough to have the chance to make a difference." Maister, supra note 170, at 71.

[205] Roland B. Smith, The Struggles of Lawyer-Leaders and What They Need to Know, NYSBA Journal 38, 40 (March/April 2009), available at http://myccl.ccl.org/leadership/pdf/landing/NYSBAJournalMarApr09.pdf.

[206] Rhode, supra note 157, at 6.

[207] Maister, supra note 170, at 71.

[208] Id. at 70.

supporter—someone not afraid to give both positive and critical feedback, and is involved enough to know when either is due."[209]

Leaders have a vibrant sense of humor, which can "deflect and diffuse tension, relieve stress, and foster collegiality. A capacity for irony and self-deprecating wit is not only appealing in itself, but also signals emotional intelligence."[210]

Leaders have strong communication skills. Because leaders are change agents, they must be able to persuade others—and to do that they must be adept at communication. This includes both sides of the communication binary: The ability to listen, and to speak and write in a way that is compelling and ultimately persuasive.[211] A survey of leaders of law and other professional services firms has identified communication skills, including the ability to listen, as among the most important leadership qualities.[212] Effective communication requires clarity about objectives,[213] understanding the audience,[214] organizing content in a way that is understandable to the audience,[215] presentation skills,[216] and preparation.[217]

Listening is a skill that is often overlooked when we think about communication. But because "leaders try to persuade followers, clients, allies, adversaries, and the broader public,"[218] leaders must be good listeners, a skill that "many law firm leaders rank as their most important skill."[219]

---

[209] Id. Managerial skills are discussed in greater detail in Chapter 8., infra.

[210] Rhode, supra note 157, at 23 (citations omitted). See also id. at 22 (leaders benefit from having a "[r]edeeming [s]ense of [h]umor").

[211] Cullen supra note 183, at 9–12 (noting "communication and persuasion" are among "key traits for leadership").

[212] Maureen Broderick, The Art of Managing Professional Services: Insights from Leaders of the World's Top Firms (2010).

[213] Rhode, supra note 157, at 68–69.

[214] Id. at 69–71.

[215] Id. at 71–77.

[216] Id. at 78–80.

[217] Id. at 80–81.

[218] Id. at 67. See also Chapter 9, infra.

[219] Id., citing Susan G. Manch with Michelle C. Nash, Learning from Law Firm Leaders 91 (2012).

4. Becoming a Leader

Leaders Are Made, Not Born

"Leaders aren't born, they are made. And they are made just like anything else, through hard work. And that's the price we'll have to pay to achieve that goal, or any goal."[220] Vince Lombardi

There is a longstanding and vigorous debate as to whether leaders are born or made. Is leadership a competency that only a few can master as a matter of inherent ability or can one, through observation, introspection, training, and hard work, develop the characters of a leader? Although some take the position that leadership is a trait that is limited to only a few, the far better position, embraced by many who have studied the issue systematically, is that leadership skills can be developed, and that each of us has the capacity to become a leader.

Compelling and diverse voices have embraced the notion that leadership is achievable by all. Professor Deborah Rhode categorically rejects the "assumption that great leaders are born not made."[221]

[M]ost leadership skills are acquired, not genetically based, and decades of experience with leadership development indicate that its major capabilities can be learned. In effect, the "best leaders are the best learners." Individuals who demonstrate leadership potential early in their careers tend to be particularly gifted learners; they are able to absorb ideas and criticisms and translate them into practical strategies.[222]

---

[220] See Kevin Kruse, 100 Best Quotes on Leadership, Forbes (October 16, 2012), available at https://www.forbes.com/sites/kevinkruse/2012/10/16/quotes-on-leadership/. See also Polden, supra note 156, at 903; Maister, supra note 170, at 71.

[221] Rhode, supra note 157, at 25.

[222] Id. (internal footnotes omitted, citing Richard D. Arvey, et al., The Determinants of Leadership Role Occupancy: Genetic and Personality Factors, 17 Leadership Quarterly 1 (2006); Bruce Avolio, Pursuing Authentic Leadership Development, in Handbook of Leadership Theory and Practice 739, 752 (2010); Warren G. Bennis & Burt Nanus, Leaders: Strategies for Taking Charge 207 (1997); Sharon Daloz, Leadership Can Be Taught (2005); James M. Kouzes & Barry Z. Posner, The Truth About Leadership (2010); Carrol Dweck, Mindset: The New Psychology of Success (2006); Douglas A.

We thus all have the potential to achieve leadership skills if we are willing to do the hard work that it takes—themes that are explored in greater specificity in Parts III and IV.

Too Early? Too Late?

Leadership is a trait that needs nurturing and development throughout one's professional life—starting *now*. It is neither just for the young nor for the old, just for the rising professional or the more experienced manager. Becoming a leader—and challenging yourself to develop greater leadership skills—is a lifelong process. It is never too late to begin to think and act like a leader, but it is also never too early.

Challenges to Leadership for Lawyers

Lawyers as leaders? To many this sounds like an oxymoron. In fact, many of the skills and characteristics commonly associated with leaders are thought to be largely absent from most lawyers. Indeed, lawyers typically are "highly skeptical, autonomous, antisocial and resistant to new ideas, have a high sense of urgency and are easily discouraged by setbacks. This places them at a considerable disadvantage when it comes to leadership and managerial tasks."[223]

Professor Rhode additionally describes what she calls the "paradox of power," which also impedes development of sustainable leadership qualities:

> Individuals reach top positions because of their need for personal achievement. Yet to perform efficiently in these positions, they need to focus on creating the conditions for achievement by others. . . . If left unchecked, the ambition, self-confidence, and self-

---

Ready, Jay A. Conger, & Linda A. Hill, Are You a High Potential?, Harv. Bus. Rev. 78, 82 (June 2010).

[223] Tom Bolt, supra note 158, citing Larry Richard, The Mind of the Lawyer Leader, Law Practice (September/October 2015), available at http://www.americanbar.org/publications/law_practice_magazine/2015/september-october/lawyer-leader.html. The same author noted that "[a]lthough lawyers are highly intelligent and astute professionals, they are inherently ill-adapted to leadership and management roles." Professor Rhode likewise has observed the "mismatch between the traits associated with leaders and those associated with lawyers." Rhode, supra note 157, at 4.

centeredness that often propel lawyers to leadership roles may sabotage their performance in those roles.[224]

These challenges may suggest that lawyers as a group are ill-equipped to achieve competence in leadership skills. The take-away instead should be that we must be superbly contemplative about ourselves and how we can adjust our behavior to succeed in becoming outstanding leaders. Those who can achieve a high level of self-reflection will quickly distinguish themselves from others who may be less self-aware.

5. In Praise of Followers

This entire discussion about leaders and leadership has an important caveat: That we all must also know how to be followers. Followers provide an enormously useful function and followership has been said to "dominate our lives and organizations."[225] While we should aim to inhabit the characteristics of leaders, we should also be good followers when the circumstances warrant. Each of us will be called upon to be followers, and for most of us followership will be a significant element of our professional lives. Followership is so crucial for organizational and individual success that it has been referred to as "inherently valuable, even virtuous."[226]

Followers are indispensable to the implementation of a leader's vision. Effective followers are those that manage themselves well, are committed to the organization and others beyond themselves, build their focus and abilities to maximize impact, and are "courageous, honest, and credible."[227]

Both leadership and followership are needed in today's legal world. In law, effective followership is essential, and this is particularly true early in one's career where working on teams, with senior attorneys, and with clients can require sublimation and execution of someone else's vision.[228]

---

[224] Id. at 5.

[225] Robert Kelley, In Praise of Followers, Harvard Business Review (November 1988), available at https://hbr.org/1988/11/in-praise-of-followers.

[226] Id.

[227] Id.

[228] See also the discussion on coachability, Section A.2., supra.

At times we should demonstrate the qualities of a leader, and there are other times when followership traits will be more valued. There is wisdom in knowing which role we should advance in any particular context.

E. QUESTIONS FOR REFLECTION[229]

1.   How coachable would you rate yourself on a scale of 1–10, with 10 being the most coachable and 1 being the least coachable? On what basis or bases did you answer this question? Do you think that your answer may be based on an unconscious level of incompetence? Why or why not?

2.   If you do not know what you do not know (as per the Dunning-Kruger effect), what mechanism(s) can you utilize to help you know what you do not know?

3.   Think of someone you admire and respect, preferably someone you have the opportunity to observe on a regular basis. Describe how you have observed and imitated things you admire about that person and how you have adapted those elements to your personality.

4.   Think about three positive habits that you have. What are they and how did you develop then? Think about three habits that you have that you would like to change. What is your strategy for changing them?

5.   Have you ever tested your IQ? If so, how did it make you feel? If not, why not? Knowing what you know after reading this chapter, do you feel differently toward your IQ? If so, why?

6.   Do your consider yourself to be a leader? Why or why not?

7.   Do you consider yourself to be a follower? Why or why not?

---

[229] For those who are not required to answer these questions (for class or a supervisor, for example), are you the kind of person who reads the questions and answers them (either in writing or in your mind)? Or do you ignore the questions altogether? This begins to tell you something about your professional persona.

8. Name a person you find it easy to follow and list three reasons why.

PART II

SELF-MANAGEMENT: PROFESSIONALISM FROM THE INSIDE

CHAPTER 4

MINDSET AND DISPOSITIONS

This chapter addresses mindsets and dispositions that characterize and drive our behavior all day, every day, and are central to developing a successful legal professional persona. These are statements of propensity that suggest what we are likely to do in particular situations,[1] attitudes, moods, intentions, and inclinations that come to define us.[2] As with other elements of one's professional persona, a healthy mindset and dispositions can be cultivated.[3]

This chapter is divided into three sections: Positive mindset; commitment to excellence; and character. Because our mindset and dispositions are interconnected, there is some inevitable overlap among the elements discussed below. They are all part of a larger whole, and all must be addressed intentionally as we develop our professional persona.

A. POSITIVE MINDSET

A positive mindset is one that is growth-based rather than fixed, that is optimistic rather than pessimistic, that embraces enthusiasm and passion, that is grounded on resilience and grit, and that is constantly curious.

1. Growth Mindset

Growth Mindset Defined

Each of us has a mindset that is either fixed- or growth-based, terms coined by the psychologist Carol S. Dweck. Those with a fixed mindset believe that their intelligence and abilities are pre-determined traits that cannot be developed or advanced. Because people with a fixed mindset do not believe that efforts

---

[1] Douglas Thomas & John Seely Brown, ACM Ubiquity—The Power of Dispositions 2 (2008), available at http://www.johnseelybrown.com/ubiquity_dispositions.pdf.

[2] See http://www.dictionary.com/browse/mindset.

[3] Deloitte Center for the Edge, Unlocking the passion of the Explorer 7 (2013), available at https://www2.deloitte.com/content/dam/insights/us/articles/unlocking-the-passion-of-the-explorer/DUP402_Worker-Passion_vFINAL3.pdf.

to learn or determination can make a difference, they do not try to improve themselves.[4] Those with a growth mindset, however, believe that their abilities and intelligence can be enhanced:[5]

> In a growth mindset, people believe that their most basic abilities can be developed through dedication and hard work—brains and talent are just the starting point. This view creates a love of learning and a resilience that is essential for great accomplishment. Virtually all great people have had these qualities.[6]

A growth mindset thus is crucial to personal development and maximization of potential.

Benefits of a Growth Mindset

A growth mindset reflects a sense of achievement orientation—the desire to do better. Those with a growth mindset think about how they can improve[7] and take on and learn from challenges. Acquiring a growth mindset includes understanding that learning and developing takes time and energy, and that things do not come easily to anyone—including those who excel academically and professionally.[8]

Those with a fixed mindset suffer from complementary deficits. Because those with a closed mindset do not believe that additional learning and effort will pay dividends, they do not attempt to improve themselves; and they spend time and energy unproductively because such individuals generally feel a need to validate themselves in the eyes of others.[9]

A growth mindset is also beneficial because it allows us to see beyond zero-sum frameworks—to imagine win-win

---

[4]   See https://mindsetonline.com/whatisit/about/index.html.

[5]   See https://www.mindsetworks.com/science/.

[6]   See https://mindsetonline.com/whatisit/about/index.html. See also Carol Dweck, What Having a "Growth Mindset" Actually Means, Harvard Business Review (January 13, 2016), available at https://hbr.org/2016/01/what-having-a-growth-mindset-actually-means.

[7]   Tyler Roberts, The power of a growth mind-set, The National Jurist 17 (Winter 2018), available at https://bluetoad.com/publication/frame.php?i=462306&p=16&pn=&ver=html5.

[8]   See https://mindsetonline.com/howmindsetaffects/mindsetforachievement/index.html.

[9]   Carol S. Dweck, Mindset: The New Psychology of Success 6 (2006).

possibilities rather than win-lose scenarios. Such a perspective is highly beneficial in law practice and other areas of life.

Professor Dweck appears to view fixed- or growth-based mindsets as binary with regard to specific situations but recognizes that one person can embrace a growth mindset in some circumstances but a fixed mindset in others. I have seen this duality in myself. Generally, I am growth-oriented, but when it comes to technology or math, my mind shuts down with the familiar refrain of one who embodies a fixed mindset.

The mindset that each of us adopts in particular situations—growth or fixed—"profoundly affects" how each of us leads our lives and builds our careers.[10] Choose growth.

2.   Optimism

"No pessimist ever discovered the secret of the stars, or sailed to an uncharted land, or opened a new doorway for the human spirit." Helen Keller[11]

Optimism is defined as "an inclination to put the most favorable construction upon actions and events or to anticipate the best possible outcome."[12] An optimistic worldview can be learned—even by attorneys.

Dispositional Versus Explanatory Optimism

There are two distinct but related approaches to measuring optimism: Dispositional optimism and explanatory optimism.

Dispositional optimism measures optimism in terms of expectancies—our sense of confidence about the attainability of our goals. People with high levels of expectancy or confidence will continue to make an effort to reach their goals, even under adverse or challenging circumstances.[13] Someone with a low level of confidence about the future does not believe that his

---

[10]   Id. at 12.

[11]   Original source unknown. See https://www.brainyquote.com/quotes/helen_keller_161286.

[12]   See https://www.merriam-webster.com/dictionary/optimism.

[13]   Martin E.P. Seligman, Learned Optimism: How to Change Your Mind and Your Life 5 (2011).

efforts will make a difference and therefore is disinclined to do his best to achieve his goals.

Explanatory optimism relates to how a person understands or explains past events, especially those that result in personal loss or defeat. Optimistic people view setbacks as temporary challenges, while pessimists view them as a reflection of helplessness or incompetence.[14]

Benefits of Optimism

There has been a recent surge of interest in optimism as a significant feature of personality and social psychology.[15] Optimism plays a defining role in the study of positive psychology, which focuses on conditions and processes that permit individuals to flourish and excel, rather than traditional psychology's focus on disorders and illnesses.[16] Whether one's explanatory style is optimistic or pessimistic has been tied closely to the likelihood of whether we achieve success, and has been referred to as "the cornerstone of resilience."[17]

Indeed, optimism offers numerous benefits: Optimists are healthier, wealthier, and more successful than pessimists. They are less likely to suffer from depression. They persevere and are determined to succeed, even in the face of drawbacks.[18] Optimists have focused problem-solving techniques,[19] and, compared with pessimists, "enjoy better moods, have a higher

---

[14] Id. at 4–5.

[15] See Catherine Gage O'Grady, Cognitive Optimism and Professional Pessimism in the Large-Firm Practice of Law: The Optimistic Associate, 30 Law & Psychol. Rev. 23, 23 (2006) ("[O]ptimism has enjoyed a heightened respect from sophisticated researchers in personality and social psychology.").

[16] See Martin E.P. Seligman & Mihaly Csikszentmihalyi, Positive Psychology: An Introduction, 55 American Psychologist 5 (January 2000), available at http://www00.unibg.it/dati/corsi/40043/82676-Positive-Psychologie-Aufruf-2000.pdf.

[17] American Bar Association, National Task Force on Lawyer Well-Being, The Path to Lawyer Well-Being: Practical Recommendations For Positive Change 52 (August 14, 2017) (internal citation omitted), available at https://www.americanbar.org/content/dam/aba/images/abanews/ThePathToLawyerWellBeingReportFINAL.pdf.

[18] See Gage O'Grady, supra note 15, at 23 (2006) (internal citations omitted). See also Todd David Peterson & Elizabeth Waters Peterson, Stemming the Tide of Law Student Depression: What Law Schools Need To Learn from the Science of Positive Psychology, 9 Yale J. Health Pol'y L. & Ethics 357, 396 (2009), available at http://digitalcommons.law.yale.edu/yjhple/vol9/iss2/2/.

[19] See Gage O'Grady, supra note 15, at 35–36 (internal citations omitted). See also Peterson & Peterson, supra note 18 at 396.

morale, and experience greater achievement, higher academic performance scores, and greater popularity."[20] A pessimistic explanatory style, to the contrary, has been linked to depression, learned helplessness,[21] and a range of other maladies.[22]

There is a special role for optimism in determining success as a lawyer. Professors Schultz and Zedeck have identified a positive correlation between lawyer success and dispositional optimism as measured on the Revised Life Orientation Test. Dispositional optimism correlates with ten of their 26 effectiveness factors for lawyers, including speaking, networking, passion, stress management, and community service.[23]

Learning Optimism

Professor Martin Seligman, the father of positive psychology, has written an entire book about learning optimism, and vigorously supports the notion that we can learn to be optimistic. Pessimism, he concludes, "is escapable."[24]

One way for those who are pessimistic to develop optimism is to use a "disputing technique" when confronted with difficulties. Such techniques instruct us to recognize challenges as the kinds of issues that others have to deal with; invalidate and dismiss pessimistic thoughts as false and unproductive; and recast the experience in a more optimistic light.[25]

---

[20] Gage O'Grady, supra note 15, at 36 (2006) (internal citations omitted).

[21] Learned helplessness is when a person mistakenly believes that she has no control over a situation. When we experience this state, we are unwilling or unable to modify the situation or solve the problem at hand. See, e.g., https://psychcentral.com/encyclopedia/learned-helplessness/.

[22] Jason M. Satterfield, John Monahan, & Martin E.P. Seligman, Law School Performance Predicted by Explanatory Style, 15 Behav. Sci. & L. 95 (1997), available at https://www.researchgate.net/publication/14057619_Law_School_Perormance_Predicted_by_Explanatory_Style; Explanatory Style (1995); Susan Nolen-Hoeksema, Joan S. Girgus, & Martin E.P. Seligman, Learned Helplessness in Children: A Longitudinal Study of Depression, Achievement, and Explanatory Style, 51 J. Personality & Soc. Psychol. 435 (1986), available at https://ppc.sas.upenn.edu/sites/default/files/lhchildrendepaches.pdf.

[23] Marjorie M. Shultz & Sheldon Zedeck, Predicting Lawyer Effectiveness: Broadening the Basis for Law School Admission Decisions, 36 L. & Soc. Inquiry 620, 635 (2011), available at http://citeseerx.ist.psu.edu/viewdoc/download?doi=10.1.1.418.7400&rep=rep1&type=pdf.

[24] Seligman, supra note 13, at 5.

[25] See Gage O'Grady, supra note 15, at 52 (internal citations omitted).

For example, imagine that you are a junior associate in a law firm. You have submitted a draft contract to your supervisor who has marked up many, many elements of the draft. A person with a pessimistic outlook would probably view those edits as an indictment of her intelligence: "He must think I am an idiot for not preparing a better draft." A more optimistic reaction would be something like this: "I now have a better understanding of the assignment and what I could have done better. This will be very useful for the next time I have to draft a contract," or "It is probably very common that young associates' work is marked up a lot. And each time he gives me feedback, I learn something." Doing so deliberately will help us ward off pessimistic reactions to events. "Credible disputing of pessimistic thinking is . . . self-maintaining because one feels better at the moment one does it."[26] It also may be helpful to visualize positive outcomes, as championship athletes do before competing.[27]

Disputing techniques are designed to make you feel better, to be sure, so that criticism or adversity does not defeat or deflate us. It is not intended, however, to immunize us to the value of constructive criticism. As discussed earlier,[28] it is important that we reflect on and internalize feedback in order to learn from it. The value of disputing techniques does not minimize that obligation—it hopefully puts you in a place from which you can appreciate the feedback for what it is, learn from it, and move on.

---

[26] Martin E.P. Seligman, Paul R. Verkuil, & Terry H. Kang, Why Lawyers are Unhappy, 23 Cardozo L. Rev. 33, 43 (2001), version available at http://www5.austlii.edu.au/au/journals/DeakinLawRw/2005/4.html. The authors posit the following example:

> In the disputing technique, the lawyer first learns to identify catastrophic thoughts she has, and the circumstances under which they occur: "I'll never make it to partner," whenever a senior member of the firm fails to return her greeting. Then she learns to treat these thoughts as if they were uttered by a rival for her job, a third person whose mission is to make her life miserable. She then learns to marshal evidence against the catastrophic thoughts, "Even though he didn't smile when I said 'hi' this morning, he praised my brief in the meeting last week. He is probably on my side and was distracted by the big case he has to argue this afternoon.

Id. at 43.

[27] See, e.g., Christopher Clarey, Olympians Use Imagery as Mental Training, The New York Times (February 22, 2014), available at https://www.nytimes.com/2014/02/23/sports/olympics/olympians-use-imagery-as-mental-training.html.

[28] See Chapter 3.A.2., supra.

Challenges to Optimism for Lawyers

Optimism is more of a challenge for many attorneys than it is for others. We are, it seems, "professional pessimists," constitutionally disinclined toward an optimistic worldview.[29] Pessimism to a point is beneficial for lawyers because it "indicates prudence, skepticism, or caution," all of which are helpful in legal practice[30] given the need to imagine and plan for worst-case contingencies.[31] There is hope, however; we can be taught to embrace a form of "flexible optimism" which allows us to know when to be pessimistic and when to be optimistic[32] and compartmentalize these views to the appropriate context.[33]

3.   Enthusiasm and Passion

"To be a good lawyer you need to have fire in the belly. I have been practicing law for more than 30 years and I still get excited about helping clients work through complex issues. When you lose that, it may be time to move on." Oliver Brahmst, Partner, White & Case LLP[34]

"Make sure you like what you do. It is easier to work hard and work well when you enjoy what you do." Eric F. Grossman, Executive Vice President and Chief Legal Officer, Morgan Stanley[35]

Something that makes young lawyers stand out is "careful selection of, and true engagement in, their chosen practice area. The best and happiest lawyers find every new project, transaction or dispute exciting

---

[29] Gage O'Grady, supra note 15, at 23.

[30] Id. at 38. See also Seligman, Verkuil, & Kang, supra note 26, at 41–42.

[31] Gage O'Grady, supra note 15, at 23. See also M. Mark Heekin, Implementing Psychological Resilience Training in Law Incubators, 1 Touro J. Experiential Learning 286, 297–98 (2016) (if lawyers are not "cognizant of all of the things that can go wrong in the legal matter for which they are engaged, they may not adequately protect the interests of their client."), available at https://digitalcommons.tourolaw.edu/cgi/viewcontent.cgi?referer=https://www.google.com/&httpsredir=1&article=1019&context=jel. See also Seligman, Verkuil, & Kang, supra note 26, at 43 (internal citation omitted).

[32] See also Seligman, Verkuil, & Kang, supra note 26, at 41–42.

[33] Gage O'Grady, supra note 15, at 29.

[34] Email from Oliver Brahmst to the author (July 16, 2018), on file with the author.

[35] Email from Eric F. Grossman to the author (July 16, 2018), on file with the author.

and as an opportunity to further develop their skill sets." Ken Schwartz, Partner, Skadden, Arps, Slate, Meagher & Flom LLP[36]

Enthusiasm and Passion Defined

Having enthusiasm and passion for work is one of the defining forces behind success.[37] Love what you do and embrace a positive attitude. It can be as simple as that.

Worker Passion Is Important but Low

Passionate workers—those that are "committed to continually achieving higher levels of performance"—can drive excellent and sustained performance improvement.[38] Passionate workers demonstrate resilience and an orientation toward learning and improvement that propels personal and organizational success, particularly in the face of market challenges and disruptions.[39] Despite these obvious benefits, fewer than 12.3 percent of U.S. workers possess worker passion.[40]

Embrace "Explorer Passion"

Explorer passion, a particular species of passion, is defined as comprising three characteristics: *commitment to domain* ("a desire to have a lasting and increasing impact on a particular industry or function"); *questing disposition* (those who "actively seek out challenges to rapidly improve their performance"); and *connecting disposition* (those who "seek deep interactions with others and build strong, trust-based relationships to gain new insight").[41] Explorers are more committed than others to continuous development and are more excited about and willing

---

[36] Email from Ken Schwartz to the author (August 7, 2018), on file with the author.

[37] Passion and engagement are listed as among the 26 effectiveness factors in the classical empirical study by Professors Marjorie M. Shultz and Sheldon Zedeck. See Shultz & Zedeck, supra note 23, at 630 (2011).

[38] Deloitte Center for the Edge, Passion at work: Cultivating worker passion as a cornerstone of talent development 4 (2014), available at https://www2.deloitte.com/insights/us/en/topics/talent/worker-passion-employee-behavior.html.

[39] Id.

[40] Id. at 4, 9 (Figure 1).

[41] Unlocking the passion of the Explorer, supra note 3, at 5. See also id. at 9–10.

to undertake new challenges.[42] They use their environments to identify new opportunities and advance their skill set.[43] Explorers are more likely to self-reflect, internalize lessons learned, adjust their behavior accordingly[44] and "deliver sustained and significant performance improvement over time."[45]

Explorers also are different from other workers because they "love their work," which has been said to be the "single best predictor of the passion of the Explorer."[46]

Passion, Not Just Ambition

Passion is not the same thing as ambition. Ambition is marked by a desire for external rewards, goals based on objective metrics, and relationships based on networking goals. A worker of passion will be motivated by intrinsic factors, oriented toward making an impact, and committed toward an industry or domain, and their relationships will be based on the desire to learn.[47] While ambition or drive sometimes is sufficient, passion is needed to excel in environments marked by change and disruption[48] such as that in which today's lawyers find themselves.[49]

Enthusiasm and Passion Are Contagious

As the old saying goes, "enthusiasm is contagious. You can start an epidemic."[50] There is in fact a great deal of truth to this. "[P]ositive affect . . . can spread among groups via emotional contagion."[51] The converse also is true. Our interactions have an "emotional subtext. . . . [W]e can make each other feel a little worse—or a lot worse. . . . Beyond what transpires in the

---

[42] Id. at 18.

[43] Id.

[44] Id. at 19.

[45] Passion at work, supra note 38, at 6.

[46] Id. at 17.

[47] Id. at 11.

[48] Id.

[49] See Chapter 2, supra.

[50] Source unknown.

[51] John D. Mayer, Richard D. Roberts, & Sigal G. Barsade, Human Abilities: Emotional Intelligence, 59 Ann. Rev. Psychol. 507, 524 (2008), available at https://www.annualreviews.org/doi/abs/10.1146/annurev.psych.59.103006.093646.

moment, we can retain a mood that stays with us long after the direct encounter ends—an emotional afterglow. . . ."[52] Mirror neurons provide the scientific explanation for the impact our emotions have on others. These neurons "reflect back on action we observe in someone else, making us mimic that action or have the impulse to do so. These do-as-she-does neurons offer a brain mechanism that explains the old lyric, 'When you're smiling, the whole world smiles with you.' "[53]

"Love the One You're with" [54]: Enthusiasm as a Self-Fulfilling Prophecy

When we fall prey to a bad mood or unhappiness with our work or some other aspect of our lives, it is easy—too easy—to fall into a rapid descent into greater unhappiness. It turns out that up to 40% of our happiness is well within our control.[55] Find even small things that can make you feel happier and focus on the positive aspects of your work and your life more generally; you will experience pleasure you did not realize you would find. I have a friend who told me that when she wakes up feeling blue, she puts on party music and dances while she showers and gets ready for work. By the time she leaves her apartment, she already feels better.

Positive emotions are important in ways that extend beyond the obvious. They contribute enormously to our overall wellbeing and competency as professionals. Positive emotions have been tied to physical wellness,[56] the ability to resist stress and depression,[57] and behavioral outcomes such as more productive workers, better performance in managerial positions, better job

---

[52] Daniel Goleman, Social Intelligence: The New Science of Human Relationships 13 (2006).

[53] Id. at 41.

[54] Stephen Stills, Love the One You're With (1970).

[55] See Sonja Lyubomirsky, Kennon M. Sheldon, & David Schkade, Pursuing Happiness: The Architecture of Sustainable Change, 9 Rev. Gen. Psychol. 111, 116 (2005), available at http://sonjalyubomirsky.com/wp-content/themes/sonjalyubomirsky/papers/LSS2005.pdf.

[56] See, e.g., Sheldon Cohen, William J. Doyle, Ronald B. Turner, Cuneyt M. Alper, & David P. Skoner, Emotional Style and Susceptibility to the Common Cold, 65 Psychosomatic Med. 652 (2003), available at http://kungfu.psy.cmu.edu/~scohen/emostyle%20printfriendly.pdf.

[57] See, e.g., Barbara L. Fredrickson, What Good Are Positive Emotions?, 2 Rev. Gen. Psychol. 300, 307 (1998), manuscript available at https://www.ncbi.nlm.nih.gov/pmc/articles/PMC3156001/.

evaluations, higher pay,[58] better cognitive organization, greater creativity and problem-solving abilities, and intellectual flexibility.[59] Finally, positive emotions are durable in that they "build resources that long outlast the feelings themselves," providing "strength to overcome future obstacles" leading to "enhanced coping skills" and "an upward spiral of positive well-being."[60]

Don't Force a Square Peg into a Round Hole

We also have to acknowledge that not every work environment is a good fit for every individual. Sometimes there is no easy fix—or any fix at all—and the solution is to seek a permanent change rather than doubling down and trying to fit a square peg into a round hole. Wisdom often lies in knowing the difference.

4.   Resilience and Grit

Resilience and Grit Defined

Resilience is the "ability to recover from or adjust easily to misfortune or change."[61] Professor Angela Duckworth, the leading authority on grit, defines it as "perseverance and passion for long-term goals."[62] Resilience thus relates to how we recover from adversity, whereas grit represents a sustained and persistent effort over longer periods of time.

Grit and resilience, however, share many dimensions—they both reflect our drive, motivation, and ability to withstand challenges and adversity. They bring together concepts discussed earlier in this section: A growth mindset that believes

---

[58] See, e.g., Sonja Lyubomirsky, Laura King, & Ed Diener, The Benefits of Frequent Positive Affect: Does Happiness Lead to Success?, 131 Psychol. Bull. 803 (2005), available at https://www.apa.org/pubs/journals/releases/bul-1316803.pdf.

[59] See, e.g., Fredrickson, supra note 57, at 307.

[60] Peterson & Peterson, supra note 18, at 405 (internal citation omitted).

[61] https://www.merriam-webster.com/dictionary/resilience.

[62] Angela L. Duckworth, Christopher Peterson, Michael D. Matthews, & Dennis R. Kelly, Grit: Perseverance and Passion for Long-Term Goals, 92 J. Personality & Soc. Psychol. 1087 (July 2007), available at https://www.researchgate.net/publication/629006 4_Grit_Perseverance_and_Passion_for_Long-Term_Goals. See also Charles Duhigg, The Power of Habit: Why We Do what We do in Life and Business 124 (grit is "the tendency to work strenuously toward challenges, maintaining effort and interest over years despite failure, adversity, and plateaus in progress.").

change through learning is possible; optimism and a worldview that embraces a level of confidence that we can achieve our goals; and passion for what we do and for doing it well.

Resilience

Resilience is the ability to adjust to challenges and change and to bounce back from adversity, and has been described as "the defining concept of [the] twenty-first century."[63] Resilient systems evolve and get stronger when challenged; resilient people "don't just bend and snap back. They manage to get stronger because of the stress."[64] This is very much the way a muscle grows: In order to develop, a muscle must be challenged with overload beyond its current limit.

Resilient individuals also have much in common with those who are growth-based and optimistic: They accept criticism more easily than others, are eager to improve themselves, have broader perspectives, enjoy collaborating, and "generally are able to accomplish more."[65] They are often seen as more successful than others, leading to satisfaction in both their personal and professional lives.[66]

Resilience can be learned,[67] and training programs abound. You can also test your own resilience level to better understand areas in which you may fall short.[68]

Grit

Grit is about a mindset based on growth, optimism, passion, and enthusiasm. Professor Duckworth describes it as follows:

---

[63] Joshua Cooper Ramo, The Age of the Unthinkable: Why the New World Disorder Constantly Surprises Us and What We Can do About It 172 (2009).

[64] Id. at 173

[65] Heekin, supra note 31, at 296.

[66] Id. The Penn Resilience Program, part of the University of Pennsylvania's Positive Psychology Center, identifies six resilience competencies: Self-awareness; self-regulation; mental agility; strengths of character; optimism; and connection. See University of Pennsylvania, Positive Psychology Center, Resilience Skill Set, available at https://ppc.sas.upenn.edu/resilience-programs/resilience-skill-set. Some of these competencies are discussed elsewhere in this and other chapters.

[67] See, e.g., https://ppc.sas.upenn.edu/resilience-programs/resilience-research.

[68] See, e.g., Manfred F.R. Kets de Vries, Assessment: How Resilient Are You?, Harvard Business Review (January 20, 2015), available at https://hbr.org/2015/01/assessment-how-resilient-are-you; see also Resilience Assessment, Resilience Alliance, available at https://www.resalliance.org/resilience-assessment.

Grit is passion and perseverance for very long-term goals. Grit is having stamina. Grit is sticking with your future, day in, day out, not just for the week, not just for the month, but for years, and working really hard to make that future a reality. Grit is living life like it's a marathon, not a sprint.[69]

Professor Duckworth's early work includes a Grit Scale designed to determine which West Point cadets would complete the initial training program, called Beast Barracks. The test was half about perseverance and half about passion,[70] and turned out to be "an astonishingly reliable predictor"[71] of who made it through Beast Barracks, results that were replicated across a range of other environments.[72] Effort, Duckworth finds, counts twice as much as talent,[73] and requires stamina and persistence—sticking with something over time, even when faced with setbacks.[74]

Grit increases over time, so we get grittier as we get older, under a theory known as "the maturity principle."[75] Maturity, gained largely from life experiences, arms us both with a capacity for and an interest in diligence.[76] Grit requires interest in what you do, practice doing it, purpose beyond yourself, and hope that things will get better.[77] As an added benefit, it turns out that gritty people are also happier people.[78]

---

[69] Angela Lee Duckworth, TED Talks Education, Grit: The power of passion and perseverance, available at https://www.ted.com/talks/angela_lee_duckworth_grit_the_power_of_passion_and_perseverance/transcript?language=en.

[70] Angela Duckworth, Grit: The Power of Passion and Perseverance 9 (2016).

[71] Id. at 10.

[72] Id. at 10–14, passim.

[73] Id. at 34. See also id. at 35–51.

[74] Id. at 53–54.

[75] Id. at 86.

[76] Id. at 87.

[77] Id. at 95–195. See also id. at 269 (to develop grit, "[y]ou can cultivate your interests. You can develop a habit of daily challenge-exceeding-skill practice. You can connect your work to a purpose beyond yourself. And you can learn to hope when all seems lost.").

[78] Id. at 270.

5. Curiosity

"I have no special talents, I am only passionately curious." Albert Einstein[79]

Attorneys should be curious, seeking out new information and novel experiences. In this way, curiosity is closely tied to intrinsic motivation.[80] Curiosity offers a host of benefits. In the short term, curiosity engages us to seek out, explore, and immerse ourselves in new situations and experiences. Over time, curiosity serves to "expand knowledge, build competencies, strengthen social relationships, and increase intellectual and creative capacities."[81] Curious people also have strong problem-solving abilities and experience comfort with new situations.[82]

B. COMMITMENT TO EXCELLENCE

"Building a strong reputation requires a lot of work, but also pays off throughout the rest of your career. As a young lawyer, you can start building a strong reputation by paying attention to detail, showing intellectual interest in new topics and focusing on the service nature of our business. And don't forget to take cues from those around you, and ask for feedback." Francesca L. Odell, Partner, Cleary Gottlieb Steen & Hamilton LLP[83]

---

[79] Original source unknown. See https://www.brainyquote.com/quotes/albert_einstein_174001.

[80] See Todd B. Kashdan & Paul J. Silvia, Curiosity and Interest: The Benefits of Thriving on Novelty and Challenge, in Curiosity and Interest 368 (2009), available at https://www.researchgate.net/publication/232709031_Curiosity_and_Interest_The_Ben efits_of_Thriving_on_Novelty_a nd_Challenge. See also Celeste Kidd & Benjamin Y. Hayden, The Psychology and Neuroscience of Curiosity, 88 Neuron. 449, 450 (November 4, 2015) (describing curiosity as a "special form of information-seeking that is internally motivated"), available at https://www.cell.com/neuron/pdf/S0896-6273(15)00767-9.pdf. Intrinsic motivation is discussed in Chapter 6.C.1., infra.

[81] Todd B. Kashdan, Melissa C. Stiksma, David J. Disabato, Patrick E. McKnight, John Bekier, Joel Kaji, & Rachel Lazarus, The five-dimensional curiosity scale: Capturing the bandwidth of curiosity and identifying four unique subgroups of curious people, 73 J. Research in Personality 130, 130 (December 2017) internal citations omitted), available at https://www.researchgate.net/publication/321471978_The_Five-Dimensional_Curiosity_Scale_Capturing_the_bandwidth_of_curiosity_and_identifying_four_unique_subgroups_of_curious_people.

[82] Derek Loosvelt, Why Employers Hire "Curious" Candidates and How to Demonstrate Curiosity in Interviews, Vault (August 14, 2017), available at https://clslegalstaffing.com/articles/why-employers-hire-curious-candidates-and-how-demo.

[83] Email from Francesca L. Odell to the author (June 28, 2018), on file with the author.

Commitment to excellence is a defining characteristic of successful people, and it is demonstrated through several characteristics: Resourcefulness; diligence and dedication; self-discipline and willpower; reliability and preparedness; craftsmanship; adaptability; creativity; and wisdom.

1. Resourcefulness

What Is Resourcefulness?

A person who is resourceful is able to use the tools—the *resources*—at her disposal to come up with solutions to problems. She can work through challenges with minimal supervision.

Why Resourcefulness for Lawyers?

Being resourceful is highly valued in the professional world, because resourceful juniors can preserve the time and energy of more senior team members.[84] When an associate darkens the door of a supervisor every time she has a question, she demonstrates a lack of resourcefulness. When you need input from a more senior person, be sure that you have used all the tools at your disposal—including colleagues—to solve the problem independently before approaching a supervisor. The same, of course, holds true for work with clients.

The Doctrine of Completed Staff Work

A partner at a major international law firm commended to me the so-called Doctrine of Completed Staff Work and requires his associates to read it when they begin working with him. (He also told me that a copy of the Doctrine of Completed Staff Work still hangs on the office wall of one of his partners—the same copy that my acquaintance gave him when the latter was a junior associate.) It so perfectly captures the essence of what it is to be a junior (although it is somewhat dated and some might disagree with a few of the particulars) that it bears quoting at length:[85]

Completed staff work is the study of a problem, and presentation of a solution, by a staff member, in such

---

[84] See Chapter 7.C.1., infra.
[85] Available at http://www.dolan-heitlinger.com/quote/stafwork.htm.

form that all that remains to be done on the part of the boss is to indicate approval or disapproval of the final action. The words "completed action" are emphasized because the more difficult the problem, the more the tendency is to present the problem to the boss in a piecemeal fashion.

It is your duty as a staff member to work out the details. You should not consult your boss in the determination of those details, no matter how perplexing they may be. You may and should consult other staff members. The product, . . . when presented to the boss for approval or disapproval, must be worked out in a finished form.

The impulse which often comes to the inexperienced staff member, to ask the boss what to do, recurs more often when the problem is more difficult. It is accompanied by a feeling of mental frustration. It is easy to ask the boss what to do, and it appears too easy for the boss to answer. Resist the impulse. You will succumb to it only if you do not know your job.

It is your job to advise the boss what she or he ought to do, not to ask your boss what you ought to do. The boss needs answers, not questions. Your job is to study, write, restudy, and rewrite until you have evolved a single proposed action—the best one of all you have considered. Your boss merely approves or disapproves.

. . . . Your views should be placed before the boss in finished form so that the boss can make them his or her views by simply signing the document. . . .

The theory of completed staff work does not preclude a rough draft, but the rough draft must not be a half-baked idea. . . . [A] rough draft must not be an excuse for shifting to the boss the burden of formulating the action.

The completed staff work theory may result in more work for the staff member but it results in more freedom for the boss. This is as it should be. Further . . . [t]he boss is protected from half-baked ideas, voluminous memos, and immature oral presentations. . . .

When you have finished your completed staff work the final test is this:

If you were the boss would you be willing to sign the paper you have prepared and stake your professional reputation on it being right?

If the answer is no, take it back and work it over, because it is not yet completed staff work.

Keep this in mind with respect to any work product you deliver to your supervisor, either orally or in writing.

2. Diligence and Dedication

What Are Diligence and Dedication?

Diligence and dedication both speak to the same thing: Working assiduously to get the job done. These terms imply a steady, earnest, and energetic effort[86] and devotion to one's pursuit.[87] These concepts require conscientiousness and attention to detail.[88]

Why Lawyer Diligence and Dedication?[89]

"Diligence," it has been said, "has many shades of meaning, depending on context, but it *always means the steady application of close attention and best efforts to the task at hand.*"[90] Diligence

---

[86] See https://www.merriam-webster.com/dictionary/diligence.

[87] See https://www.merriam-webster.com/dictionary/dedication.

[88] Attention to detail is one of the top ten capabilities most important for starting lawyers based on the results of a study of 24,000 practicing attorneys around the country. See Institute for the Advancement of the American Legal System, Foundations for Practice: The Whole Lawyer Character Quotient 26 (July 2016), available at http://iaals. du.edu/sites/default/files/reports/foundations_for_practice_whole_lawyer_character_quo tient.pdf.

[89] Diligence is listed as one of the 26 effectiveness factors in the classical empirical study by Professors Shultz and Zedeck. See Shultz & Zedeck, supra note 23.

[90] Daisy Hurst Floyd & Paul A. Haskins, Diligence, Essential Qualities of the Professional Lawyer 117 (2013) (emphasis added). Diligence is one area in which the internalization of habits, as discussed in supra Chapter 3 "Legal Professional Persona Building Blocks," is particularly important. "A notion of constancy resides at the core of diligence. . . . [The] constant state of compliance, across thousands of discrete acts of diligence over a career, cannot occur in a vacuum. It must be a function of a diligent frame of mind—a deeply ingrained habit of mind that makes diligent actions reflexive and automatic for that lawyer, every time." Id. at 118.

in this way can be seen as "vigilance in action."[91] Diligence is particularly important because a duty of diligence is expressly codified in rules of professional responsibility.[92]

Diligence means that we pay meticulous attention to detail at all times.[93] These things matter. Notions of diligence and dedication include setting up and following a set of processes to manage work—everything from client inquiries, deadlines, organizing documents,[94] client development,[95] timekeeping and other administrative tasks, and the range of other responsibilities that are part of a lawyer's work. They include dotting the i's and crossing the t's.

The Role of Initiative

"Volunteer—be the person who wants to do more, who is willing to push himself. Show a strong work ethic—run your engine hot and convey that to others." Eric F. Grossman, Chief Legal Officer, Morgan Stanley[96]

One thing that makes young lawyers stand out is "a commitment to doing the job right and having a take charge attitude—no matter the challenge." Ken Schwartz, Partner, Skadden, Arps, Slate, Meagher & Flom LLP[97]

Initiative means taking charge and acting strategically to resolve challenges,[98] and is an important element of diligence and dedication. Taking the initiative often requires foresight, and it requires us to view our jobs broadly, to see where there is

---

[91] Id.

[92] See American Bar Association Model Rule of Professional Conduct: Rule 1.3 (Diligence), available at https://www.americanbar.org/groups/professional_ responsibility/publications/model_rules_of_professional_conduct/rule_1_3_diligence. html.

[93] Diligence and having a strong work ethic are among the top ten capabilities most important for starting lawyers based on the results of a study of 24,000 practicing attorneys around the country. See Foundations for Practice: The Whole Lawyer Character Quotient, supra note 88, at 26.

[94] See Chapter 5.B.1., infra.

[95] See Chapter 7.D.1., infra.

[96] Email from Eric F. Grossman to the author (July 16, 2018), on file with the author.

[97] Email from Ken Schwartz to the author (August 7, 2018), on file with the author.

[98] See https://www.merriam-webster.com/dictionary/initiative.

a need, and to jump in when appropriate. Be proactive. Identify problems and propose solutions. Anticipate needs and address them without being told.

One of the questions I ask students in my externship seminar involves the role of initiative: "You, a junior associate, are copied on an email from Charles Client to Betty Boss, the partner to whom you report. What do you do?" An answer I hear too often is that since the message was not directed to the associate, there is nothing for the associate to do. This misses the point completely. Instead of this passive response, be proactive and think about what you can do to help the partner respond. If you are not sure, ask.

Build Something

Taking initiative also includes big-ticket items that can be career game-changers. A partner at a large international law firm that I spoke with while writing this book told me that one of the benchmarks for advancement to partner at his firm is whether an associate undertakes efforts to build something. This could be a training program for juniors, a diversity initiative, or something else. This lawyer mentioned that in response to this expectation, one lawyer created a new practice area within the firm that would more fully service existing clients. That new practice area is thriving, and that attorney is now an equity partner.

3. Self-Discipline and Willpower

What Is Self-Discipline and Willpower?

Self-discipline is defined as "correction or regulation of oneself for the sake of improvement."[99] Notions of discipline are closely related to the concept of willpower, defined as "energetic determination"[100] and "the ability to resist short-term temptations in order to meet long-term goals."[101]

---

[99] https://www.merriam-webster.com/dictionary/self-discipline.

[100] https://www.merriam-webster.com/dictionary/willpower.

[101] American Psychological Association, What You Need to Know about Willpower: The Psychological Science of Self-Control (2012), available at http://www.apa.org/helpcenter/willpower.aspx.

Why Self-Discipline and Willpower for Lawyers?

The most famous experiment regarding self-discipline and willpower is the so-called marshmallow test, designed and conducted by psychologist Walter Mischel. In this test, pre-school aged children were allowed to choose a treat—for instance a marshmallow—and eat it immediately, or wait in their seats until the facilitator returned to the room, after which they would be rewarded for their forbearance with two marshmallows.[102] Although the marshmallow test was designed to determine when willpower emerged in children, numerous longitudinal studies confirm a range of significant long-term benefits of willpower: Significantly higher SAT scores, better social cognitive and emotional coping in adolescence, higher educational achievement, higher sense of self-worth, and better ability to cope with stress.[103] The study concludes that resisting temptation "is an essential component of social and cognitive development"[104] and is "more important than IQ in predicting academic success."[105]

How to Build Self-Discipline and Willpower

Self-discipline and willpower are tied to habit; willpower is a crucially important keystone habit for individual success.[106] And "the best way to strengthen willpower. . . is to make it into

---

[102] See Walter Mischel, The Marshmallow Test: Understanding self-control and how to Master It (2014).

[103] See Walter Mischel, Ozlem Ayduk, Marc G. Berman, B. J. Casey, Ian H. Gotlib, John Jonides, Ethan Kross, Theresa Teslovich, Nicole L. Wilson, Vivian Zayas, & Yuichi Shoda, "Willpower" over the life span: decomposing self-regulation, 6 Soc. Cogn Affect Neurosci 252 (April 2011), available at https://www.ncbi.nlm.nih.gov/pmc/articles/PMC3073393/.

[104] Id. at 252.

[105] American Psychological Association, What You Need to Know About Willpower, The Psychological Science of Self-Control 2 (2012), available at http://www.apa.org/helpcenter/willpower.pdf.

[106] Duhigg, supra note 62, at 131 ("Dozens of studies show that willpower is the single most important keystone habit for individual success."). See also id. at 133 (noting that "if you knew how to avoid the temptation of a marshmallow as a preschooler . . . you also knew how to get yourself to class on time and finish your homework. . .").

a habit."[107] Willpower thus is something that we can learn to develop[108] and can be reinforced with practice.[109]

4.   Reliability and Preparedness

Reliability and preparedness both relate to getting the job done, consistently and well.

What Is Reliability?

Being reliable means that if you say you will get something done, it will get done, and it will get done by the time promised. It implies showing up on time, responding to people promptly, following through on promises, and otherwise being the kind of person others can depend on. Reliability demands that you promise only what you are certain you can deliver and that you deliver what you promise.[110] Being reliable also suggests that your work will demonstrate a consistent level of quality, so that others can trust both the performance and the work product. People have confidence in those who establish themselves as reliable.

Reliability also means taking responsibility or ownership over tasks and projects and being accountable when something goes wrong. Reliable people do not blame others and they do not proffer excuses. People who are reliable do not feel or act like victims.

Being reliable is a matter of trust. Reliability is something that is earned based on experience; when others see that you consistently deliver quality work on time, you will be rewarded with a reputation as a reliable person.

---

[107] Id. at 131.

[108] Id.

[109] American Psychological Association, What You Need to Know About Willpower, The Psychological Science of Self-Control 1 (2012), available at http://www.apa.org/helpcenter/willpower.pdf.

[110] One writer urges us to "[t]hink of your work as a contract. Before agreeing to anything, be sure you understand the terms and conditions. If the deadline or expectation is unrealistic, address it." Chrissy Scivicque, How to Be a More Reliable Professional, Forbes (June 28, 2011), available at https://www.forbes.com/sites/work-in-progress/2011/06/28/how-to-be-a-more-reliable-professional.

Why Lawyer Reliability?

Studies show that a lack of reliability is the number one career limiting behavior.[111] Supervisors need reliable people who they can depend on so thoroughly that they can truly forget about the task. As to people who are not fully reliable, a boss retains "psychological ownership" over a task, which is a burden on her time and mental energy.[112]

What Does It Mean to Be Prepared?

To be prepared is to be ready for a purpose or activity.[113] The closely related word preparedness means a state of readiness, and often applies in case of war or other emergency situations.[114] Preparedness is intimately connected to reliability because the extent to which you are reliable depends largely on how prepared you are.

Why Lawyer Preparedness?

I like the crisis connotation of the word preparedness because it endows our readiness with an appropriate sense of urgency. Being prepared is crucial for lawyers, whether it is for a court hearing, negotiation, deposition, client meeting, or a meeting with a supervisor or colleague. Failing to be prepared reflects a level of disrespect toward others and toward our work more broadly. It also leaves us vulnerable to failure—when we are not prepared we cannot possibly perform at our best.

Consider the following true story: A young lawyer is to give a presentation to her practice group at a meeting scheduled to begin at 8:30 a.m. She arrives a few minutes past 8:30, has no printed notes, and when she tries to retrieve her presentation notes from her laptop, she finds that her computer battery is dead. This lawyer is ill-prepared in the extreme, and her lack of

---

[111] See VitalSmarts, Stuck in a Dead-End Career? Your Career-Limiting Habit is to Blame (May 26, 2011), available at https://www.vitalsmarts.com/press/2011/05/stuck-in-a-dead-end-career-your-career-limiting-habit-is-to-blame/.

[112] Joseph Grenny, Almost All Managers Have at Least One Career-Limiting Habit, Harvard Business Review (July 5, 2016), available at https://hbr.org/2016/07/almost-all-managers-have-at-least-one-career-limiting-habit.

[113] See https://www.merriam-webster.com/dictionary/prepare.

[114] See https://www.merriam-webster.com/dictionary/preparedness.

readiness is probably all that anyone in attendance can remember about her presentation.

5. Craftsmanship

What Is Craftsmanship?

Craftsmanship refers to skill in carrying out tasks and connotes a sense of artistry and pride in one's work.[115] Craft involves "neither rules nor theory, but rather a kind of working technique, know-how, or tacit knowledge."[116] It means striving for accuracy and a "desire for exactness."[117]

Why Lawyer Craftsmanship?

Because law is an exalted profession, it may be easy to dismiss the notion of craftsmanship as an integral element of the work of a lawyer. But craftsmanship is essential to our professional identity. Treating our work as craft offers benefits to the way we approach and perform our work. A craftsman works with pride, looking "to the past with faithfulness, seeking inspiration, guidance, and foundation" while focusing "on the future, endeavoring to create something useful, comely, and lasting. . . ."[118]

The great Karl Llewellyn emphasized the

> concept of craft, of craft-tradition, of craft-responsibility, and of craftsmanship not as meaning merely the high artistry of God's gift, but as including the uninspired but reliable work of the plain and ordinary citizen of the craft. The existence of a craft means the existence of some significant body of working knowhow, centered on the doing of some perceptible kind of job. This working knowhow is in some material degree transmissible and transmitted to the incomer.[119]

---

[115] See https://dictionary.cambridge.org/us/dictionary/english/craftsmanship.

[116] Brett G. Scharffs, Law as Craft, 54 Vand. L. Rev. 2245, 2324 (2001), available at http://coloradomentoring.org/wp-content/uploads/2013/09/Scharffs-BG-Law-as-Craft-54 -Vand.-L.-Rev.-2245-November-2001.pdf.

[117] Arthur L. Costa & Bena Kallik, Preface, Learning and Leading with Habits of Mind: 16 Essential Characteristics for Success xxi (2008).

[118] Scharffs, supra note 116, at 2249.

[119] Karl N. Llewellyn, The Common Law Tradition 214 (1960).

What a beautiful concept! Take pride in and be attentive both to the "high artistry" *and* the "uninspired but reliable work of the plain and ordinary citizen of the craft," which forms a substantial part of the work of an attorney,[120] a goal to keep well in sight.

6.   Adaptability

What Is Adaptability?

Adaptability refers to the capability to adjust to new conditions or new uses or purposes.[121]

Why Lawyer Adaptability?

Adaptability of course is best known with reference to Charles Darwin's seminal work *On the Origin of Species* in which he demonstrates that the species most likely to survive are not necessarily the strongest, but those most adaptable to changes in their environment.[122] Darwin's work has great currency for today's lawyers, given the remarkable pace of change in the marketplace for legal work.[123] Those individuals and firms that can anticipate and understand these changes and modify their behaviors and approaches to meet the current and future climate will be successful and flourish. Those who cannot adapt to new realities inevitably will become extinct.[124] Adaptability thus is essential in the larger picture of changing market dynamics.

Adaptability is also crucial in the daily life of an attorney. Adaptability requires mental agility and the need to constantly re-assess and when necessary re-engineer strategies based on

---

[120] See the discussion of Humility later in this chapter.

[121] See https://en.oxforddictionaries.com/definition/adaptable.

[122] Charles Darwin, On the Origin of Species (1859).

[123] See Chapter 2.B., supra.

[124] See Legal Executive Institute, 2017 Report on the State of the Legal Market 2–3 ("As an analogy for the challenge faced by law firms in today's radically changed market environment . . . the survival of the most adaptable seems particularly fitting. At the end of the day, the firms that continue to prosper will most likely be those that are able to adapt most successfully to the evolving demands of their clients and the changed conditions of the marketplace. Those firms that are unable to do so will most likely become endangered species."), available at https://legalsolutions.thomsonreuters.com/law-products/ns/solutions/peer-monitor/report-on-the-state-of-the-legal-market-repository?CID=TRSite.

unexpected circumstances or new facts, which arise continuously.

I experienced firsthand the need for adaptability in law practice. When I took my first deposition as a junior associate, I felt well-prepared, armed with a comprehensive list of questions for the plaintiff I was to depose. But I was too rigidly wedded to my prepared questions and failed to follow up on interesting things the deponent said in response to some of those questions. This is a common rookie mistake. If I had been truly prepared *and* suitably flexible, I would have been comfortable enough to go "off script" and I would have adjusted my questions to her answers. Preparedness without adaptability is limiting.

7.   Creativity and Enterprising Spirit

When asked to describe lawyers, few people would respond with the word "creative." But creativity can be an enormously valuable tool for lawyers and, because many lawyers lack creativity, being creative can be a meaningful differentiator.[125]

What Is Creativity?

Creativity often is mistakenly confused with artistry. While those who are gifted in the arts often are creative, they do not have a monopoly. Creativity comes in numerous shapes and sizes. Creativity at its core refers to the ability to solve problems using novel or non-obvious solutions.[126]

Why Lawyer Creativity?

When we are creative, we see solutions rather than problems and opportunities rather than obstacles.[127] Creativity has been linked to memory and learning more broadly, and researchers have found that high potential individuals are marked by a "catalytic learning capability" defined as "the capacity to scan for new ideas, the cognitive capability to absorb

---

[125] Creativity is listed as one of the 26 effectiveness factors in the classical empirical study by Professors Shultz and Zedeck. See Shultz & Zedeck, supra note 23.

[126] See https://en.oxforddictionaries.com/definition/creativity.

[127] Tina Seelig, inGenius, A Crash Course on Creativity 4 (2012).

them, and the common sense to translate that new learning into productive action. . . ."[128]

Lawyers benefit from creativity in several ways. Most important, creativity can enable attorneys to devise unique approaches or novel solutions to client problems, business deals, or litigation matters. Creativity can also aid in client development and retention, which is of increasing importance in the current climate for legal services, in which commodity work largely is disappearing.

A former student, a partner at a mid-sized law firm in New York City, once told me about how her creativity led her to secure a career-changing corporate client: The client, at the time served by one of the New York's largest firms, wanted to structure a deal in a way that its attorneys said was impossible. My former student, who knew the general counsel, asked for one weekend to try to figure out a way to structure the transaction in a way that would achieve the company's goals. The GC, believing that the big law firm's attorneys would have figured out a solution if there had been one, reluctantly agreed. When two days later she came up with a way to structure the deal, she walked away with the business formerly held by one of New York's most venerable firms. That is creativity.

Can Creativity Be Learned?

Creativity can be learned; it is possessed by the gifted and by the rest of us, and it is an "endless, renewable resource" that "we can tap into at any time."[129] Our brains are made to engage in creative problem solving and we should view everything as "an opportunity for ingenuity."[130]

How to Maximize Creativity

Creativity does not come naturally to many of us. Lawyers are trained to think in a rigid, analytic manner that may impede creative impulses.

---

[128] Douglas A. Ready, Jay A. Conger, & Linda A. Hill, Are You a High Potential?, Harvard Business Review (June 2010), available at https://hbr.org/2010/06/are-you-a-high-potential.

[129] Seelig, supra note 127, at 7.

[130] Id. at 8.

We must learn to welcome freewheeling and spontaneous thought, to let the "madman" inside each of us do his work.[131] This inner madman, it turns out, is often suppressed by our more reasoned and disciplined internal critic, which censors and filters out ideas that seem too implausible. Julia Cameron, the influential author of *The Artist's Way*, urges us to outrun our "inner Censor"—"that nasty voice that tries to discount what we are doing."[132] The Censor impedes the flow of creative ideas by judging and critiquing our creative output, often without adequate deliberation.[133] Scientific evidence supports the notion that brain activity is affected during the creative process, shutting down the normal inhibition of new ideas.[134]

Allow yourself time to ruminate over ideas, even those that seem a little far-fetched. When trying to come up with novel solutions, unplug and give your mind license to roam. Practice boredom, which allows the mind space to contemplate.[135] Suppress your internal censor and allow yourself to be open to ideas, no matter how implausible they may seem initially.

Know When Not to Be Creative

Much of legal work is analytical and rule-bound, and of course our system of law is based on precedents. Creativity does not mean failing to comply with court rules or professional norms; it does not mean making legal arguments that disregard settled precedent. Creativity in our profession has its limits.

---

[131] See Bryan A. Garner, Legal Writing in Plain English 10–15 (2d ed. 2013). Garner credits English professor Dr. Betty Flowers with the notion of the madman. He describes the madman as the "imagination" and "creative impulse" that each of us has. See also Sarah Green, Interview with Bryan Garner, Improve Your Business Writing, Harvard Business Review (February 28, 2013), available at https://hbr.org/ideacast/2013/02/improve-your-business-writing.html.

[132] Julia Cameron, Outrunning your Censor (March 6, 2014), available at http://juliacameronlive.com/2014/03/06/outrunning-your-censor/.

[133] Id.

[134] See Seelig, supra note 127, at 8–9.

[135] Manoush Zomorodi, Bored and Brilliant: How Spacing Out Can Unlock Your Most Productive and Creative Self (2017).

8. Wisdom

What Is Wisdom?

To be wise is to have insight, an "ability to discern inner qualities and relationships" and exercise good judgment.[136] Aristotle famously wrote of practical wisdom as the master virtue,[137] encompassing other virtues such as loyalty, self-control, courage, fairness, generosity, gentleness, friendliness, and truthfulness.[138] One who has the ability to apply these virtues in concrete, practical situations has practical wisdom.[139]

More colloquially, we can think of practical wisdom as the "right way to do the right thing in a particular circumstance, with a particular person, at a particular time."[140] One writer has identified seven fundamental elements of wisdom:[141]

- *Perceptiveness*—"seeing, linking, and reflecting on features, factors, dimensions, anomalies, inconsistencies, and repercussions that others might overlook."[142]

- *Foresight*—"imagining, modeling, visualizing, and predicting future behavior and events."[143]

- *Creativity*—"making associations among seemingly unrelated ideas, products, events, entities, and individuals and solving problems with new associations."[144]

- *Fairness*—"forgoing personal gain to meet ethical standards of equality and equity and leading other

---

[136] See https://www.merriam-webster.com/dictionary/wisdom.

[137] Aristotle, Nicomachean Ethics 101 (C.D. Reeve 2014).

[138] Id. at 101–02.

[139] Id. at 102.

[140] Barry Schwartz & Kenneth Sharpe, Practical Wisdom: The Right Way to Do the Right Thing 85 (2010).

[141] Randall Kiser, Soft Skills for the Effective Lawyer 190–224 (2017).

[142] Id. at 190.

[143] Id.

[144] Id. at 191.

people to follow standards that fulfill expectations of fairness and justice."[145]

- *Judgment*—"exhibiting knowledge, objectivity, proportion, sensitivity, and humaneness in making complex evaluations and decisions."[146]

- *Self-Renewal*—"knowing when our knowledge and mental models have become invalid and learning how to renew our minds and bodies to foster wisdom."[147]

- *Courage*—"risking physical or emotional harm by compelling yourself to act for the benefit of others or to comply with your highest expectations of yourself."[148]

How to Develop Wisdom in Decision-Making

Wisdom is integral to the myriad decisions—large and small—that each of us makes each day within our professional spheres. Here are some critical steps to decision-making that reflects wisdom:

- *Analyze Facts*—Develop a feel for synthesizing facts, sifting through facts to separate those that are important and reliable from those that are not, be curious about what additional facts might be helpful, and determine a hierarchy of credibility for facts needed to exercise sound judgment.

- *Include Various Perspectives*—Consider whether your understanding of a situation may be shaped by any internal biases.[149] When time permits, ask others for their views so that you can incorporate an array of perspectives into your decision-making process. This has the additional benefit of getting buy-in from stakeholders.

---

[145] Id.
[146] Id.
[147] Id.
[148] Id.
[149] See Chapter 7.B.5., infra.

- *Understand the Timing*—Be sure that you have an appropriate sense of the timing for decisions that need to be made so that you can react accordingly.

- *Perform a Situational Analysis*—Think about your options using an "if . . . then . . ." formulation. Carefully consider all options from the perspective of various stakeholders. Fully assess the risks and benefits of each possible course of action.

- *Engage Your Instincts*—Do not discount your "gut feeling." Wisdom has an important intuitive element. High potential individuals generally have refined instincts, dynamic sensors that arm them with a "well-tuned radar that puts a higher premium on quality results."[150] Beyond a simple sense of judgment, they have "a feel for timing, an ability to quickly read situations, and a nose for opportunity. . . . [and] for being in the right place at the right time."[151] This is the essence of wisdom, and we get more of it as we gain experience.[152]

- *Learn from Your Decisions*—Practical wisdom has "a strong experiential component."[153] Learning from experience is a true element of wisdom and can enhance our judgment immensely. It is important to reflect on decisions we have made, both the good and the bad.[154]

A Few Additional Words About Instinct

As attorneys trained in rigorous disciplined analysis we may be dispositionally inclined to dismiss the importance and value of instinct. This would be a mistake. Instinct is not witchcraft but instead is an intuition based on experience and refined over time. Instinct forms an important part of our "moral fabric. . .

---

[150] Ready, Conger, & Hill, supra note 128.

[151] Id. See also Scharffs, supra note 116, at 2269 ("The expert. . . develops a feel for what needs to be done in a given situation. . . . Through long practice and experience, [we] develop a feel for how to respond to situations, each of which is unique and different, but each of which reflects patterns found in earlier experiences.").

[152] See the additional brief discussion of instinct below.

[153] Scharffs, supra note 116 at 2269.

[154] See Chapter 3.A.2., supra.

stitched out of the dozens—hundreds—of decisions" that we make each day.[155] Our instinct reflects that moral fabric; of the many decisions we make on a daily basis, most of them are made within "fractions of seconds."[156]

C. CHARACTER

Character refers to features or attributes that make up and distinguish an individual.[157] I chose "Character" as the title of this section because the word evokes a state of being, an approach that is simplistic in its fidelity to doing the right thing in the right way at the right time. In that spirit, this section discusses gratitude; dignity; discretion; humility; confidence; authenticity; integrity; humor; and elegance. Demonstrate your essence—your character—in everything you do.

1. Gratitude

Show Gratitude Often

When someone does a favor for us, minor as it may be, we must demonstrate genuine appreciation, regardless of the outcome. The efforts of others should never be taken for granted or received with a sense of entitlement.

Why Show Gratitude?

Demonstrating appreciativeness is important because it is quite simply the right way to treat others.

There is in addition a far more selfish reason to recognize efforts undertaken by others on your behalf. An example is instructive: A few years ago, I introduced an acquaintance to an attorney friend who in turn introduced that acquaintance to another attorney, who hired her at his law firm. The acquaintance herself never thanked me for the connection, and in fact did not even inform me that she had gotten a position. When she reached out to me about two years later for a favor,

---

[155] Patrick J. Schiltz, Legal Ethics in Decline: The Elite Law Firm, the Elite Law School, and the Moral Formation of the Novice Attorney, 82 Minn. L. Rev. 705, 719 (1998), available at http://coloradomentoring.org/wp-content/uploads/2013/09/Schiltz-P-Legal-Ethics-in-Decline-The-Elite-Law-Firm-The-Elite-Law-School-and-the-Moral-Formation-of-the-Novice-Attorney-82-Minn.-L.-Rev.-705-February-19981.pdf.

[156] Id. at 719–20.

[157] See https://www.merriam-webster.com/dictionary/character.

can you guess what the first thing was that I remembered about her?

Do not let a lack of gratitude become a trademark, something by which you are remembered.

How to Show Gratitude

There are myriad ways in which gratitude can be expressed. Typically, gratitude does not require a significant or tangible expression; an email, call, or handwritten note is sufficient to demonstrate to the other that you recognize that she exerted time and effort on your behalf and that you are appreciative. If someone's secretary or assistant helped you, make sure to acknowledge that person's efforts as well.

2. Dignity

Dignity means acting in a manner that is worthy of respect or honor, a goal toward which every legal professional should strive. This includes being composed and acting with a level of seriousness appropriate to any specific situation, both in our personal and professional lives. All our actions should be dignified to enhance our own professionalism and for the benefit of the organizations with which we are affiliated and the profession more broadly. Acting in a dignified manner includes treating others with respect and honor. Never shame or publicly criticize others.

3. Discretion

Lawyers routinely work with confidential and other sensitive information, and being discreet is a core requirement of our ethical obligations and something that should be a fundamental element of our legal professional persona. But the need for discretion goes well beyond ethical prescriptions; we should be judicious across a range of circumstances even when confidentiality is technically not required.[158]

---

[158] Keeping information confidential is one of the top ten capabilities most important for starting lawyers based on the results of a study of 24,000 practicing attorneys around the country. See Foundations for Practice: The Whole Lawyer Character Quotient, supra note 88, at 26.

Because knowledge often equates with power, some people like to demonstrate to others the extent of their power by disclosing information that should not be shared. This reflects a lack of discretion that in turn undermines the trust and confidence others have in us.

4. Humility

"[I]f you meet a really humble man . . . [h]e will not be thinking about humility: he will not be thinking about himself at all."[159]

Most people do not associate humility with lawyers, but humility is an important element of the legal professional persona.

Humility Defined

The essence of humility is a belief that you can learn something from someone else. Humility also enables us to perform tasks that we might think are menial or beneath our level of education or experience.

Benefits of Humility

Humility Makes Us Open to Ideas—Humility allows us to recognize the limits of our abilities and knowledge and opens us to ideas and other ways of doing things. When we are humble we may actually learn things!

Humility Enables Relationships—Humility makes us better listeners and thus helps us develop stronger relationships with others. It is an approach to life that is strongly appealing to others.

Humility Gives Us License to Admit We Made a Mistake—Humility allows us to admit to mistakes and acknowledge discrepancies and inconsistencies in our own thoughts and actions. It enables us to take responsibility for what we do. Eric Grossman, the Chief Legal Officer of Morgan Stanley, praises

---

[159] C.S. Lewis. Mere Christianity, Book 3, Chapter 8, The Great Sin 128 (1952), available at https://www.dacc.edu/assets/pdfs/PCM/merechristianitylewis.pdf.

the need to be "thoughtful, open to ideas, and unafraid to change your mind,"[160] in other words, to be humble.

Humility Helps Us Do the Routine Work Inevitable in Law Practice—Contrary to what is portrayed in the movies and on television, much of the work of attorneys is mundane and sometimes it is downright boring.[161] Yet such tasks are important—to the firm, to clients, and to one's professional development. Humility lets us get our hands dirty, and to do so without complaint or compromise.

When I was a litigation associate, I worked with a brilliant junior attorney—brilliant in the sense that she was intellectually gifted (having graduated at the top of her class from an elite law school), exceptionally poised, and a talented writer and orator. She exceeded my abilities in all of these areas. Yet she was unwilling or unable to perform some of the less exotic tasks that are part of the everyday work of most attorneys. When it came time to prepare an important brief for filing, she failed to perform the mundane charge of compiling tables of authorities and contents and finalizing citations to the record and legal authorities. Despite her enviable and undeniable talents, her career was short-lived, a casualty of a lack of humility to undertake some of the more tedious but essential aspects of practice.

5. Confidence

"Whether you think you can, or you think you can't—you're right."[162]

---

[160] Email from Eric F. Grossman to the author (July 16, 2018), on file with the author.

[161] See Patrick J. Schiltz, On Being A Happy, Healthy, and Ethical Member of an Unhappy, Unhealthy, and Unethical Profession, 52 Vand. L. Rev. 871, 911 (1999), a version of which is available at http://faculty.law.miami.edu/mcoombs/Schlitz.htm ("Most of a lawyer's working life is filled with the mundane. . . . Your life as a lawyer will be filled with dictating letters and talking on the phone and drafting memoranda and performing 'due diligence' and proofreading contracts and negotiating settlements and filling out time sheets.") (internal citations omitted). See also id. at 928 ("most big firm lawyers—especially firm associates—spend the bulk of their professional lives working on run-of-the mill matters.")

[162] Commonly attributed to Henry Ford, see, e.g., https://www.goodreads.com/quotes/978-whether-you-think-you-can-or-you-think-you-can-t--you-re, although there is a debate over the origin of this quotation. See https://quoteinvestigator.com/?s=Whether+you+.

Confidence Defined

Confidence is a feeling of power over a situation, a person's belief in his own efficacy or ability to achieve goals. Confidence is having and projecting a sense of what you know, what you can do, and your ability to do something with competence.

Importance of Confidence

As the opening quotation of this section suggests, confidence is a self-fulfilling prophecy. If you feel confident, you are more likely to succeed; if you lack confidence, you are less likely to succeed. Importantly, confidence also impacts how others perceive you. If you are confident, others will believe that you are competent. A lack of confidence makes it difficult for others to believe that you can get the job done. Think about it: Would you ever hire an attorney—or anyone else for that matter—who demonstrably lacks confidence?

Appearing More Confident

How can we appear confident even when we do not feel competent? When faced with a challenging task or assignment, recall other times when you initially felt overwhelmed by or fearful that you might not be able to complete a task and take comfort in the fact that you managed the task well. When you accomplish something, allow yourself to take pride in a job well done. This will create a memory that you can draw on when you lack confidence with respect to a new project or event. Finally, act confident by standing straight and tall and otherwise projecting an air of composure and self-assurance.

Remember the Dunning-Kruger Effect

While confidence is important, it bears recalling the Dunning-Kruger effect discussed earlier.[163] Our inability to appreciate our own levels of (in)competence signals a need to be extremely thoughtful about the level of confidence that we should project, the need for continuous learning and development, and the need to embrace a deep awareness that self-assessments are inherently flawed.

---

[163] See Chapter 3.A.2., supra.

Confidence, Not Arrogance

Some see a thin line between confidence and arrogance, and of course that is a line we do not want to cross. An arrogant person is one who has a condescending sense of superiority over others and a need to be better than others. Someone who is confident is comfortable with who she is and does not need to put others down to feel good about herself and her abilities. Confident people also have the humility to understand that they can learn from others, a trait often missing from those who are arrogant.

It may be that the meaningful difference between those who are confident and those who are arrogant is *deference*. It is not the confidence that makes some people bullies or arrogant—it is confidence paired with a lack of deference toward the knowledge, skills, and abilities of others that leads to arrogance.[164]

Confidence, Not Malpractice

It should go without saying that lawyers should be mindful of the duty of competent representation[165] and should not use confidence as a pretext to provide representation in areas in which she is not competent.

6. Authenticity

"Be yourself. Everyone else is already taken."[166]

Authenticity Defined

The notion of authenticity is just what it sounds like—that each of us should strive to be true to our own personality, spirit, values, and character, and that we should be original, rather than fake or a replica of someone else. Authenticity instructs

---

[164] Tim David, Confident or Cocky, Psychology Today (December 19, 2016), available at https://www.psychologytoday.com/us/blog/the-magic-human-connection/201612/confident-or-cocky.

[165] American Bar Association Model Rules of Professional Conduct: Rule 1.1 (Competence), available at https://www.americanbar.org/groups/professional_responsibility/publications/model_rules_of_professional_conduct/rule_1_1_competence.html.

[166] This quotation is widely attributed to Oscar Wilde, but there is disagreement as to whether in fact he ever said it. See https://quoteinvestigator.com/2014/01/20/be-yourself/.

that we should act in a way that feels natural and comfortable, even if adjusted for professional circumstances.

In the context of a professional persona, authenticity demands an integration of our professional identity and our personal identity; these should be two integrated elements rather than two completely different beings. Your professional persona should incorporate aspects and be an outgrowth of your personality rather than being something completely foreign to yourself.[167]

Benefits of Authenticity

When we are authentic, we are better at what we do.[168] To be inauthentic requires time and energy that could better be spent on other things. Being authentic is also tied to being happier.[169] Have you ever been in an uncomfortable situation in which for whatever reason you felt like you were trying to be someone or something you are not? If you have been, you probably recall that as a very awkward and unhappy situation. An example with which many of us can associate is the situation faced by closeted gay or transgender friends, family members, or acquaintances. The efforts required to hide identity from others is a form of inauthenticity that generally takes significant effort and causes much unhappiness.

Authenticity Requires Intellectual Integrity Balanced with Flexibility

Authenticity includes an element of intellectual integrity— recognizing the importance of being true to one's own thinking and opinions. But authenticity should not be a pretext for being inflexible or unwilling to be open to differing views, and we must not allow authenticity to stymie our development. A rigid self-concept is counterproductive. "Without the benefit of . . . valuable external perspectives we get from experimenting with new [ ] behaviors. . . , habitual patterns of thought and action

---

[167] See also Chapter 1.C., supra.

[168] Daisy Hurst Floyd, The Authentic Lawyer: Merging the Personal and the Professional, in The Essential Qualities of the Professional Lawyer 20 (2013).

[169] Id.

fence us in."[170] While each of us should have a clear sense of self, "a too rigid self-concept becomes an anchor that keeps us from sailing forth."[171]

Achieving Authenticity Reminds Us That Our Professional Persona Evolves

Achieving authenticity does not happen overnight and may require a period of adjustment as we assume different roles in different organizations at different times in our careers and lives.[172] The evolving nature of professional identity also reflects changes in our personal persona; authenticity can mean appreciating that who we are at the age of 50 is not the same as who we were at the age of 25 or 30. It also means understanding that we change due to a range of reasons (marriage, children, parental care, or illness or other traumas) and the need to be attuned to the interplay between self and professional identity as we change and react to change.

Challenges to Lawyer Authenticity

Legal education and law practice present challenges to achieving authenticity. Legal education tends to compartmentalize the qualities needed by great lawyers by focusing on legal analysis and other skills directly related to "thinking like a lawyer," often at the expense of other tools, such as helping to integrate personal values with new lawyering skills. Law firm practice, with its increased specialization and heavy focus on revenue generation, also may reinforce behaviors that are at odds with true authenticity.

Do Not Take Authenticity Too Far

Authenticity does not mean that we should speak without filter or boundaries, or that we should wear our emotions—particularly our fears and vulnerabilities—on our sleeve. Authenticity often requires us to adapt our personal tendencies

---

[170] Herminia Ibarra, The Authenticity Paradox, Harvard Business Review (January–February 2015), available at https://hbr.org/2015/01/the-authenticity-paradox.

[171] Id.

[172] "By viewing ourselves as works in progress and evolving our professional identities through trial and error, we can develop a personal style that feels right to us and suits our organizations' changing needs." Id.

in a range of specific professional (and personal) contexts. We must balance authenticity with the demands of any particular situation. Making intentional choices is key.

7. Integrity[173]

Integrity has several different meanings that are relevant to our mindset as legal professionals.

One meaning of integrity is closely related to authenticity. The words integrity, integrate, integral, and integer (as in numbers) all derive from the Latin word *integer*, which means "whole."[174] Integrity thus suggests a sense of personal wholeness or cohesion, an internal consistency of character exemplified by consistency between the values one holds and professes and his actions. People with integrity act in predictable ways because they act consistent with a core set of values. Integrity builds trust and confidence because others understand that a person with integrity has a level of internal consistency and acts in a manner consonant with that inner code.

The more commonly understood meaning of integrity refers to being honest and having a strong moral compass.[175] In this sense, integrity means "soundness of moral principle and character, as shown by one person dealing with others . . . , and fidelity and honesty in the discharge of trust; it is synonymous with 'probity,' 'honesty,' and 'uprightness.' "[176] The ideal of integrity is deeply engrained in our professional ethics and underlies our reputation as professionals. Our integrity is crucial to our professional persona and must be closely guarded.

A professional with whom I work and whom I admire greatly believes that integrity is the single most important feature of one's legal professional persona. I have given this a great deal of thought, and think she may well be on to something. Integrity, in both its meanings, brings together many of the other values

---

[173] Integrity and trustworthiness are among the top ten capabilities most important for starting lawyers based on the results of a study of 24,000 practicing attorneys around the country. See Foundations for Practice: The Whole Lawyer Character Quotient, supra note 88, at 26. Integrity also is listed as one of the 26 effectiveness factors in the classical empirical study by Professors Shultz and Zedeck. See Shultz & Zedeck, supra note 23.

[174] See https://en.oxforddictionaries.com/definition/integrity.

[175] See https://en.oxforddictionaries.com/definition/integrity.

[176] See https://thelawdictionary.org/integrity/.

discussed in this section—authenticity, soundness, strength, dependability, durability, and reliability, as well as morality, virtue, and trustworthiness that are essential parts of our professionalism. We should embrace integrity in all of its multi-dimensional facets.

8.   Humor

Attorneys should take their work seriously but should also embrace humor when appropriate. Humor has the effect of releasing stress and deflecting uncomfortable situations. Humor makes us and those around us happy. In fact, humor has been found scientifically to offer a range of both long-term and short-term benefits.[177] Humor can be self-deprecating but it may never be used at the expense of others. Laughter, a common byproduct of humor, itself promotes a number of benefits, among them social intelligence.[178] Laughter also can energize us, enable us to persevere, and recover from stressful situations.[179]

9.   Elegance

Elegance is a state of mind reflecting timeless traditions and style, a refined grace. There are countless ways in which we can demonstrate elegance, and to do so is often very easy. Here is one example: Recently my undergraduate university put me in contact with a very successful alum, currently the general counsel of a large global company. We were scheduled to have lunch and his assistant contacted me that morning to reschedule, letting me know that my would-be lunch companion had been called away on an urgent company matter. Later that day I received an email from the general counsel himself, expressing his personal apology for the schedule change. That is elegance.

---

[177] See, e.g., Alexandra Michel, The Science of Humor Is No Laughing Matter, Observer, Association for Psychological Science, (April 2017), available at https://www.psychologicalscience.org/observer/the-science-of-humor-is-no-laughing-matter.

[178] As Daniel Goleman writes, "laughter may be the shortest distance between two brains, an unstoppable infectious spread that builds an instant social bond." Goleman, supra note 52, at 45. See also Michel, supra note 177 (describing laughter as "an important adaptation for social communication").

[179] See Michel, supra note 177.

Be elegant when opportunities arise. Others will notice, and they will remember.

D. QUESTIONS FOR REFLECTION

1. Imagine that you are training for a marathon. You have tendonitis for the third time in three months. What are your thoughts about that injury?

2. You have to prepare a memorandum. You are on your third draft, and each time the partner comes back to you with comments. What are your attitudes toward your work? What are your attitudes toward your supervisor?

3. What about your work or studies keeps you awake at night out of excitement? What keeps you awake at night out of anxiety?

4. How often do you use the Internet to learn about an issue that you know little or nothing about? What makes you do that? What does that tell you about your level of curiosity?

5. Imagine that you are going through a period of boredom with your work or studies. What strategies have you tried to get more excited about what you are doing?

6. Name an area in which you have tremendous self-discipline and willpower. Why does that come easy? Name an area in which you lack sufficient self-discipline. What is your strategy for improving in that area?

7. Name 5 things you can do with a paperclip. How many of these things did you come up with on your own (as opposed to looking on the Internet)?

8. When was the last time you expressed gratitude to someone? What compelled you to do that? In what way(s) did you demonstrate your appreciation?

9. You are a junior attorney. Your supervisor has asked you to complete a task that you feel could be done by a secretary. What would you do, and why?

CHAPTER 5

TIME MANAGEMENT AND ORGANIZATION

Time management and organization are closely related to productivity and are of profound importance to our professional persona. Failing to manage our time in order to honor our commitments seriously compromises our credibility and ability to meet our goals. Hand-in-hand with time management is organization. There is no single approach to organization that works for all of us (I have enormously successful colleagues whose offices are cluttered and those whose offices are neat in the extreme). Whatever the style, your ability to do your work productively depends on knowing where things are and how to use them effectively. At the end of the day, time management and organization are intrinsically linked: Being organized is critical to successful time management.

What follows are some tips for managing time and organizing ourselves to be as efficient and effective as possible.

A. TIME MANAGEMENT

"Time is really the only capital that any human being has, and the thing that he can least afford to waste or lose." Thomas Edison[1]

Time management is a challenge for many lawyers given the significant demands and fast pace associated with legal work. The task has become intensified due to some of the changes to the profession discussed in Chapter 2 and the ubiquity of mobile devices that make us accessible at all times. Each of us has many things to juggle in both our personal and professional lives, making how we spend our time "a key strategic decision."[2]

---

[1] Original source unknown. See http://www.thomasedison.com/quotes.html.

[2] Peter Bregman, An 18-Minute Plan for Managing Your Day, Harvard Business Review (July 20, 2009), available at https://hbr.org/2009/07/an-18minute-plan-for-managing.

1. Time Management Basics

This section addresses two elements of time management—being on time and being timely with assignments; and the notion of time as a valuable commodity, which each of us possesses in equal measure.[3]

Be on Time and Be Timely[4]

It should go without saying, yet it needs to be said, that a professional is always on time and timely. Being on time and being timely applies to the full range of commitments each of us has on a daily basis—meetings, conference calls, the submission of documents to a more senior attorney or client, and any other obligations that we have to meet as part of our professional lives. For all of these activities, we must be on time and timely—it is a simple matter of respect.

Be on Time—For personal meetings, conference calls, and similar kinds of commitments, being on time means being ready to participate by the time the event is scheduled to begin. Do not amble in at the time a meeting is called for, still needing to remove your coat, choose a seat, and take out your computer or pen and paper. Take account of possible commuting delays or delays that you may find at the security or reception desk. As Oscar Wilde says, "[t]o expect the unexpected shows a thoroughly modern intellect."[5] In today's world, the "unexpected" may take many forms.

Be Timely—Being timely means that assignments are delivered by the time they are due. Obviously, this applies to court deadlines and also to materials that a client or another attorney is expecting to receive.

Being on Time and Being Timely Is About Respect—Being on time and being timely ultimately is about respect toward

---

[3] This discussion puts aside weighty issues like mortality.

[4] Arriving on time for meetings, appointments and hearings is one of the top ten capabilities most important for starting lawyers based on the results of a study of 24,000 practicing attorneys around the country. See Institute for the Advancement of the American Legal System, Foundations for Practice: The Whole Lawyer Character Quotient 26 (July 2016), available at http://iaals.du.edu/sites/default/files/reports/foundations_for_practice_whole_lawyer_character_quotient.pdf.

[5] Oscar Wilde, An Ideal Husband, Third Act.

others. No one should have to wait for us, whether it is for a meeting to begin or for an assignment to be delivered.

Imagine that I have an appointment scheduled to take place in my office at 10:00 a.m. I have planned my morning activities to accommodate that meeting, and I am wrapping up other projects at about 9:50 to allow myself a few minutes to prepare for the 10:00 meeting. At 9:58 I am ready to receive the person I expect at 10:00. But the appointed hour comes and goes. It is 10:10 and I do not know whether the person will arrive, so I pivot to a new project. At 10:15 the person arrives. This person has wasted my time *and* disrupted my work on the new project, causing me further inefficiencies.

Or imagine that I am waiting for documents to be delivered from a few different people by 3:00 p.m. I have set aside the next hour to compile and review those documents before sending them to a client. Two of the three people from whom I am expecting material submit their work on time; the third does not. The time I set aside to compile and review the material has been compromised. I will have to find another time to do that before they are due to the client, unsettling other commitments.

A mature professional knows how to plan ahead to be sure that she will be on time and timely. A mature professional processes her own work in a way that does not unnecessarily create unreasonably short deadlines for others. She always informs others well in advance when she will not be on time or timely, and she does not do this often. She does not wait until the last minute to get things done, recognizing that doing so runs unnecessary and unreasonable risks. She does not impede the ability of others to be their best and most productive selves.

Time as a Valuable Commodity: The Great Equalizer

"Five hundred twenty-five thousand, six hundred minutes." Jonathan Larson[6]

When it comes to time, there are two givens: First, just about everyone feels that there is not enough time to do the things we need and want to do; second, each of us is given the

---

[6]   Jonathan Larson, Seasons of Love (1996).

gift of 168 hours per week.[7] In this way, time is the great equalizer. It also means that time is a precious commodity and, like money, should be spent and invested wisely and deliberately. Unlike money, however, time is non-renewable; we cannot borrow time, and we cannot do anything to increase the amount of time in a given day or week. Each of us should make thoughtful decisions about how to spend the time that we have.

2. Your Time Budget

One way to be more deliberate about our use of time is to generate and stick to a time budget. Just like a financial budget, a time budget can help us to be more thoughtful about how we use precious resources.

Create a Time Budget

Each of us should have a time budget. A first step in creating any budget is to perform an audit to see how you have been spending your resources. If you have ever used a financial budget or other planning tool, you may have been surprised by the amount of money you spend on designer coffee or taxis. Similarly, if you were to perform a time audit, you might be surprised to find how much time you spend on non-professional social media, mindless television, or random Internet browsing. Knowing how much time you spend on specific things can give us better control over how we use our time.

Just as with a financial budget, decide how much time you need or want to use for particular items. Be sure to include 7 or more hours for sleep per night and time for family, friends, commuting, personal care, fitness, and other commitments. Then try to schedule other things that you need and want to do into your calendar.

The Importance of Scheduling

Scheduling time is important for two reasons: First, research confirms that when we schedule specific tasks or

---

[7] See Scott Behson, Relax, You have 168 Hours This Week, Harvard Business Review (August 1, 2014), available at https://hbr.org/2014/08/relax-you-have-168-hours-this-week.

activities, we are much more likely to complete them.[8] Second, setting aside chunks of time—a process known as "batching"— allow us to get more done than trying to do several things at once.[9]

Beware the "Planning Fallacy"

When planning, be alert to the fact that we have a scientifically proven tendency to underestimate the amount of time we need to complete particular projects, even when we have specific experience that suggests that a task will require more time.[10] Keep this in mind as you devise your time budget and build a cushion into your schedule to accommodate errors in calculations due to the planning fallacy.

3.   Make Planning Your Day a Ritual

Undertake an Intellectual Mise-en-Place

As discussed earlier,[11] habits can help us make better use of our time. There is a cooking ritual known as *mise-en-place* ("everything in its place"), the planning phase of every meal in which the chef studies the recipe, thinks through the tools and equipment he will need, and ensures that he has the ingredients ready in the right proportion before even beginning to boil water. This practice is not simply a time saving tool but "a state of mind."[12] The advance planning associated with *mise*, as the ritual is known, means that the chef does not have to search for or measure out ingredients as he works, allowing him to focus his full attention on the dish he is preparing.[13] This kind of deliberation and preparation can be enormously helpful to the

---

[8]   See Bregman, supra note 2 (discussing research showing that specifying the time and place of an activity made it significantly more likely that the task would be completed).

[9]   See the discussion of multitasking, Section 6., infra.

[10]   Roger Buehler, Dale Griffin, & Michael Ross, Exploring the "Planning Fallacy": Why People Underestimate Their Task Completion Times, 67 J. Personality and Soc. Psychol. 366 (1994, available at http://web.mit.edu/curhan/www/docs/Articles/biases/67_ J_Personality_and_Social_Psychology_366,_1994.pdf).

[11]   See Chapter 3.B.2., supra.

[12]   Ron Friedman, How to Spend the First 10 Minutes of Your Day, Harvard Business Review (June 19, 2014), available at https://hbr.org/2014/06/how-to-spend-the-first-10-minutes-of-your-day.

[13]   Id.

rest of us. Planning out our work offers us an "intellectual mise-en-place"[14] that promises greater productivity.

The 18-Minute Planning Ritual

In order to make the most of our time we should undertake a daily three-part ritual:[15]

- *Step 1—Set Plan for the Day (5 minutes)*: Write down what you want to do that day, and then schedule those items into specific time slots on your daily agenda.[16]

- *Step 2—Refocus Each Hour (1 minute per hour)*: Set an alarm for each hour so that you can quickly assess how you spent the last hour in light of your plans. Do what you can to recommit to your goals for the remainder of the day. This helps each of us manage our time rather than letting time manage us.[17]

- *Step 3—Review the Day (5 minutes)*: At the end of the day, review your progress toward the goals you set out in the morning and decide what, if anything, you might have done to keep more closely on track with your plan for the day.

Make Goals Specific and Action-Based

The goals we set out for ourselves, especially those that are immediate or short-term, should be as specific as possible. The more we can break down projects into very specific action items, the easier it is to prioritize them (see below), delegate some, and accomplish the rest.

Lawyers of course are service providers and ultimately much of what we do is dictated by client needs (which often come at the last minute) and the demands of more senior attorneys. For that reason we must retain flexibility in how we plan our

---

[14] Id.

[15] Bregman, supra note 2.

[16] Id.

[17] Id.

days. But having an idea of when we will complete specific tasks is the best way to spend the time over which we do have control.

4.   Do Not Let the Urgent Hijack the Important

"I have two kinds of problems: the urgent and the important. The urgent are not important and the important are never urgent." Dwight D. Eisenhower[18]

The so-called Eisenhower principle has become a well-known tool for organizing work and ordering priorities. This principle has been refined and popularized by Stephen Covey in *The Seven Habits of Highly Effective People*. Under this principle, tasks are evaluated along two axes:[19]

Urgent and Important	Not Urgent but Important
Urgent but Not Important	Not Urgent and Not Important

Important activities are those that contribute to our long-term goals and values. Urgent activities are those that demand our immediate attention. We usually deal with urgent matters immediately because the consequences of not dealing with them swiftly tend to be immediate. Urgent activities put us in a reactive mode.

It is exceptionally easy to confuse urgent tasks with those that are important. We all have felt frustration "when the urgent crowds out the important."[20] This has never been truer than it is today, with general expectations that we will react instantaneously to whatever form of communication we receive.

Having a better understanding of the nature of urgent and important tasks can help each of us be more intentional about how we prioritize, delegate, and otherwise manage various assignments.

---

[18]   See https://quoteinvestigator.com/2014/05/09/urgent/. Eisenhower apparently paraphrased J. Roscoe Miller, former President of Northwestern University. See id.

[19]   Interactive matrices are available on a number of sites. See, e.g., http://contentstrategyonline.com/assets/productivity-tools/Eisenhower-Decision-Matrix.pdf.

[20]   Michael D. Watkins, The Urgent vs. The Important, Harvard Business Review (March 21, 2007), available at https://hbr.org/2007/03/the-fire-within.

Urgent and Important

The quadrant composed of urgent and important tasks is known as the quadrant of necessity. These are high priority items that must be done now and that could not have been anticipated or planned for. Because of the nature of activities that are urgent and important, we must be flexible enough to accommodate them. Examples of urgent and important activities are crises and last-minute demands from others that must be fulfilled. What should not be included in this quadrant are deadline-driven projects with sufficient advance notice; tasks that begin as important but not urgent should not be delayed until they become urgent. This is where strategic time management is of paramount importance.

Not Urgent but Important

Tasks that are important but not urgent make up the so-called quadrant of quality. This is where we should be spending the majority of our time, as these are the activities that allow us to complete important work and help us achieve our personal and professional goals. The tasks that fall within the quadrant of quality are those that are most crucial for our long-term success but are often neglected or deferred. Examples of not urgent but important tasks include strategic planning and thinking and other projects that help us advance our goals, relationship building, recreation, fitness, and personal care.

One personal strategy that I use to deal with important but non-urgent tasks is to set time aside on my calendar to work on specific longer term projects. I designate these times as "DND" to signal to my staff that I should not be disturbed during these times absent some reason that is both important and urgent. These chunks of time prove immensely valuable as I attempt to complete important but non-urgent projects. This book would never have been written had I not had the discipline to set aside time exclusively for this project.

Urgent but Not Important

Urgent but not important tasks are distractions. Although they are often important to other people, they typically do not help us achieve our own goals. We should try to minimize the intrusions occasioned by urgent but not important tasks by scheduling a time to do them efficiently, consolidating them when possible, drawing boundaries, or delegating when appropriate. Urgent but not important activities include unscheduled phone calls, meetings, and personal visits. Pleasers in particular often find themselves spending too much of their time in this quadrant.

Not Urgent and Not Important

Tasks that are not urgent and not important are frivolous ways of spending time. They are time wasters, and each of us should make conscious decisions about how much time we spend on matters that lack both importance and urgency.

5.   Avoid Procrastination

"Only put off until tomorrow what you are willing to die having left undone." Pablo Picasso[21]

To procrastinate is "to put off intentionally and habitually" something that should be done.[22] Procrastination is often done against one's better judgment.[23] When we procrastinate, we pass the task to our future self[24] and unintentionally convert non-urgent tasks into urgent tasks.[25] In this way, there can be significant costs to procrastinating; "Evidence suggests that the habit of leaving things until the last minute generally results in low-quality work performance and reduced well-being. For example, students who routinely procrastinate consistently get lower grades."[26]

There are several factors that may lead us to procrastinate: A personal lack of organization or structure; we find the task unpleasant; anxiety about a project arising out of a fear of failure and lack of confidence about the task; or a temporal delay

---

[21] Original source unknown. See https://www.goodreads.com/quotes/27001-only-put-off-until-tomorrow-what-you-are-willing-to.

[22] https://www.merriam-webster.com/dictionary/procrastinate.

[23] Shahram Heshmat, The 5 Most Common Reasons We Procrastinate, Psychology Today (June 17, 2016), available at https://www.psychologytoday.com/us/blog/science-choice/201606/the-5-most-common-reasons-we-procrastinate.

[24] Id.

[25] See Section 4, supra.

[26] Heshmat, supra note 23.

between the task and any reward for completing the project or punishment for failing to complete the work.[27]

I myself experienced procrastination while writing this book. Anyone who has ever worked with me knows that I am not a procrastinator; to the contrary, I am rather compulsive about getting things done well in advance. However, while working on this book I went through uncharacteristic periods of procrastination, and I know exactly why that happened: I was anxious about the scope of the project. I used a few tactics to get past my anxiety: Breaking the project into discrete and more manageable parts (for example, rather than thinking to myself "Today I will write Chapter 5," I thought "Today I will write about the importance of being on time and timely."); promising drafts of certain portions of the book to colleagues who offered to read it at various stages, which forced upon me a level of accountability; and allowing myself some small reward (a day off, for instance), after completing some defined section of the book. These are some tools that we can use if we find ourselves falling into a pattern of procrastination.

6. Limit Multitasking

We live in an age of multitasking. We are constantly connected to our phones and computers, and in some cases our watches. We are incessantly barraged by emails, phone calls, text messages, and similar forms of communication. Most people expect instantaneous access and immediate replies, making us instinctively want to do many things at once.

Many believe that multitasking makes us more productive but scientific studies suggest otherwise.[28] In fact, multitasking as we might imagine it does not truly exist—we do not do several things at once, but instead we move between tasks, a process known as "task shifting."[29] The "mental juggling" required when we move between and among tasks results in a significant loss

---

[27] Id.

[28] Paul Atchley, You Can't Multitask, So Stop Trying, Harvard Business Review (December 21, 2010), available at https://hbr.org/2010/12/you-cant-multi-task-so-stop-tr.

[29] See Harold Pashler, Task Switching and Multitask Performance, in Stephen Monsell and Jon Driver, Control of Cognitive Processes: Attention and Performance XVIII 275 (2000), paper available at http://citeseerx.ist.psu.edu/viewdoc/download?doi=10.1.1.408.7509&rep=rep1&type=pdf.

of productivity.[30] Studies show that reorientation to a task can lead to a loss of efficiency of up to 40 percent.[31] Multitasking also has been tied to reduced long-term memory and creativity[32] and increased stress.[33]

When possible, close your office door and do the electronic equivalent.[34] Try to focus on a single task for at least 18 minutes (the time at which our attention starts to wane).[35] Limit how often you switch between tasks to increase your overall productivity.

B. ORGANIZATION

Organization is a critical aspect of one's professional persona and allows greater work efficiency and effectiveness. Being organized allows us to manage our time more effectively, know what we have to do, prioritize action items, and construct a plan for getting those tasks done.[36]

Most legal professionals have organizational systems that they used in other work or study contexts, and to the extent those methods have served you well, they certainly can be adapted to the practice of law. To the extent that you do not have effective systems that can handle the demands of law practice, this is the time to develop and implement them. Even if you are very good at remembering things, you should develop systems *now*. As you need to remember more and more, and as you simultaneously get older and experience the forgetfulness that often comes with aging, counting on your memory will serve you

---

[30] American Psychological Association, Multitasking: Switching Costs (March 20, 2006), available at http://www.apa.org/research/action/multitask.aspx (summarizing research).

[31] Atchley, supra note 28.

[32] Id.

[33] Kostadin Kushlev & Elizabeth W. Dunn, Checking email less frequently reduces stress, 43 Computers in Human Behavior 220 (2015), available at https://happylabubc.files.wordpress.com/2010/11/kushlev-dunn-email-and-stress-in-press1.pdf.

[34] Atchley, supra note 28.

[35] Id.

[36] Organizing and managing one's own work and the work of others is listed as one of the 26 effectiveness factors in the classical empirical study by Professors Marjorie M. Shultz and Sheldon Zedeck. See Marjorie M. Shultz & Sheldon Zedeck, Predicting Lawyer Effectiveness: Broadening the Basis for Law School Admission Decisions, 36 L. & Soc. Inquiry 620, 630 (summer 2011), available at http://citeseerx.ist.psu.edu/viewdoc/download?doi=10.1.1.418.7400&rep=rep1&type=pdf.

less and less well and the need for reliable systems will become increasingly important.

1. Workspace and File Organization

Physical Workspace: Neat or Messy?

"If a cluttered desk is a sign of a cluttered mind, of what, then is an empty desk a sign?" Albert Einstein.[37]

Most legal professionals deal with a lot of paper, and managing the flow of documents each of us handles on a daily basis can be vexing.

People disagree as to whether a neat desk is important. Some believe that a paperless desk surface and minimalist surrounding is most beneficial to productivity. There is, however, scientific evidence to suggest that messiness can promote creative thinking ability.[38] Others have argued that the time and energy needed to organize workspace outweighs its value.[39] Alternatively, to the extent that clients and more senior colleagues visit your office, there is value to having a neat working area because perception matters.[40] (When I was a junior associate, I was given a really easy tip from a more senior colleague: When meeting with a client, always show up with your paperwork in a folder bearing the client's name and matter number. It makes an impression on the client.) At the end of the day, what each of us does is a matter of personal habit and preference; there is no one-size-fits-all approach to organization.

---

[37] Original source unknown. See, e.g., David Burkus, When To Say Yes To The Messy Desk, Forbes (May 23, 2014), available at https://www.forbes.com/sites/davidburkus/2014/05/23/when-to-say-yes-to-the-messy-desk/.

[38] Kathleen D. Vohs, Joseph P. Redden, & Ryan Rahinel, Physical Order Produces Healthy Choices, Generosity, and Conventionality, Whereas Disorder Produces Creativity, 24 Psychological Science 1860 (August 1, 2013), available at http://journals.sagepub.com/doi/pdf/10.1177/0956797613480186. For a discussion of why creativity is important for lawyers, see Chapter 4.B.7., supra.

[39] Andrew Tate, 5 reasons creative geniuses like Einstein, Twain and Zuckerberg had messy desks—And why you should too, Canva, available at https://www.canva.com/learn/creative-desks/.

[40] See Kelly Lynn Anders, The Importance of Personal Organization, in Essential Qualities of the Professional Lawyer 242 (2013).

Electronic Files Must Be Organized

The messy-desk-leads-to-genius-levels-of-creativity argument has no applicability when it comes to electronic files. Electronic files must be organized in a clear and intelligible way. Any benefit associated with a messy workspace simply does not apply to electronic files.

Transparency

Whatever system we use to organize paper and electronic files must be intelligible and transparent to others. This allows colleagues to locate materials that may be needed in an emergency and also protects clients in the case of unforeseen circumstances that may befall us. If you have ever had a colleague rushed to the hospital unexpectedly—as I have—you know the importance of a transparent system of organization.

2. To Do Lists

To do lists, whether done by hand or on an electronic device, are essential tools for legal professionals. To do lists enable us to capture the many details we need to remember and to prioritize them. Keep your lists up-to-date and comprehensive. Break activities down into discrete, smaller tasks to ensure that you can better appreciate the complexity of each project and so that projects seem more manageable. To be sure, not everyone uses such lists, but everyone needs to have some system for keeping track of projects and deadlines that works for them.

3. Calendar

Every attorney and law student must have a calendar that is meticulously up-to-date. Missing meetings, conference calls, or deadlines is a rapid and surefire way to lose credibility and appear unprofessional with superiors, clients, colleagues, and others. Ideally your calendar will be electronic so that others who need to access it can do so. As with tasks, do not rely on your memory. Remember to schedule specific tasks and interim deadlines into your calendar, integrating deadlines that others have for work owed to you to be sure that the workflow proceeds on schedule. Keep yourself—and others on the team—accountable for meeting both interim and final deadlines.

C. QUESTIONS FOR REFLECTION

1. Do an analysis of how you spend your time on one relatively normal day. Did anything surprise you? What can you do to clear more time for important tasks?

2. Is there something you really want to do but do not do because you are procrastinating? Why do you think that is? How can you get past it?

3. Keep a record of how often you say or think, "I don't have time" in a given week about something you need or want to do. Does this surprise you? What can you do about it?

4. How would you describe your personal organizational style? What about this style works for you? What could be improved?

CHAPTER 6

WELLBEING AND SUSTAINABILITY

"Much has been said about the plight of lawyers today—
a depressed, anxious, suicidal, alcoholic group—and
those are the ones with jobs." Daniel S. Bowling, III[1]

The concept of lawyer wellbeing may seem like an
oxymoron. Research confirms, time and again, that lawyers
suffer disproportionate to the general population from a range of
maladies such as depression, stress, anxiety, burnout, and drug
and alcohol abuse. We think about and idealize suicide. We eat
poorly, sleep too little, and exercise infrequently. We divorce at
elevated rates. We are not happy. There is much to lament.

There is some good news, however. For one thing, there is a
great deal that we can do to control our own wellbeing. Each of
us should take responsibility for developing our own personal,
sustainable path to wellbeing. In addition, organizations like
law firms—which have good reason for caring deeply about their
workers' health and happiness—can take steps to improve
wellbeing among their ranks. Finally, in recent years, addictions
and mental health issues that commonly afflict lawyers have
come to the forefront. We recognize the issues and talk about
them; they are no longer the taboo subjects of years past.[2] There
now are confidential resources that struggling attorneys can
utilize to assist them.

This chapter discusses the concept of wellbeing; the state of
lawyer wellbeing; why wellbeing is important from both a
personal/family/societal and business perspective; how we can
achieve better wellbeing for ourselves and promote wellbeing
within organizations; and the need to develop a plan for a
personal, sustainable path to wellbeing.

---

[1] Daniel S. Bowling, III, Lawyers and Their Elusive Pursuit of Happiness: Does it
Matter?, 7 Duke F. L. & Soc. Change 37, 37 (2015), available at https://scholarship.law.
duke.edu/cgi/viewcontent.cgi?article=1057&context=dflsc.

[2] See, e.g., Joseph Milowic III, Quinn Emanuel Partner Suffers From Depression
and He Wants Everyone to Know, New York Law Journal (March 28, 2018), available at
https://www.law.com/newyorklawjournal/2018/03/28/quinn-emanuel-partner-suffers-
from-depression-and-he-wants-everyone-to-know/.

A. WHAT IS "WELLBEING" AND WHY DOES IT MATTER?

1. What Is Wellbeing?

Wellbeing is a multidimensional concept that embraces several discrete but interconnected elements:[3]

- *Physical Wellness*—Developing a lifestyle of regular physical activity, proper diet and nutrition, sufficient sleep, and recovery; minimizing the use of addictive substances; seeking help for physical health when needed.

- *Emotional/Mental Health*—Recognizing the importance of emotions and developing an ability to identify and manage our own emotions in a way that enables us to support our own mental health and to make informed decisions about when to seek mental health help.

- *Occupational Pursuits*—Cultivating personal satisfaction, growth, and enrichment in work, and achieving financial stability.

- *Intellectual Endeavors*—Continuous learning and the pursuit of creative or intellectually challenging activities that foster ongoing development; and monitoring cognitive wellness.

- *Spirituality (in Whatever Form)*—Developing a sense of meaningfulness and purpose in all aspects of life.

---

[3] The notion of wellbeing "is multi-dimensional and includes, for example, engagement in interesting activities, having close relationships and a sense of belonging, developing confidence through mastery, achieving goals that matter to us, meaning and purpose, and a sense of autonomy and control, self-acceptance, and personal growth. This multi-dimensional approach underscores that a positive state of well-being is not synonymous with feeling happy or experiencing positive emotions. It is much broader." American Bar Association, National Task Force on Lawyer Well-Being, The Path to Lawyer Well-Being: Practical Recommendations for Positive Change 9–10 (August 14, 2017) (hereinafter National Task Force on Lawyer Well-Being), available at https://www .americanbar.org/content/dam/aba/images/abanews/ThePathToLawyerWellBeing ReportFINAL.pdf.

- *Social*—Feeding the human need to develop a sense of connection and having a well-developed support network.

The American Bar Association's National Task Force on Lawyer Well-Being identifies the benefits that can be derived through wellbeing to include physical health, mental flourishing, making contributions to society, focus on client care, feeling connected and a sense of belonging, willingness to seek help when needed, engagement at work, continual intellectual growth, emotional intelligence, and experiencing a sense of meaning and purpose.[4]

Lawyer wellbeing involves a process of continuous improvement in each of these areas.[5] Each of us thus should be habitually attuned to maximizing the various facets of wellbeing as we develop our legal professional persona.

2. Why Wellbeing Matters[6]

Wellbeing is important for a range of personal and professional reasons.

The Personal/Family/Community Case for Wellbeing

Each of us deserves to be as happy and healthy as our dispositions permit; the quest for happiness should not be seen as a weakness but instead viewed as an essential element of self-actualization. The importance of happiness has an impressive and longstanding pedigree, which includes Aristotle ("[h]appiness is the meaning and purpose of life, the whole end of human existence"[7]) and our Declaration of Independence.[8]

---

[4] Id. at 73.

[5] Id. at 9.

[6] Stress management, and self-development is listed as one of the 26 effectiveness factors in the classical empirical study by Professors Marjorie M. Shultz and Sheldon Zedeck. See Marjorie M. Shultz & Sheldon Zedeck, Predicting Lawyer Effectiveness: Broadening the Basis for Law School Admission Decisions, 36 L. & Soc. Inquiry 620, 630 (summer 2011), available at http://citeseerx.ist.psu.edu/viewdoc/download?doi=10.1.1. 418.7400&rep=rep1&type=pdf.

[7] Aristotle, Nicomachean Ethics § 7 (Jonathan Barnes ed., 1984). See also id. (happiness is the "noblest . . . thing in the world.").

[8] Declaration of Independence para. 2, available at https://www.archives.gov/ founding-docs/declaration-transcript.

Wellbeing additionally carries implications that go beyond our own lives, and is an important feature of our relationships with family, friends, colleagues, and the larger communities in which we live.[9]

The Business Case for Wellbeing

For those who cannot or will not accept the personal case, there is a compelling business case to be made for individual wellbeing. Simply stated, individuals who want to excel in their careers should monitor and address their own wellbeing; and firms and leaders—even those motivated purely by self-interest and the bottom line—also have good reasons for creating a culture that advances lawyer wellbeing. The business case has several discrete components, including attorney competence, emotional contagion, and the need to limit attorney attrition.

Lack of Wellbeing Compromises Lawyer Competence

"Employee well-being and performance go hand in hand." Jade Wood & Bailey Nelson[10]

Positive emotions and happiness are not just about psychological effects—they are also associated with behavioral outcomes such as more productive workers, better performance in managerial positions, better job evaluations, and higher pay.[11] Our mental and physical health is integrally tied to our professional endeavors, and the various physical and psychological issues experienced by many lawyers impact our ability to work effectively, efficiently, and competently. In a nutshell, "[t]o be a good lawyer, one has to be a healthy"[12] and a

---

[9]   Martin E.P. Seligman, Paul R. Verkuil, & Terry H. Kang, Why Lawyers Are Unhappy, 23 Cardozo L. Rev. 33, 34 (2005) (lawyer "dysfunction entails societal, as well as personal, costs."), version available at http://www5.austlii.edu.au/au/journals/DeakinLawRw/2005/4.html. See also id. at 53 ("Given their role in a public profession they can also injure their clients by failing to provide adequate representation.").

[10]   Jade Wood & Bailey Nelson, Gallup Blog, The Manager's Role in Employee Well-Being (November 29, 2017), available at http://news.gallup.com/opinion/gallup/222833/manager-role-employee.aspx.

[11]   See Sonja Lyubomirsky, Laura A. King, & Ed Diener, The Benefits of Frequent Positive Affect: Does Happiness Lead to Success?, 131 Psychol. Bull. 803, 846 (2005).

[12]   Task Force on Lawyer Well-Being at 1. See also Frederic S. Ury & Deborah M. Garskof, Health and Wellness, in Essential Qualities of the Professional Lawyer 219 (2013) ("When a lawyer becomes overwhelmed with stress and strain, not only does career satisfaction suffer, so does his or her ability to perform"). See also id. at 9 (wellbeing enables us to make "responsible decisions" that affect our clients).

happy lawyer.[13] The importance of wellbeing is corroborated by the fact that a growing number of law firms have implemented wellness programs.[14]

When our wellbeing is undermined, our most important asset—the human capital that each of us possesses—is weakened[15] and we are unable to do our best work, which raises "troubling implications for many lawyers' basic competence."[16] Unhappy attorneys fall short of their potential, creating costs for them, their firms, and their clients.[17]

Numerous studies have demonstrated the relationship between wellbeing and lawyer performance. A lack of work-life balance has been tied to declining work product;[18] employee engagement has been linked to client satisfaction, lower turnover, and higher productivity and profitability;[19] health, happiness, and job satisfaction have been tied to job performance,[20] with "[h]appier, healthier lawyers" being found to "equate to better risk, fewer claims, and greater profitability."[21] Happy employees translate into a panoply of specific productivity benefits, including creativity, effective decision-making, interpersonal relations, leadership, managerial potential, income, and negotiating ability.[22]

---

[13] "[A] happy lawyer is a better lawyer and a more effective, ethical advocate for her clients." Bowling, supra note 1, at 45.

[14] See Ryan Lovelace, Akin Gump Adds On-Site Counseling as Firms Fret Over Mental Health, National Law Journal (May 15, 2018), available at https://www.law.com/nationallawjournal/2018/05/15/akin-gump-adds-on-site-counseling-as-firms-fret-over-mental-health/; Martha Neil, Kirkland & Ellis to offer 'emotional fitness' training at all law firm offices, ABA Journal (May 4, 2016) available at http://www.abajournal.com/news/article/kirkland_ellis_to_offer_emotional_fitness_training_at_all_law_firm_offices/. See also Staci Zaretsky, Some Law Firms Try to 'Eliminate Stigma' From Attorneys Struggling With Mental-Health Issues, Above the Law (May 22, 2017), available at https://abovethelaw.com/2017/05/some-law-firms-try-to-eliminate-stigma-from-attorneys-struggling-with-mental-health-issues/.

[15] National Task Force on Lawyer Well-Being, supra note 3, at 8.

[16] National Task Force on Lawyer Well-Being, supra note 3, Executive Summary.

[17] Seligman, Verkuil, & Kang, supra note 9, at 33.

[18] New York State Bar Association, Report of the Task Force on the Future of the Legal Profession 78 (April 2, 2011), available at https://www.nysba.org/futurereport/.

[19] National Task Force on Lawyer Well-Being, supra note 3, at 8.

[20] Id. at 8.

[21] Id. at 43.

[22] See Peter H. Huang & Rick Swedloff, Authentic Happiness and Meaning at Law Firms, 58 Syracuse L. Rev. 335, 337 (2008) (and citations therein), available at https://

Wellbeing also has been linked to lawyers' ability to comply with their obligations to deliver competent and ethical representation.[23] Substance abuse, depression, and other mental impairments are major factors leading to disciplinary action and claims of malpractice.[24] It has been estimated that up to 70% of disciplinary proceedings and malpractice claims against lawyers involve substance abuse and/or depression.[25]

Wellbeing—or Lack Thereof—Results in Emotional Contagion

Institutional concern for member wellbeing provides great "bang for the buck" for firms because of the principle of emotional contagion.[26] It turns out that happiness has an infectious effect on those around us. But emotional contagion works both ways—unhappy, stressed, and demoralized attorneys will also spread their disaffect to others within the organization. Law firms with a reputation for having happy associates also may find their recruiting efforts enhanced,[27] as borne out by the familiar law firm Quality of Life rankings.[28]

Lack of Wellbeing Leads to Attorney Attrition

A lack of wellbeing among associates leads to attrition, which results in a strain on human and financial resources within the firm and disruption for clients. There is a good deal of dissatisfaction with the practice (which has increased in

---

papers.ssrn.com/sol3/papers.cfm?abstract_id=1086675. See also id. at 336 ("Unhappy lawyers may loaf at work or otherwise be unproductive.").

[23] National Task Force on Lawyer Well-Being, supra note 3, at 8.

[24] Ury & Garskof, supra note 12, at 225, citing John P. Ratnaswamy, Substance Abuse and Attorney Discipline, The Bencher (Sept.–Oct. 2011).

[25] Douglas B. Marlowe, Alcoholism, Symptoms, Causes & Treatments, in Stress Management for Lawyers 104 (2d ed. 1987).

[26] See https://psychology.iresearchnet.com/social-psychology/emotions/emotional-contagion/.

[27] See Task Force on the Future of the Legal Profession, supra note 18, at 77–78.

[28] See Staci Zaretsky, Vault Rankings: The Best Law Firms To Work For In America (2019), available at https://abovethelaw.com/2018/06/vault-rankings-the-best-law-firms-to-work-for-in-america-2019/. See also Huang & Swedloff, supra note 22, at 336. I am a member of a listserv of law firm professional development staff who regularly lament the difficulties associated with attorney retention. The issue of attrition is one that clearly has caught the attention of law firms.

recent years)[29] leading to attrition, which is a major concern for law firms,[30] both because attrition is costly and because it is unsettling and annoying to clients.

Attrition Is Costly to Law Firms—Turnover is expensive, as demonstrated by numerous estimates of the cost of attrition to law firms:

- Turnover costs more than $25 million for a 400-attorney firm.[31]

- Firms spend an average of $12,000 in recruiting and training each associate they hire. That figure increases to $62,000 for law firms with more than 250 employees.[32]

- Firms spend between $500,000 and $700,000 identifying, recruiting, paying, and supporting an attorney during the first three years of hire.[33]

- Law firms do not recover their initial investment in an associate until close to three years from the date of hire.[34]

When firms invest so much in hiring and training associates, attrition has an obvious negative effect on the bottom line; when

---

[29] Catherine Gage O'Grady, Cognitive Optimism and Professional Pessimism in the Large-Firm Practice of Law: The Optimistic Associate, 30 Law & Psychol. Rev. 23, 24 (2006) (internal citations omitted).

[30] "Associate attrition is currently in the stratosphere." The Lawyer Whisperer, Associates are fleeing law firms in droves. These are the Top 3 reasons why (October 24, 216), available at https://www.thelawyerwhisperer.com/question/associates-are-fleeing-law-firms-in-droves-these-are-the-top-3-reasons-why/.

[31] Assessing Lawyer Traits & Finding a Fit for Success: Introducing the Sheffield Legal Assessment 3, available at http://therightprofile.com/wp-content/uploads/Attorney-Trait-Assessment-Study-Whitepaper-from-The-Right-Profile.pdf. This includes a $250,000 cost to recruit one first year associate. Id. at 4.

[32] Robert Half News Release, One-Quarter of Firms to Expand First-Year Associate Hiring (September 20, 2017), available at http://rh-us.mediaroom.com/2017-09-20-One-Quarter-Of-Law-Firms-To-Expand-First-Year-Associate-Hiring.

[33] See Report of the Task Force on the Future of the Legal Profession, supra note 18, at 76.

[34] Report of the Task Force on the Future of the Legal Profession, supra note 18, at 75, citing Peter Giuliani, Parting May Be Sweet Sorrow, But It's Getting More Expensive, N.Y. ST. B.A.J. 32 (May 2006).

attorneys are retained their time can be leveraged to help increase profit margins.[35]

Turnover Is Annoying to Clients—Clients understandably find attorney attrition to be disruptive.[36] John J. Flood, former Vice President and Associate General Counsel of NASD, notes the disruptive impact of attorney turnover and its impact on his company's hiring decisions:

> Some firms try to hide attrition. In one case, the chief partner, a trial lawyer, and two associates disappeared in an 18-month period and we were only told about one. I won't use that firm again. It's wasting my time to have to re-tell the story, what my corporation is about, what our history is.[37]

Linda Madrid, former General Counsel at CarrAmerica, likewise notes that it is "frustrating when outside counsel don't provide consistent lawyers. . . [N]othing [is] worse than investing in and relying on someone, and then having that person pulled out."[38]

Clients care not only about the disruption to work occasioned by turnover: They also want to work with law firms that are humane toward their associates, believing that associates who are treated well ultimately provide better representation. Linda Madrid notes that even worse than the disruption to work from attorney attrition is the belief that attrition reflects that

> the firm isn't treating them well enough to keep them. We have tried to look at how our outside counsel treat their young lawyers. . . including demands in terms of billing. These are all issues that we think ultimately have an impact on the services we receive.[39]

---

[35] Report of the Task Force on the Future of the Legal Profession, supra note 18, at 76.

[36] Id. at 74–75.

[37] Joan C. Williams, Cynthia Thomas Calvert, & Holly Cohen Cooper, Better on Balance? The Corporate Counsel Work/Life Report, 10 Wm. & Mary J. Women & L. 367 (2004), available at https://docplayer.net/26667320-Better-on-balance-the-corporate-counsel-work-life-report.html. See also National Task Force on Lawyer Well-Being, supra note 3, at 8.

[38] Williams, Thomas Calvert, & Cohen Cooper, supra note 37, at 367.

[39] Id.

For these reasons, employers and managers should care deeply about promoting and preserving employee wellbeing.

B. THE STATE OF, REASONS FOR, AND CHALLENGES TO LAWYER WELLBEING

1. The State of Attorney Wellbeing: A Long Way to Go

The toxic effects of the physically, intellectually, and emotionally demanding nature of many law-related jobs has been well documented. The National Task Force on Lawyer Well-Being finds a profession "falling short" with respect to wellbeing.[40] There is rampant dissatisfaction within the profession and the level of dissatisfaction has increased over the past decades.[41] In particular, the profession faces the following specific and alarming challenges to lawyer wellbeing:[42] 21–36% of attorneys are problem drinkers; 28% of attorneys suffer from depression; 19% of attorneys suffer from anxiety; 23% of attorneys demonstrate signs of elevated stress; and 25% of attorneys suffer from work addiction. Attorneys also experience elevated levels of suicide, sleep deprivation, work-life conflict, job dissatisfaction, and attrition. Attorneys commonly avoid seeking help.

These findings are not novel or new.[43] Numerous studies spanning decades confirm that lawyers consistently are the unhappiest of all professionals and suffer disproportionately from chronic stress and high rates of depression and substance abuse. A 2013 report notes the "profound ambivalence" that

---

[40] National Task Force on Lawyer Well-Being, supra note 3, at 1.

[41] See Susan Daicoff, Lawyer Be Thyself: An Empirical Investigation of the Relationship Between the Ethic of Care, the Feeling Decisionmaking Preference, and Lawyer Wellbeing, 16 Va. J. Soc. Pol'y & L. 87, 90 n. 9 (2008–09), available at https://papers.ssrn.com/sol3/papers.cfm?abstract_id=2442368.

[42] National Task Force on Lawyer Well-Being, supra note 3, at 73.

[43] In particular, these findings are not tied to the current economic challenges facing the profession. Even in the 1980s, the so-called Golden Age for law hiring, law students and lawyers suffered from inordinately high levels of distress. See G. Andrew H. Benjamin, Alfred Kaszniak, Bruce Sales, & Stephen B. Shanfield, The Role of Legal Education in Producing Psychological Distress Among Law Students and Lawyers, 11 Am. B. Found. Res. J. 225, 226 (1986), available at https://www.jstor.org/stable/828178?seq=1#page_scan_tab_contents.

many lawyers have toward their work.[44] Here is one somewhat dated but chilling account:

> In a country where the depression rate is ten times higher today [2009] than it was in 1960, lawyers sit at the unenviable zenith of depressed professionals. Of all professionals in the United States, lawyers suffer from the highest rate of depression after adjusting for socio-demographic factors, and they are 3.6 times more likely to suffer from major depressive disorder than the rest of the employed population. Lawyers are also at a greater risk for heart disease, alcoholism and drug use than the general population. In one sample of practicing lawyers, researchers found that 70% were likely to develop alcohol-related problems over the course of their lifetime, compared to just 13.7% of the general population; of these same lawyers, 20% to 35% were "clinically distressed," as opposed to only 2% of the general population. With such disproportionate levels of unhappiness, it is not surprising that the profession itself is suffering. Alcoholism or chemical dependency is the cause of the majority of lawyer discipline cases in the United States, and a growing disaffection with the practice of law pushes 40,000 lawyers to leave the profession every year.[45]

2. Reasons for Lawyer Dysfunction and Challenges to Lawyer Wellbeing

It All Begins in Law School

No one who has studied law will be surprised to learn that the dysfunction experienced by many in the legal profession can be traced to law school. Studies demonstrate that before law school, subjects were similar to the normal population along an array of responses (such as obsessive-compulsive behavior,

---

[44] David L. Chambers, Overstating the Satisfaction of Lawyers, 39 Law & Soc. Inquiry 1, 1 (2013), available at https://repository.law.umich.edu/cgi/viewcontent.cgi?referer=https://www.google.com/&httpsredir=1&article=1871&context=articles.

[45] Todd David Peterson & Elizabeth Waters Peterson, Stemming the Tide of Law Student Depression: What Law Schools Need To Learn From the Science of Positive Psychology, 9 Yale J. Health Pol'y, L. & Ethics 357, 358 (2009) (internal citations omitted), available at http://digitalcommons.law.yale.edu/yjhple/vol9/iss2/2/.

interpersonal sensitivity, depression, anxiety, hostility, phobic anxiety, paranoid ideation, and social alienation and isolation), which become elevated significantly during law school. These maladies continue into the professional careers of the subjects.[46] Significantly, these findings are unique to law students and do not apply similarly across graduate students in other disciplines,[47] earning law schools the dubious distinction of being labeled "unique producers of depression."[48]

A recent Survey of Law Student Well-Being finds troublesome rates of alcohol use, anxiety, depression, and illegal drug use.[49] Nearly half of the respondents report needing help but very few actually seek it.[50] Law school student wellbeing surveys reflect pervasive binge drinking and risk for alcoholism and suicidal thoughts.[51] At least one study finds that more than 40% of law students meet the criteria for clinically significant levels of psychological distress.[52] This study also reveals that law students report a significantly higher level of drug and alcohol use than college and high school graduates generally, and that their alcohol use progressively increases during their three years of law school.[53]

Students themselves have taken stock of the toll that law school takes on them and their peers. Student leaders from 13 leading U.S. law schools publicly have pledged to broaden mental health initiatives on their campuses and to seek to reduce the stigma often attached to seeking help. The student

---

[46] See Benjamin, Kaszniak, Sales, & Shanfield, supra note 43.

[47] See, e.g., Marilyn Heins, Shirley N. Fahey, & Roger C. Henderson, Law Students and Medical Students: A Comparison of Perceived Stress. 33 J. Legal Educ. 511, 511–14 (1983).

[48] Corie Rosen Felder, The Accidental Optimist, 21 Va. J. Soc. Pol'y & L. 63, 66 (2014).

[49] Jerome M. Organ, David B. Jaffe, & Katherine M. Bender, Suffering in Silence: The Survey of Law Student Well-Being and the Reluctance of Law Students to Seek Help for Substance Use and Mental Health Concerns, 66 J. Legal Educ. 116, 127–36 (Autumn 2016), available at https://jle.aals.org/home/vol66/iss1/13/.

[50] More than 40% of law students needed help for poor mental health but only about half sought it out. Id. at 140.

[51] Id. at 139–40. See also Peterson & Peterson, supra note 45, at 358–59 (internal citations omitted).

[52] See id. at 358–59, citing Lynda L. Murdoch, Psychological Distress and Substance Abuse in Law Students: The Role of Moral Orientation and Interpersonal Style 87 (November 2002) (unpublished Ph.D. dissertation, Simon Fraser University).

[53] Id. at 358–59.

leaders pointedly observe the challenges facing law students (and practitioners), which stems from the

> damaging stereotypes that law school must be a grueling and overwhelming ordeal to adequately prepare students for legal practice. The toll on students' mental health has become an accepted characteristic of law school life rather than properly recognized as an impediment to our success. . . . Moreover, law school culture as well as character and fitness inquiries into mental health treatment history can encourage self-medication in the form of alcohol consumption and substance abuse, rather than healthy longterm treatment. We must be vigilant to stop the internalization of these misguided mental health norms in our law schools. . . . Poor student or practitioner health is not a necessary byproduct of a rigorous legal education and needs to be treated as the scourge of the profession that it is. Students left behind are not failures of personal strength. They are testaments to our collective failure to uplift one another and raise the standards of our trade.[54]

There are a number of reasons to explain the suffering occasioned by law school. Legal education places a virtually singular value on rigorous, objective analytic thinking, minimizing the perceived utility of other kinds of thinking. Much of law student and lawyer unhappiness has been tied to the rigorous analytical approach inherent in teaching students to think like lawyers.[55] This approach, many argue, tends to deplete creativity and compels students to value "consistency over ambiguity, rationality over emotion, and rules over social context."[56]

It is no wonder that law students begin to exhibit signs of distress during their studies[57] given this method of thinking,

---

[54] https://images.law.com/contrib/content/uploads/documents/292/LawSchoolsMH Pledge-1-copy.pdf.

[55] Jean Stefancic & Richard Delgado, How Lawyers Lose Their Way: A Profession Fails Its Creative Minds xi–xiii (2005).

[56] Id. at xi.

[57] See Lawrence S. Krieger, Psychological Insights: Why Our Students and Graduates Suffer, and What We Might Do About It, 1 J. Ass'n Legal Writing Directors

coupled with the heavy workload (which often results in isolation from family and friends); new and challenging ways of reading (case law); the crushing competition for grades, journal membership, clerkships and other top jobs, and other external standards of success (which often leads to isolation from classmates); as well as the Socratic method, which induces stress and exposes ignorance (or perceived ignorance).[58]

Many also experience a form of cognitive dissonance when they enter law school. So many of us decide to pursue a career in law because of service-oriented values, values that dissipate during and are largely anomalous to law study.

Lawyers as a Group Are Highly Competitive

Adding to the challenges of attorney wellbeing, lawyers as a group tend to be inherently competitive people. This may be especially true of those attracted to large firm practice:

> Big firm lawyers . . . have spent almost their entire lives competing to win games that other people have set up for them. First they competed to get into a prestigious college. Then they competed for college grades. Then they competed for LSAT scores. Then they competed to get into a prestigious law school. Then they competed for law school grades. Then they competed to make the law review. Then they competed for clerkships. Then they competed to get hired by a big law firm.

258, 261–62 (2002), available at https://ir.law.fsu.edu/cgi/viewcontent.cgi?article=1099& context=articles. See also Kennon M. Sheldon & Lawrence S. Krieger, Does Legal Education Have Undermining Effects on Law Students? Evaluating Changed in Motivation, Values and Well-Being, 22 Behav. Sci. & L. 261 (2004), available at http:// citeseerx.ist.psu.edu/viewdoc/download?doi=10.1.1.555.7527&rep=rep1&type=pdf; Eli Wald & Russell G. Pearce, 9 U. St. Thomas L. J. 403, 423–24 (2011), available at https:// ir.lawnet.fordham.edu/cgi/viewcontent.cgi?article=1625&context=faculty_scholarship; Cynthia Fuchs Epstein, Knowledge for What?, 49 J. Legal Educ. 41, 41 (1999), citing Deborah L. Rhode, Missing Questions: Feminist Perspectives on Legal Education, 45 Stan. L. Rev. 1547 (1993) and Michael Burns, The Law School as a Model for Community, 10 Nova L. J. 329 (1986), available at https://www.jstor.org/stable/42893582; Daisy Hurst Floyd, We Can Do More, 60 J. Legal Educ. 129, 130–32 (2010), available at https:// jle.aals.org/home/vol60/iss1/8/.

[58] The Socratic method leads to student alienation because it "relies on adversarial relationship between professor and student." Wald & Pearce, supra note 57, at 424–25.

> Now that they're in a big law firm, what's going to
> happen? Are they going to stop competing? Are they
> going to stop comparing themselves to others? Of course
> not. They're going to keep competing—competing to bill
> more hours, to attract more clients, to win more cases,
> to do more deals. They're playing a game. And money is
> how the score is kept in that game.[59]

The competitive nature of law students and lawyers thus may present a chicken-and-egg kind of problem. Our competitive nature draws us to law school and law practice, both of which reinforce and intensify our natural competitiveness, resulting in a vicious cycle. This cycle is further exacerbated by the intense pressure and competition for clients.[60]

The Adversarial Nature of the Legal System

The competitive qualities inherent to many attorneys are further underscored by the fact that law is an adversarial system, a notion that is introduced early on in our law study, as appellate decisions form the mainstay of legal education, especially in first year doctrinal courses. This system of course revolves around conflict. And as agents of others, much of our work is as advocates promoting particular positions.[61] Lawyers, embedded in an adversarial system like to win, an inclination that becomes problematic when bled into other areas of our lives.[62]

---

[59] Patrick J. Schiltz, On Being a Happy, Healthy, and Ethical Member of an Unhappy, Unhealthy, and Unethical Profession, 52 Vand. L. Rev. 871, 906 (1999) (internal citations omitted), a version of which is available at http://faculty.law.miami. edu/mcoombs/Schlitz.htm.

[60] See Chapter 2.B.1., supra.

[61] Lawrence S. Krieger, What We're Not Telling Law Students—And Lawyers— That They Really Need to Know: Some Thoughts-in-Action Toward Revitalizing the Profession From Its Roots, 13 J. L. & Health 1, 24–25 (1998–89), available at https://ir. law.fsu.edu/cgi/viewcontent.cgi?article=1100&context=articles.

[62] See Peterson & Peterson, supra note 45, at 401.

C. HOW TO ACHIEVE GREATER WELLBEING

1. What We Can Do as Individuals

Each of us needs to take personal responsibility for our own wellbeing. Our professional commitments should always be undertaken with reference to and in light of our health, happiness, and sense of balance.

Based on the obstacles to wellbeing identified above,[63] it may seem that lawyers—by nature or by virtue of the process of legal education—are hard-wired to be unhappy and unhealthy. This is not true. However, it may mean that we must work a little harder than others to achieve a state of wellbeing. In particular, it is important to be reflective about how our work affects us and how we can maintain our wellbeing. And because the challenges associated with our work may make us inclined to skimp on elements of personal wellness, it is important that we develop strong habits that promote our wellbeing.

What follows are some of the basic components of a wellbeing plan. Much of this is common sense, but because so many of us neglect these essential elements of wellbeing, they need to be emphasized with the hope that each of us will be more purposeful about ensuring that we build and maintain our physical and psychological resources.

Eat Well

A nutritious, balanced diet is important for physical and mental health. Eating well can be difficult because fast food and other unhealthy choices are often more accessible to those of us on a busy schedule. Eating healthy food is also often more expensive than eating unhealthy food, which may be a concern for many law students and others on a budget. It is well worth the extra resources needed to eat well. Here are a few specific suggestions:

Be Deliberate About How and What We Eat—When in a hurry, many of us do not think enough about what we put into our bodies. Developing a habit of being more conscious about our

---

[63] Section B.2., supra.

food choices can make a difference, and need not consume much time. Those of us who have dietary restrictions imposed by health concerns, religious beliefs, or ethical or moral principles do this all the time. Developing a habit of being conscious of what we consume is a practice that would serve each of us well.

Snack Well—Be sure to have healthy snacks available (for example, nuts, fresh or dried fruit, a low-sugar protein bar) that you can eat on the run or when you are stuck behind your desk so that you avoid the temptations of fast food and vending machines.

Take Time for Breakfast—Cliché as it sounds, breakfast is the most important meal of the day. Eating breakfast will boost your metabolism for the entire day, giving you more energy and allowing you to burn more calories.[64]

Limit Sugar Content—Sugary treats and simple carbohydrates make for great and easy comfort food but ultimately increase insulin production, lower your blood sugar, and give you a surge in appetite and craving for the same kind of food.[65] Most of us enjoy these foods from time to time but we should be careful not to indulge in them too often.

Get Enough Sleep

Surprisingly, science has yet to come up with a comprehensive understanding for why we need sleep, although numerous theories have been advanced.[66] Nevertheless, there is widespread agreement on the importance of sleep and the fact that sleep deprivation will affect us in a number of vital ways. The absence of quality and adequate sleep has been linked to depression, cognitive impairment, decreased concentration, and burnout, and these impairments can be profound.[67] In some circles there may be a conviction that sleeping little is a sign of

---

[64] Gregory L. Jantz, The Most Important Keys to a Healthy Diet, Psychology Today (January 6, 2015), available at https://www.psychologytoday.com/blog/hope-relationships/201501/the-most-important-keys-healthy-diet.

[65] Id.

[66] See, e.g., Why Do We Sleep, Anyway?, Healthy Sleep (December 18, 2007), available at http://healthysleep.med.harvard.edu/healthy/matters/benefits-of-sleep/why-do-we-sleep (naming the restoration, energy conservation, and brain plasticity theories of sleep).

[67] National Task Force on Lawyer Well-Being, supra note 3, at 53.

sturdiness or commitment, but the downside implications of skimping on sleep are significant.

The benefits of sufficient sleep include improved learning and the ability to pay attention, make decisions, and be creative; sleep deficiency alters brain activity and makes it difficult for us to make decisions, solve problems, control emotions, and cope with change.[68] Each and every one of these implications relates to an important part of what lawyers do, strengthening the case for the need for legal professionals to get adequate sleep.

There are still others who may suffer from insomnia or other serious sleep disorders. Although many of us suffer from sleeplessness from time to time, in particular in response to situational pressures, if it becomes chronic, it is time to seek professional help.

Are you one of the many people who believe that they do not need a lot of sleep? Chances are you are mistaken. Only 1–3 percent of the population, described as the "sleepless elite," needs fewer than 6 hours of sleep per night.[69] These "natural 'short sleepers' " are energetic, outgoing, and ambitious without much sleep, naps, or caffeine.[70] Lucky them! The problem is that many of us think that we are natural short sleepers when in fact we are not. Out of every 100 people who think they are natural short sleepers, only 5 are. The other 95 need the recommended 7 (or more) hours of sleep per night.[71]

Take Other Periods of Rejuvenation

In addition to sleep, we need other periods of downtime to recover from the demands of our work and minimize the risk of depression, exhaustion, and burnout.[72] These can be vacations, but even shorter evening, weekend, or midday breaks can help.[73]

---

[68] National Heart, Lung, and Blood Institute, Why is Sleep Important?, available at https://www.nhlbi.nih.gov/health-topics/sleep-deprivation-and-deficiency.

[69] See Melinda Beck, The Sleepless Elite: Why Some People Can Run on Little Sleep and Get So Much Done, The Wall Street Journal (April 5, 2011), available at https://www.wsj.com/articles/SB10001424052748703712504576242701752957910.

[70] See id.

[71] See id.

[72] National Task Force on Lawyer Well-Being, supra note 3, at 53, and citations therein.

[73] Id. A former colleague and I would occasionally take long lunches together when time permitted. We called them "mini-vacations," and they worked!

Taking breaks of whatever duration has been tied to increased productivity and creativity.[74] We perform best and most productively when we "alternate between periods of intense focus and intermittent renewal."[75]

It is important that these periods of rejuvenation truly allow us to disconnect. One study reports that more than 60 percent of us who take vacations check email and/or voicemail while on vacation, undermining the quality of the rejuvenation period.[76]

Develop and Commit to a Fitness Plan

When it comes to managing our time,[77] exercise is often viewed as a luxury that many of us forgo. But physical activity is important to promoting several measures of wellbeing, including mental health, brain functioning, and energy levels. Physical exercise, particularly aerobic exercise, has been found to be effective at alleviating symptoms of depression and dementia, and is associated with improvements in memory, attention, verbal learning, and cognitive processing.[78] Exercise also can improve confidence and discipline,[79] and helps us manage stress[80] by reducing the amounts of stress hormones and increasing the body's production of endorphins.[81]

---

[74] Jackie Coleman & John Coleman, The Upside of Downtime, Harvard Business Review (December 6, 2012), available at https://hbr.org/2012/12/the-upside-of-downtime.

[75] Tony Schwartz, The Productivity Paradox: How Sony Pictures Gets More Out of People by Demanding Less, Harvard Business Review (June 2010), available at https://hbr.org/2010/06/the-productivity-paradox-how-sony-pictures-gets-more-out-of-people-by-demanding-less.

[76] Travel Leaders Group, More than 62% of Americans Regularly "Check In" with Work While Vacationing, According to New Survey (May 16, 2017).

[77] See Chapter 5.A., supra.

[78] National Task Force on Lawyer Well-Being, supra note 3, at 53–54, and citations therein. See also Ury & Garskof, supra note 12, at 226, citing Benefits of Regular Physical Activity, Mayo Clinic (July 23, 2011), available at https://www.mayoclinic.org/healthy-lifestyle/fitness/in-depth/exercise/art-20048389. (finding that exercise improves health, mood, and energy, and helps you sleep better).

[79] Ury & Garskof, supra note 12, at 227, citing Press Release, Harvard Health Publishing, Benefits of exercise—reduces stress, anxiety and helps fight depression, Harvard Men's Health Watch (February 2011), available at https://www.health.harvard.edu/press_releases/benefits-of-exercisereduces-stress-anxiety-and-helps-fight-depression.

[80] Id. at 226 (2013), citing Gretchen Reynolds, Why Exercise Makes You Less Anxious, N.Y. Times Well Blog (November 18, 2009), available at https://well.blogs.nytimes.com/2009/11/18/phys-ed-why-exercise-makes-you-less-anxious/.

[81] Id. at 226–27 (2013), citing Press Release, Harvard Health Publications, Benefits of exercise—reduces stress, anxiety and helps Fight depression, Harvard Men's Heath

If, as is the case with many of us, you are not in the habit of getting physical exercise, start with modest goals—take the stairs more often, walk when possible, and stand rather than sit when you can.

If you have trouble getting started with an exercise routine, find a friend or colleague to exercise with. This creates an incentive and keeps you accountable. Try to set aside a fixed time to do your exercise. You do not need to do much to make a difference—doing even two and a half hours of moderately intense aerobic activity and two hours of strength training each week is helpful.[82] And because exercise releases endorphins, you might find that you crave even more physical activity—making exercise one very healthy addiction!

Learn How to Manage Stress

Stress is inevitable in the life of most people, especially lawyers. In mild or moderate levels, stress can be a positive force.[83] But when stress becomes overwhelming, it can lead to negative consequences, such as burnout, depression, anxiety, substance abuse; physical conditions such as cardiovascular, inflammatory, and other illnesses; and cognitive decline, such as impaired attention, concentration, memory, and problem-solving ability.[84] All of these negative outcomes can compromise our capacity to practice law effectively.[85]

Stress is an internal feature that we can regulate and control through out attitudes toward and perceptions of outside stressors.[86] While we cannot always affect external stressors, we do have the ability to control how we deal with them. Many of us attribute stress to external influences but in fact stress refers to our *reactions* to specific external factors. When stressful factors are out of your control, do not internalize them—that would

---

Watch (February 2011), available at https://www.health.harvard.edu/press_releases/benefits-of-exercisereduces-stress-anxiety-and-helps-fight-depression.

[82] Jantz, *supra* note 64.

[83] National Task Force on Lawyer Well-Being, *supra* note 3, at 51 ("When stress is perceived as a positive, manageable challenge, the stress response actually can enable peak performance.") (internal citations omitted).

[84] *Id.* (internal citations omitted).

[85] *Id.* (internal citations omitted).

[86] Professor Lawrence Krieger refers to stress as a "profoundly subjective" determination. Krieger, *supra* note 61, at 28.

simply be a waste of resources with no corresponding perceptible benefit. Take deliberate account of what your stressors are and think consciously of how to minimize your reaction to them. Be productive and organized to alleviate the feelings of stress they elicit. Try mindfulness, as discussed below.

Avoid or Eliminate Unhealthy Addictions

Addictions common to lawyers and law students include alcohol and drug abuse but also perfectionism[87] and workaholism,[88] maladies that we often experience but do not view as the addictions that they are. If you find that you have a strong need for perfection, regularly overextend yourself, fear criticism, constantly seek approval and affirmation from others, mistrust your own feelings, and find it difficult to identify and express your emotions, you may suffer from these disorders.[89] Acknowledge and challenge these feelings, and if necessary, seek help.

Get Help if You Need It

Be attuned to your own physical and psychological health. Each of us is in a position to recognize signs of distress and changes in our health. Do not ignore these warnings. Engage in a continuous process of monitoring and evaluating yourself. Trust your instincts. We should also listen to thoughtful observations made by loved ones and trusted colleagues, who at times are better able than we are to spot warning signs. This is particularly important because lawyers as a group are reluctant to seek help.[90]

---

[87] It has been said that "perfectionism transforms into a feeling that nothing is good enough." Leslie A. Gordon, How lawyers an avoid burnout and debilitating anxiety, ABA Journal (July 2015), available at http://www.abajournal.com/magazine/article/how_lawyers_can_avoid_burnout_and_debilitating_anxiety.

[88] Workaholism has been defined as "a compulsive drive to work at the expense of other aspects of a person's life. The workaholic, like other addicts, loses control of his or her life and becomes habitually dependent on work." Benjamin L. Sells, Workaholism, 79-DEC ABA J. 70, 70 (1993). See the discussion, infra, regarding the need to develop and cultivate interests beyond work.

[89] See Krieger, supra note 61, at 33.

[90] See, e.g., Andrea Ciobanu & Stephen M. Terrell, Out of the Darkness: Overcoming Depression among Lawyers, 32 GP Solo (2015), available at https://www.americanbar.org/content/dam/aba/publications/gp_solo_magazine/march_april_2015/gp m_v032n02_15mar_apr.authcheckdam.pdf. Jerome M. Organ, David B. Jaffe, & Katherine M. Bender, Suffering in Silence: The Survey of Law Student Well-Being and

If you see changes in your own wellbeing, or someone you trust has identified such changes, seek help. If your concerns relate to mental health issues or alcohol, drugs, gambling, or other addictive behaviors, make use of confidential lawyer assistance programs available in every U.S. state and territory.[91]

Monitor Your Hours

Lawyers may be unhappy for myriad reasons, but the punishing time commitment demanded by law practice seems to top the list.[92] The long hours that most lawyers devote to work are exhausting, and that is what truly defeats us. These time commitments, when "all-consuming," leave little time or energy for anything else,[93] including friends and family and other things that we value.

Beyond the actual hours worked, the fact that the work of attorneys in private practice is divided into billable and non-billable units leads to an "economically reductive view of work" that is inherently unsatisfying to many.[94]

Consistent with the discussion above,[95] there is a business case to be made for not working excessive hours. Studies have shown that "long hours spent in the office do not always yield the best work product."[96] This is a straightforward function of the economic law of diminishing returns.[97] To put this in the language of working hours, there is a point at which adding hours to the workday or workweek will begin to yield smaller and smaller or even diminishing returns in terms of output. Studies have confirmed that working less can lead to greater

---

the Reluctance of Law Students to Seek Help for Substance Use and Mental Health Concerns. 66 J. Legal Educ. 116 (2016), available at https://jle.aals.org/home/vol66/iss1/13/.

[91] For a list of lawyer assistance programs by state, see https://www.americanbar.org/groups/lawyer_assistance/resources/lap_programs_by_state.html.

[92] Schiltz, supra note 59, at 888–89.

[93] Id. at 915.

[94] Sells, supra note 88, at 71.

[95] See Section A.2., supra.

[96] Ury & Garskof, supra note 12, at 221.

[97] See Encyclopedia Britannica, Diminishing Returns, available at https://www.britannica.com/topic/diminishing-returns.

productivity,[98] leading some companies to move from a 40- to a 30-hour workweek.[99] Rather than being "badges of honor,"[100] excessive hours properly should be seen as counterproductive.

All of which begs the question: Do lawyers have any meaningful control over their hours? Sometimes we do and sometimes we do not. There may be times when we do have control but take on projects that we really do not have time for out of fear of appearing uncooperative or weak; we sometimes work more hours than we really need to on projects that could be done more efficiently. We must find the sweet spot at which we provide outstanding service while preserving our ability to do so on a long-term basis.[101]

To the extent that we genuinely do not have control over our hours and they become unmanageable and unhealthy in our current work environment, this may be a sign that it is time to consider other options. There is great wisdom in knowing when to move on.

Seek Intrinsic Rather than External Motivation and Rewards

Our motivations matter and can affect our wellbeing. When our motivations are intrinsic, we engage in activities for the purpose of gaining satisfaction from the activity itself or to further goals that are important to us, such as self-improvement

---

[98] See, e.g., Jon Youshaei, How Many Hours Is The Optimal Workweek? Fewer Than You Think (May 3, 2016), available at https://www.forbes.com/sites/jonyoushaei/2016/05/03/how-many-hours-is-the-optimal-workweek-fewer-than-you-think/#40ae25fe60e3; C.W., Proof that you should get a life, The Economist (December 9, 2014), available at https://www.economist.com/free-exchange/2014/12/09/proof-that-you-should-get-a-life.

[99] See, e.g., Charlotte Graham-McLay, A 4-Day Workweek? A Test Run Shows a Surprising Result, The New York Times (July 19, 2018), available at https://www.nytimes.com/2018/07/19/world/asia/four-day-workweek-new-zealand.html;   Peter Kotecki, Companies are shortening the 40-hour workweek to increase employee productivity—here's how it's going around the world, Business Insider (July 26, 2018), available at https://www.businessinsider.com/employee-productivity-experiments-companies-shortening-the-workweek-2018-7; Simon Kuper, Why the 30-hour work week is almost here, FT Magazine (February 14, 2018), available at https://www.ft.com/content/78c5cebe-111b-11e8-940e-08320fc2a277; Karen Turner, Amazon is piloting teams with a 30-hour workweek, The Washington Post (August 26, 2016), available at https://www.washingtonpost.com/news/the-switch/wp/2016/08/26/amazon-is-piloting-teams-with-a-30-hour-work-week/?noredirect=on&utm_term=.985de77c743f.

[100] Bowling, supra note 1, at 43.

[101] See Section D., infra.

and personal satisfaction. Intrinsic motivations further our wellbeing. Extrinsic motivations, however, such as those driven by the desire for money, prestige, power, or other rewards, or to relieve a sense of guilt or fear, are inimical to wellbeing and are likely to produce frustration and anxiety.[102]

The issue of money is a serious one for many attorneys along a number of dimensions. Many lawyers stay in jobs that do not promote their wellbeing because they feel trapped by financial responsibility. Earning lots of money may lead to a vicious cycle under which we measure our value by our salary, and that is a value that can never measure up:

> If you fall into the trap of measuring your worth by money, you will always feel inadequate. There will always be a firm paying more to its associates than yours. There will always be a firm with higher per-partner profits than yours. There will always be a lawyer at your firm making more money than you.[103]

Another problem with the high earning potential associated with many areas of law practice is the "hedonic treadmill"[104] on which we ride once we become accustomed to the increased standard of living made available by high salaries and bonuses. Studies show that the happiness associated with earnings is fairly transitory. In an analysis of data from more than 6,000 lawyers and law students, researchers find that the external rewards that are highly valued by lawyers and students, such as law school grades, law school rank, law journal membership, and income after graduation, correlate weakly or not at all with a sense of wellbeing.[105] As we get more money, our desires increase accordingly, leading to "a treadmill that never ends, even for

---

[102] Krieger, supra note 57, at 260–61.

[103] Schiltz, supra note 59, at 921.

[104] Philip Brickman & Donald T. Campbell, Hedonic Relativism and Planning the Good Society, in Adaptation-Level Theory: A Symposium 287, 289 (1971). See also Daniel Kahneman, Alan B. Krueger, David A. Schkade, Norbert Schwarz, & Arthur A. Stone, A Survey Method for Characterizing Daily Life Experience: The Day Reconstruction Method, 306 Science 1776, 1779 (2004), available at http://science.sciencemag.org/content/306/5702/1776.

[105] See Lawrence S. Krieger & Kennon M. Sheldon, What Makes Lawyers Happy? A Data-Driven Prescription to Redefine Professional Success, 83 Geo. Wash. L. Rev. 554 (2015), available at https://ir.law.fsu.edu/cgi/viewcontent.cgi?referer=https://www.google.com/&httpsredir=1&article=1093&context=articles.

billionaires."[106] Beyond a fairly low level of income, making or having more money apparently does not make us happier.[107]

Engage in Mindfulness

Mindfulness is the ability to be fully present in the moment with an awareness of what we are doing and how we are feeling, of resting the mind in the present rather than getting caught up in worries about other things.[108] Mindfulness "provides a heightened awareness of whatever event is occurring in your life in the present moment, and how you are thinking, feeling and experiencing the event."[109]

Mindfulness has the ability to make us calm because our focus on the present limits the likelihood that we will be overwhelmed by external events.[110] It also makes us better listeners because it increases our focus. For this reason, mindfulness has been called "the essence of engagement."[111]

To many, mindfulness may conjure images of chanting and crystals. I myself have been skeptical of these kinds of techniques, but there is powerful scientific evidence to support that mindfulness offers a range of benefits both physical and

---

[106] Daniel Goleman, Social Intelligence: The New Science of Human Relationships 311 (2006), citing Daniel Kahneman, Alan B. Krueger, David A. Schkade, Norbert Schwarz, & Arthur A. Stone, A Survey Method for Characterizing Daily Life Experience: The Day Reconstruction Method, 306 Science 1776, 1779 (2004), available at http://science.sciencemag.org/content/306/5702/1776. Or, as Bruce Springsteen writes, "[p]oor man wanna be rich, rich man wanna be king, and a king ain't satisfied 'til he rules everything." Bruce Springsteen, Badlands (1978).

[107] See Daniel Kahneman, Alan B. Krueger, David Schkade, Norbert Schwarz, & Arthur A. Stone, Would You Be Happier If You Were Richer? A Focusing Illusion, 312 Science 1908 (June 30, 2006), available at http://science.sciencemag.org/content/312/5782/1908.full; Mike Rudin, The science of happiness, BBC News (April 30, 2006), available at http://news.bbc.co.uk/2/hi/programmes/happiness_formula/4783836.stm.

[108] See, e.g., Merriam-Webster Dictionary, defining mindfulness as "the practice of maintaining a nonjudgmental state of heightened or complete awareness of one's thoughts, emotions, or experiences on a moment-to-moment basis." https://www.merriam-webster.com/dictionary/mindfulness.

[109] Jan L. Jacobowitz, Mindfulness and Professionalism, in Essential Qualities of the Professional Lawyer 231 (2013).

[110] "Mindfulness is the basic human ability to be fully present, aware of where we are and what we're doing, and not overly reactive or overwhelmed by what's going on around us." What is Mindfulness, Mindful, https://www.mindful.org/what-is-mindfulness/ (October 8, 2014).

[111] Interview with Ellen Langer, Mindfulness in the Age of Complexity, Harvard Business Review (March 2014), available at https://hbr.org/2014/03/mindfulness-in-the-age-of-complexity.

mental related to learning, cognition, memory, executive control, emotional regulation, empathy, stress management, anxiety, focus, productivity, and happiness and overall wellbeing. Mindfulness also has been found to hone interpersonal skills, increase empathic accuracy, and reduce cognitive rigidity, thereby promoting creative thinking.[112]

The National Task Force on Lawyer Well-Being agrees that there are substantial benefits to attorneys engaging in mindfulness meditation:

> Mindfulness meditation is a practice that can enhance cognitive reframing (and thus resilience) by aiding our ability to monitor our thoughts and avoid becoming emotionally overwhelmed. A rapidly growing body of research on meditation has shown its potential for help in addressing a variety of psychological and psychosomatic disorders, especially those in which stress plays a causal role. One type of meditative practice is mindfulness—a technique that cultivates the skill of being present by focusing attention on your breath and detaching from your thoughts or feelings. Research has found that mindfulness can reduce rumination, stress, depression, and anxiety. It also can enhance a host of competencies related to lawyer effectiveness, including increased focus and concentration, working memory, critical cognitive

---

[112] See Jan L. Jacobowitz, The Benefits of Mindfulness for Lawyers, ABA Young Lawyers Division (August 9, 2017), available at https://www.americanbar.org/groups/young_lawyers/publications/tyl/topics/work-life/the_benefits_mindfulness_lawyers/; Alvin Powell, Researchers study how it seems to change the brain in depressed patients, The Harvard Gazette (April 9, 2018), available at https://news.harvard.edu/gazette/story/2018/04/harvard-researchers-study-how-mindfulness-may-change-the-brain-in-depressed-patients/; Mindfulness: The Science, available at http://www.mindfulnessforlawyers.com/science/. Liz Mineo, With mindfulness, life's in the moment, The Harvard Gazette (April 17, 2018), available at https://news.harvard.edu/gazette/story/2018/04/less-stress-clearer-thoughts-with-mindfulness-meditation/; Manoj K. Bhasin, John W. Denninger, Jeff C. Huffman, Marie G. Joseph, Halsey Niles, Emma Chad-Friedman, Roberta Goldman, Beverly Buczynski-Kelley, Barbara A. Mahoney, Gregory L. Fricchione, Jeffrey A. Dusek, Herbert Benson, Randall M. Zusman, & Towia A. Libermann, Specific Transcriptome Changes Associated with Blood Pressure Reduction in Hypertensive Patients After Relaxation Response Training, 24 J. Alt. & Comp. Med. 486 (2018), available at https://www.ncbi.nlm.nih.gov/pubmed/29616846; Richard Chambers, Barbara Chuen Yee Lo, & Nicholas B. Allen, The Impact of Intensive Mindfulness Training on Attentional Control, Cognitive Style, and Affect, 32 Cognitive Therapy and Research 303 (June 2008), available at https://link.springer.com/article/10.1007/s10608-007-9119-0.

skills, reduced burnout, and ethical and rational decision-making. . . . Evidence also suggests that mindfulness can enhance the sense of work-life balance by reducing workers' preoccupation with work.[113]

Importantly, mindfulness allows us to think before reacting, providing a delay—a "pause"—between an event and our response.[114] In this way, we can be more deliberate than reactive to difficult situations.

Although it appears that law firms have been slow to embrace mindfulness training, numerous corporate giants offer mindfulness training for their employees, including Google, General Mills, Aetna, Target, Apple, Barclays, General Electric, Goldman Sachs, KPMG, McKinsey & Company, Unilever,[115] and Nike, as well as the U.S. military and the NFL Seattle Seahawks.[116] This is ample evidence that mindfulness is widely recognized as a means to greater presence on the job and increased productivity.

Mindfulness resources abound, and there are a number of Internet-based guided meditations.[117] Meditation does not have to be done seated cross-legged, with eyes closed and palms out; we may engage in contemplative behavior while walking, eating, or as part of our before bedtime or waking up ritual—or virtually any other time. What is important is that we embrace the basic premise behind mindfulness: Slow down; be fully present in what we are doing, especially with regard to our work;[118] and let

---

[113] National Task Force on Lawyer Well-Being, supra note 3, at 52–53 (internal citations omitted). For a summary of the science showing the benefits of mindfulness see http://www.mindfulnessforlawyers.com/science/ (also listing corporations that have mindfulness programs for their employees).

[114] Jacobowitz, supra note 109, at 232.

[115] See Kimberly Schaufenbuel, Why Google, Target, and General Mills Are Investing in Mindfulness, Harvard Business Review (December 28, 2015), available at https://hbr.org/2015/12/why-google-target-and-general-mills-are-investing-in-mindfulness; http://www.mindfulnessforlawyers.com/science/.

[116] See Mindfulness: The Science, available at http://www.mindfulnessforlawyers.com/science/.

[117] See, e.g., Google's Search Inside Yourself Leadership Institute, with guided mindfulness exercises available at https://siyli.org/resources/category/guided-meditation.

[118] Personally, I do not think it undermines my wellbeing if while doing the laundry or washing dishes my thoughts turn to a work matter or to my upcoming vacation. Mindfulness enthusiasts might disagree. Each person should find and practice her own style of mindfulness.

go of unproductive thoughts or worries that distract our focus and compromise our ability to do our very best work.

Develop and Nurture Outside Interests

It is important to cultivate interests beyond our professional lives. Having an escape from the issues we focus on day in and day out will make us happier and provides periods of rejuvenation. Researchers have found that mastery experiences that allow us to challenge ourselves outside of work promote recovery, as do other activities that permit psychological detachment and relaxation.[119]

Developing and nurturing outside interests also can actually make us better at what we do.[120] When our identity is expressed solely through work, "the big loser . . . is the work itself. . . . When we ask work to provide us with an identity, we ask too much."[121]

Cultivating outside interests gives us broader perspective and allows us to view issues (whether legal or interpersonal or something else) with greater range. Have you ever thought about why federal courts in the U.S. are primarily courts of general jurisdiction rather than specialized courts that are common in many U.S. states and countries around the world? One powerful reason in support of the use of courts of general jurisdiction, despite their relative inefficiency, is that the range of cases a federal judge hears helps enlarge his perspective and ability to cross-fertilize ideas from various fields.[122] The same is true for the rest of us.

---

[119] See National Task Force on Lawyer Well-Being, supra note 3, at 53, citing Anne M. Brafford, Positive Professionals: Creating High-Performing, Profitable Firms Through the Science of Engagement (2017); Verena C. Hahn, Carmen Binnewies, Sabine Sonnentag, & Eva J. Mojza, Learning How to Recover from Job Stress: Effects of a Recovery Training Program on Recovery, Recovery-Related Self-Efficacy, and Well-Being, 16 J. Occup. Health Psychol. 202 (2011), available at https://www.ncbi.nlm.nih.gov/pubmed/21463049.

[120] See Ury and Garskof, supra note 12, at 222 ("Becoming more versatile and well-rounded is likely to enhance, not decrease, your productivity and career longevity.").

[121] Sells, supra note 88, at 72.

[122] See Jed Rakoff, Are Federal Judges Competent? Dilettantes in An Age of Economic Expertise, 17 Fordham J. Corp. & Fin. L. 1, 10 (2012), available at https://ir.lawnet.fordham.edu/jcfl/vol17/iss1/1/ (supporting the federal court model of courts of general jurisdiction, arguing among other things that "even the best of judges in

Cultivate Meaningful Relationships

Loneliness is rampant in the United States. Nearly 40% percent of Americans report being lonely,[123] and loneliness has been described as "the most common pathology" in the nation.[124] Loneliness is a scourge that impacts health as well as our productivity,[125] and weakens our ability to work cooperatively and to manage information properly.[126] Conversely, spending time with friends, relatives, and partners is found to be the activity that gives us the greatest pleasure.[127] It may come as no surprise that lawyers outrank other professionals on a loneliness scale,[128] highlighting the need for each of us to develop significant personal relationships.

Understand and Evaluate Your Personal Agenda

The link between professional and personal personae discussed above[129] also reminds us of the need for a personal agenda as we move through our careers (and our lives). A personal agenda is basically a plan for what we want to achieve and how we plan to accomplish it. This ensures that we do not get entrenched in a career path accidentally, or for reasons that do not truly satisfy us. Many of us know attorneys who are caught up in jobs that do not suit them and who remain for the wrong reasons—money, security, or inertia, to name a few. Such attorneys may realize too late that they are dissatisfied—their

---

specialized courts tend to develop a tunnel vision, oblivious to developments in other parts of the law that should impact their decisions.").

[123] See Cigna U.S. Loneliness Index (2018), available at https://www.multivu.com/ players/English/8294451-cigna-us-loneliness-survey/docs/IndexReport_1524069371598-173525450.pdf; Shawn Achor, Gabriella Rosen Kellerman, Andrew Reece, & Alexi Robichaux, America's Loneliest Workers, According to Research, Harvard Business Review (March 19, 2018), available at https://hbr.org/2018/03/americas-loneliest-workers-according-to-research.

[124] Achor, Kellerman, Reece, & Robichaux, id.

[125] See id.

[126] See Debra Cassens Weiss, Lawyers rank highest on 'loneliness scale,' study finds, ABA Journal (April 3, 2018), available at http://www.abajournal.com/news/article/ lawyers_rank_highest_on_loneliness_scale_study_finds.

[127] See Daniel Kahneman, Alan B. Krueger, David A. Schkade, Norbert Schwarz, & Arthur A. Stone, A Survey Method for Characterizing Daily Life Experience: The Day Reconstruction Method, 306 Science 1776, 1779 (2004), available at http://science. sciencemag.org/content/306/5702/1776.

[128] See Cassens Weiss, supra note 126.

[129] See Chapter 1.C., supra.

financial security is tied up with the firm, they do not have a portable book of business that will enable them to find comparable employment, or it just seems like too much trouble to change course. Do not let this happen to you.

It is important to take the time occasionally to assess what you want from your professional life and your life more broadly; to ask the difficult question of whether your current arrangement advances those interests; and what you can do to refocus on your goals if there is a dissonance between where you want to go and where you are headed. This ultimately is important not just for your personal identity but also because it will enable you to maximize your potential professionally.

2. What Employers/Managers Can Do

Because wellness is critical to strong attorney performance, law firms would do well to promote a culture that prioritizes self-care and care for others and that encourages struggling attorneys to seek help. Firms should communicate to their attorneys that taking care of oneself is not a sign of weakness but a way to make yourself a better professional; and that there is no stigma to needing and seeking assistance for physical or psychological concerns.

A 2016 study by sociologists at the University of Toronto confirms that organizations have a significant role in promoting personal wellbeing. The utility of individual solutions to common lawyer maladies is limited because of certain law practice realities: First, the source for such dysfunction rests largely in the top-down way in which law firms are managed. Second, the typical law firm climate exalts extreme work hours and provides little control, especially to attorneys at junior levels.[130] For this reason, law firms should take a "systematic perspective" to building structural resilience.[131]

Employers also should do what they can to promote employee engagement, which promotes mental health, job

---

[130] Jonathan Koltai, Scott Schieman, & Ronit Dinovitzer, The Status-Health Paradox: Organizational Context, Stress Exposure, and Well-being in the Legal Profession, available at http://journals.sagepub.com/doi/pdf/10.1177/0022146517754091.

[131] National Task Force on Lawyer Well-Being, supra note 3, at 52 (internal citation omitted).

satisfaction, reduced turnover, performance, and profitability, and results in diminished stress and burnout.[132] Part of engagement is trying to pair work assigned to employees with what they like to do and what they feel good at, whenever possible. When employees believe that they have the opportunity to do the kind of work they do best and enjoy doing, they will be more productive and more likely to stay.[133]

Law firms and other employers should look for other ways to promote lawyer (and other employee) wellbeing, which will have a positive impact on productivity and ultimately on the bottom line. Firms with reputations for being "nice places to work" will also benefit in their recruitment and retention efforts. With intense competition, young talent can exercise some agency and choose workplaces that understand this. The market pressure for talent in this way can generate a virtuous cycle.

D. CREATING A SUSTAINABLE APPROACH TO WELLBEING

Each individual's personal approach to wellbeing must be sustainable. Sustainability principles, most commonly associated with environmental issues, discourage us from consuming or destroying resources at a faster pace than we can replenish them. Each of us can take valuable lessons from the environmental playbook. At the heart of sustainability principles is the notion that we as individuals can and should make choices and investments in our personal wellbeing that promise positive rates of return for us and the communities in which we live. Short-term trade-offs like eating poorly, not exercising, and sleeping too little are wasteful of our own human capital.

Have you ever said to yourself: "I will get my life back on track after I write this paper," or "I will start eating well and exercising after this deal," or "I will find more time for my family

---

[132] Id. at 50.

[133] See generally Gemma Robertson-Smith & Carl Markwick, Employee engagement: A review of current thinking (2009), available at https://www.employment-studies.co.uk/system/files/resources/files/469.pdf; Daniel Sgroi, Happiness and productivity: Understanding the happy-productive worker (October 2015), available at http://www.smf.co.uk/wp-content/uploads/2015/10/Social-Market-Foundation-Publication-Briefing-CAGE-4-Are-happy-workers-more-productive-281015.pdf.

after this brief"? If you find yourself doing this too often, you are probably not living in a sustainable manner. The current state of lawyer (and law student) wellbeing suggests that many of us lead lives that lack sustainability.

Sustainability includes the cultivation of personal habits that enable us to live fully in the present without compromising the future, to maximize our own health and sense of joy and minimize our individual toxic footprint. Our lives should both feel good at the moment *and* lay a solid foundation for future wellness and growth. When we put short-term rewards ahead of long-term benefits, when we expend more energy than we acquire, we compromise sustainability.

The basic question in determining your own personal sustainability is whether you can keep doing the same thing you are doing indefinitely. The notion of sustainability encourages us to discern when depletions occur so that we can nurture the necessary growth and replenishment. Adopting sustainable approaches to our own lives helps produce resilience and long-term benefits to the associations within which we operate (families, workplaces, and communities). This is a form of enlightened self-interest that each of us should embrace.

Take the time to think about your own footprint. If, in your eagerness to be more productive in the short-term, you create negative effects for the future (too much stress, health issues, problems in relationships), your approach may not be sustainable. If you burn the candle at both ends in a way that compromises your future health, productivity, and valued relationships, your approach may not be sustainable. If, in an attempt to gain security and avoid uncertainty, you leave yourself without viable options for the future, your approach may not be sustainable. If you do not continue to develop and challenge yourself professionally in order to cultivate possibilities for future engagement and greater challenge, your approach may not be sustainable. By cultivating a practice of mindfulness in everyday living, we can be fully present in what we do and become astute observers of our surroundings and ourselves. Mindfulness in the context of sustainability efforts involves developing a conscious appreciation for cause and effect, both for the present and the future.

E. QUESTIONS FOR REFLECTION

1. How would you describe your current state of wellbeing? What tools do you use to enhance your wellbeing? What area or areas would you like to improve? What is your plan for doing so?

2. Name three stressors that impact your wellbeing and how you manage them.

3. Name three things that you enjoy doing that are not school- or work-related and how you plan time for them.

PART III

RELATIONSHIPS: PROFESSIONALISM WITH THE OUTSIDE

CHAPTER 7

WORKING WITH OTHERS

"Lawyering is a service business and I think the best lawyers—and the happiest lawyers—enjoy serving and collaborating with others. They are trusted by colleagues, clients, tribunals and adversaries. They look for holistic, sustainable solutions to problems, not just tactical victories. They take great pleasure in doing their best work. They communicate well 'up' and 'down' within their own organizations and with clients." Grant Hanessian, Partner, Baker & McKenzie LLP[1]

"Relationships with others are the foundation of what lawyers do: A combination of courtesy, social intelligence, and awareness of cultural and generational differences are bound to define a lawyer's weight and success—or lack thereof." Javier El-Hage, Chief Legal Officer, Human Rights Foundation[2]

The practice of law at its very core is about relationships—relationships with colleagues, clients, adversaries, the court, and the public. This chapter discusses some fundamental elements of relationships and suggestions for building specific kinds of relationships that are common in and essential to law practice.

A. FOUNDATIONS FOR WORKING WITH OTHERS

This section discusses four foundational principles for working with others: Civility; reliability, responsibility, and accountability; collaboration; networking; and the importance of mentors and sponsors. They are foundational because they cut across all of the various constituencies with whom lawyers work and are basic building blocks upon which other relationship skills are based.

---

[1] Email from Grant Hanessian to the author (July 13, 2018), on file with the author.

[2] Email from Javier El-Hage to the author (July 8, 2018), on file with the author.

1. Civility[3]

Civility "is the mark of an accomplished and superb professional." Justice Anthony Kennedy[4]

Civility Defined

I almost sub-titled this section "Don't Be a Jerk" because it sums up well what civility requires. It is not that hard. To be somewhat more concrete, here is my favorite description of an attorney who seems eminently civil, written by his protégé:

> I recall how Fitzmaurice would take strident letters or briefs that I had drafted and tone them down. I recall how Fitzmaurice would run into an attorney who had treated him shabbily and greet the attorney warmly. I recall how Fitzmaurice would time and again refer clients and files to young lawyers in our firm who were having trouble attracting business. I recall how Fitzmaurice never blamed others for his mistakes, but often gave others credit for his accomplishments. I recall how often Fitzmaurice took the blame for mistakes that I and other young attorneys made. I recall how Fitzmaurice, at the conclusion of a trial or hearing, would walk over to the client of his adversary and say, "I just want you to know that your attorney did a terrific job for you." In short, what I best recall about Fitzmaurice were not occasions of great moral heroism, but his "quiet, everyday exhibitions of virtue."[5]

Complaints about the decline of civility in the legal profession have been reported for years but seem to get more

---

[3] Treating others with courtesy and respect is one of the top ten capabilities most important for starting lawyers based on the results of a study of 24,000 practicing attorneys around the country. See Institute for the Advancement of the American Legal System, Foundations for Practice: The Whole Lawyer Character Quotient 26 (July 2016), available at http://iaals.du.edu/sites/default/files/reports/foundations_for_practice_whole_lawyer_character_quotient.pdf.

[4] Anthony M. Kennedy, Law and Belief, 34 Trial 23, 25 (1998).

[5] Patrick J. Schiltz, Legal Ethics in Decline: The Elite Law Firm, the Elite Law School, and the Moral Formation of the Novice Attorney, 82 Minn. L. Rev. 705, 738 (1998), available at http://coloradomentoring.org/wp-content/uploads/2013/09/Schiltz-P-Legal-Ethics-in-Decline-The-Elite-Law-Firm-The-Elite-Law-School-and-the-Moral-Formation-of-the-Novice-Attorney-82-Minn.-L.-Rev.-705-February-19981.pdf.

acute and urgent.[6] Ever more disciplinary proceedings are being lodged against lawyers for incivility.[7] But standards of civility go well beyond the absence of the kind of outrageous behavior demonstrated by lawyers subject to disciplinary behavior.[8] Civility is a general disposition, an orientation toward others. Yale Law School Dean Anthony T. Kronman describes a civil person as one who is marked by "politeness and a high-minded determination not to descend from principles to personalities."[9] My friend and colleague Judge Gerald Lebovits defines civility to include "courtesy, decency, fairness, integrity, and similar hallmarks of virtue . . . being honorable toward opposing counsel, toward clients, toward the court, toward witnesses, toward colleagues, toward everyone."[10] Truly, it is not difficult.

Civility Requires Introspection

When confronted with uncivil behavior, take a moment to consider whether your own actions in any way contributed to the unprofessional conduct. You might be surprised to find that you share some of the responsibility for eliciting such behavior.[11] If this is the case, accept your role in the incident and take action to avoid such behavior in the future.

Take a Breath

It is sensible to think and take a breath—and a break— before replying when you feel angry. It is at these times that you run the risk of saying or doing something that might be uncivil.

---

[6] See, e.g., National Task Force on Lawyer Well-Being, The Path to Lawyer Well-Being: Practical Recommendations for Positive Change 15–16 (August 14, 2017), available at https://www.americanbar.org/content/dam/aba/images/abanews/ThePathTo LawyerWellBeingReportRevFINAL.pdf.

[7] See Jayne R. Reardon, Civility as the Core of Professionalism, in Essential Qualities of the Professional Lawyer 43–44 (2013). See also G.M. Filisko, You're Out of Order! Dealing with the Costs of Incivility in the Legal Profession, ABA Journal (January 2013), available at http://www.abajournal.com/magazine/article/youre_out_of_order_dealing_with_the_costs_of_incivility_in_the_legal.

[8] See, e.g., Matter of Zappin, N.Y. App. Dev. (1st Dept., March 8, 2018), available at https://law.justia.com/cases/new-york/appellate-division-first-department/2018/2018-ny-slip-op-01564.html.

[9] Anthony T. Kronman, Civility, 26 Cumb. L. Rev. 727, 727 (1996), available at http://digitalcommons.law.yale.edu/cgi/viewcontent.cgi?article=2054&context=fss_papers.

[10] Id.

[11] See id. ("And civility often requires clear, active reflection on one's own contributions to difficult situations, rather than just those of others. . . .").

Eric Grossman, the Chief Legal Officer of Morgan Stanley, offers what he calls the 24-hour rule: "Whenever possible, do not respond within 24 hours when you think someone has wronged you."[12] This gives you time to be more thoughtful about and measured in your response. Immediate responses are prone to be unduly intemperate.

Civility Is Consistent with Zealous Advocacy

Civility is fully consistent with and serves a lawyer's duty of zealousness. The American Bar Association Model Rules of Professional Responsibility reinforce the need for civility even in adversarial settings:

> A lawyer is not bound . . . to press for every advantage that might be realized for a client. . . . The lawyer's duty to act with reasonable due diligence does not require the use of offensive tactics or preclude the treating of all persons involved in the legal process with courtesy and respect.[13]

Why Be Civil?

There are myriad benefits associated with civility and significant consequences associated with incivility. Perhaps most important, a lawyer's professional reputation is tied closely with civil activity.[14] Being civil even may make us happier.[15]

Incivility, on the other hand, carries a number of serious drawbacks:[16]

---

[12] Email from Eric F. Grossman to the author (July 16, 2018), on file with the author.

[13] Comment [1] on Rule 1.3 of the Model Rules of Professional Conduct, available at https://www.americanbar.org/groups/professional_responsibility/publications/model_rules_of_professional_conduct/rule_1_3_diligence/comment_on_rule_1_3.html. See also Peter R. Jarvis & Katie M. Lachter, The Practical Case for Civility, in Essential Qualities of the Professional Lawyer 50 (2013) ("On many occasions, the cause of civility compels a search for common interests with an adversary rather than an emphasis on the usually more evident areas of disagreement.").

[14] See Reardon, supra note 7, Essential Qualities of the Professional Lawyer 42.

[15] "Lawyers who behave with civility . . . report higher personal and professional rewards. Conversely, lawyer job dissatisfaction is often correlated with unprofessional behavior by opposing counsel." Reardon, supra note 7, Essential Qualities of the Professional Lawyer 41.

[16] See Jarvis & Lachter, supra note 13, at 50–51.

- Acting in uncivil ways makes us angry, and we do not do our best work when angry.

- We also do not do our best listening when angry.

- Incivility begets incivility. Stop the carnage.

- Incivility causes delays which results in unnecessary expense for the parties and the legal system.

- Incivility is vexing to others, for instances judges and juries, on whose good graces we depend.

- Incivility leads to bar and malpractice complaints.[17]

A lack of civility is extremely short sighted and destined to result in negative repercussions to any attorney who demonstrates such behavior.

2.   Reliability, Responsibility, and Accountability

Reliability

Reliability means being dependable and is crucial to the practice of law. In this highly interdependent world, it is important that colleagues, clients, and others know that you can be depended on, and that you will do what you say you will do within the time frame promised or within a reasonable time.

Responsibility and Accountability

We should always take responsibility and remain accountable for our actions. Mistakes will happen—this is inevitable.[18] It is how we handle ourselves in the face of mistakes that defines us as a person who is or is not accountable and responsible. Mistakes that are acknowledged and handled

---

[17] "A surprisingly large number of bar complaints and legal malpractice claims can be traced to lawyers' failing to exhibit the common courtesy of returning client phone calls or responding to emails or letters on a timely basis." Id. at 52–53 (2013). See, e.g., *In re Law Firm of Wilens and Baker*, 9 A.D. 3d 213, 214 (1st Dep't 2004) (censuring entire law firm for "rude and uncivil conduct to a client").

[18] Lawrence S. Krieger, What We're Not Telling Law Students—And Lawyers— That They Really Need to Know: Some Thoughts-in-Action Toward Revitalizing the Profession From Its Roots, 13 J. L. & Health 1, 12–13 (1999), available at https:// engagedscholarship.csuohio.edu/jlh/vol13/iss1/3/ ("good, valuable people make mistakes as a normal part of human life, . . . mistakes reflect transitory imperfections in what one is doing, rather than fundamental flaws in what one intrinsically is.").

directly can be forgiven; conversely, when one becomes defensive or tries to deflect responsibility for an error, the impact of mistakes are increased.

Some time ago I had a scheduled meeting with two students. Neither appeared at the appointed hour, so I sent an email asking what happened. Student A appeared in my office about 10 minutes later with a profuse and what appeared to be heartfelt apology. She was immediately forgiven and our working relationship continued apace. Student B wrote back stating that we did not have an appointment. When confronted with an email confirming the meeting, the excuses followed. Student B made several feeble attempts to justify her mistake, continuing to waste both of our time over what could have been concluded with a simple apology.

In conversations I have had with practitioners, I have heard excuses for the late submission of assignments or failure to be on time for meetings as farfetched as "I was in Chicago and forgot about the time difference," "the wind was very strong so it took longer to get here," "the subway is always delayed!," "I was upset about Anthony Bourdain's suicide," and "I missed the deadline because a colleague told me that the project was to be submitted on Tuesday." These are irresponsible responses to errors, which are much more significant than and compound the initial mistake. Hearing these excuses I am reminded of the old saying, "It's not the crime, it's the cover up."[19]

Excuses for mistakes are cowardly and reflect a lack of character. Take ownership over and responsibility for mistakes. Do not blame others. Apologize with grace and sincerity. Ask how you can make up for the shortcoming. Try to ensure that it does not happen again.

3.   Collaboration

Because of the nature of legal practice, collaboration will inevitably be a significant part of the work of most legal professionals, and it is important to understand how to work effectively with others. Sometimes, our role in collaborations will

---

[19] The exact origin of this saying cannot be verified but it is said to date to the Watergate break in. See https://www.maryferrell.org/pages/Watergate.html.

be more as leaders, and sometimes it will be more as followers.[20] What follows is a discussion of what collaboration is, its importance, elements of effective collaboration, and finally some words of caution about collaboration "overload."[21]

Collaboration Defined

Collaboration or teamwork is defined as two or more people working together toward a shared goal. Collaboration is essential to success in the legal profession.

The Importance of Collaboration

"Law school is about individual achievement. Yet . . . clients' complex problems require masterful collaboration." Orrick[22]

A collaborative spirit is highly desirable and often associated with organizational and individual success. People are the most important asset of virtually any organization, and this is particularly true with respect to professional service firms.

It is a familiar refrain that we can do more together than we can do separately. Exchanges with others, for instance, can stimulate creativity and offer a sounding board, an opportunity to question our underlying assumptions. Working with others— particularly those that are different from us—allows us an opportunity to engage in genuinely inclusive thinking.[23]

For lawyers, the benefits of teamwork are particularly striking because law can be practiced only in relationship to others.[24] The strong value of collaboration in the legal profession

---

[20] See Chapter 3.D.5., supra.

[21] This is a nod to Rob Cross, Rob Rebele, & Adam Grant, Collaborative Overload, Harvard Business Review (January–February 2016), available at https://hbr.org/2016/01/collaborative-overload, discussed later in this section.

[22] See https://www.orrick.com/Innovation.

[23] See Section B.5., infra.

[24] See Daisy Hurst Floyd, The Authentic Lawyer: Merging the Personal and the Professional, in Essential Qualities of the Professional Lawyer 28 (2013).

has been broadly recognized[25] and borne out by empirical data.[26] Research demonstrates the importance of cohesion among team members in law firms; when there is a high level of cohesion among attorneys, client attrition is minimized when the relationship partner or other person responsible for work coordination departs.[27] Collaboration is also highly beneficial to cross-selling services within the firm, which in many firms is a huge prospect for growth.[28]

Collaborative lawyering goes beyond working with teams of lawyers and embraces non-lawyers (clients, who may range from the most sophisticated businesses to the more naïve and unschooled individual clients, and experts in a range of fields (finance, economics, technology and other sciences, to name a few)). This has never been truer; as clients pursue value-oriented approaches to legal services by unbundling tasks and using alternative providers for commoditized services,[29] the need for attorneys to collaborate increases exponentially.[30]

---

[25] Marjorie M. Shultz & Sheldon Zedeck, Predicting Lawyer Effectiveness: Broadening the Basis for Law School Admission Decisions, 36 Law & Soc. Inquiry 620, 632 noted 5 (2011), available at http://citeseerx.ist.psu.edu/viewdoc/download?doi=10.1.1.418.7400&rep=rep1&type=pdf (identifying "working with others" as one of eight categories of effectiveness factors).

[26] See, e.g., Heidi Gardner, Effective Teamwork and Collaboration, in Managing Talent for Success: Talent Development in Law Firms 150–54 (2013) (finding that well-functioning teams produce "higher value" and "more sophisticated" work).

[27] See Michelle Rogan, How Strong Internal Networks Can Save Client Relationships, Insead Knowledge (July 13, 2015), available at https://knowledge.insead.edu/strategy/how-strong-internal-networks-can-save-client-relationships-4147.

[28] See, e.g., David H. Freeman, Growth Trends for 2016: A Disconnect Between Aspiration and Execution, Legal Management (April 12, 2016), available at http://www.davidfreemanconsulting.com/wp-content/uploads/2016/04/Growth-Trends-for-2016_-A-Disconnect-Between-Aspiration-and-Execution-_-Legal-Management.pdf (noting that cross-selling was ranked as the second highest priority in a survey of law firm rate growth initiatives).

[29] See Chapter 2.B.2., supra.

[30] "The adoption by clients of a value-oriented approach to selecting and paying the legal services providers has substantial implications on who will deliver those services, and how they will go about doing so. For example, value-based billing encourages increased collaboration and cooperation between lawyers (and law firms) and clients." Report of the Task Force on the Future of the Legal Profession, New York State Bar Association 21 (April 2, 2011), available at https://www.nysba.org/futurereport/.

Elements of Effective Collaboration

Given the significance to organizations and individuals of collaboration, it is important to understand what makes for effective collaboration:

- *Open Dialogue*—Open and honest communication among team members is essential to meaningful collaboration.

- *Clear Expectations*—Team members must share a vision about goals, expectations, roles, means of communication, timing and deadlines, and other features of the collaboration. This serves to avoid misunderstandings and to maintain member accountability.

- *Receptivity*—All members of a team must be open and receptive to feedback and must genuinely reflect on their behaviors that may compromise the effectiveness of the collaboration. This is particularly true for leaders (or perceived leaders) of teams.

- *Eliminate or Minimize the Participation of Disruptive Team Members*—Those who are poor communicators, self-centered, domineering, irresponsible, or defensive make poor team members. These individuals are best in roles in which collaboration is not at a premium.

- *Psychological Safety*—Promoting a sense of psychological safety is critical to successful collaborative work. Google's Project Aristotle,[31] a paean to Aristotle's quote "the whole is greater than the sum of its parts," concludes that the feeling of psychological safety of the members was "by far the most important"[32] predictor of teamwork success. When team members feel psychological safety, they are comfortable asking questions and taking risks,

---

[31] Guide: Understand team effectiveness, available at https://rework.withgoogle.com/guides/understanding-team-effectiveness/steps/introduction/?gclid=EAIaIQobChMIsZWi2dHY2wIVQVmGCh2V0Qs4EAAYASAAEgJwEvD_BwE.

[32] Id.

even given the possibility of seeming ignorant, incompetent, negative, or disruptive. Psychological safety gives team members comfort that they will not be ridiculed or punished for asking a question, offering an idea, or making a mistake. Project Aristotle discusses the work of Harvard Professor Amy Edmonson, who first coined the term "team psychological safety" and who suggests these ideas for fostering team psychological safety:[33]

o   Frame the work as an exercise in learning rather than simply an exercise in execution.

o   Acknowledge your own shortcomings.

o   The leader or perceived group leader should "[m]odel curiosity and ask lots of questions."[34]

• *Dependability*—Project Aristotle lists the dependability of team members as the second most important factor in determining collaborative success.[35] Dependability refers to whether team members can be counted on to reliably complete tasks on time.[36]

The Downside of Collaboration: Collaboration Overload[37]

Despite the many advantages of teamwork, collaborative efforts have a cost in the increased burden collaboration puts on workers, leading to stress, burnout, and turnover.[38] The effects of what has been called "escalating citizenship"[39] further burden top performers who in the end have little time for the "deep work" that is so critical for individual and organizational success[40] and which is the antithesis of our collaborative culture.

---

[33]   See id.

[34]   Id.

[35]   Id.

[36]   Id. See also the discussion of reliability, Chapter.4.B.4., supra.

[37]   See Cross, Rebele, & Grant, supra note 21.

[38]   Id.

[39]   Mark C. Bolino, Anthony C. Klotz, William H. Tunley, & Jason Harvey, Exploring the dark side of organizational citizenship behavior, 34 Organiz. Behav. 542, 544 (2012), available at https://onlinelibrary.wiley.com/doi/full/10.1002/job.1847.

[40]   Cal Newport, Deep Work: Rules for Focused Success in a Distracted World.

When this occurs, collaboration may turn a "virtuous cycle" into a "vicious cycle."[41] Presumably because they are stereotyped as more nurturing and cooperative, women may assume a disproportionate burden than do their male counterparts when it comes to collaboration.[42]

In the end, in any particular context, we should intentionally balance the need to collaborate and the benefits of collaboration against the downsides.

4. Networking

"Keep your relationships. Work and friends mix. There is no such thing as work/life balance. It is all life." Eric F. Grossman, Executive Vice President and Chief Legal Officer, Morgan Stanley[43]

Networking seems to be the buzzword of the day. Everyone is told to network. We should network to find a job (or a new job); we should network to develop clients and build a book of business; we should network to expand our professional horizons; we should network to learn from a range of people with differing experiences.

All of this is true,[44] but few speak about how to network effectively, and in particular to those that might not have a lot of experience in or comfort with the art. Here are a few key suggestions:[45]

- Networking is effective largely because it results in the flow of information. We live in a society that is governed by information. The larger the size of your network, the more valuable information will flow to you, giving you opportunities that simply would be impossible without that flow of information.

---

[41] Cross, Rebele, & Grant, supra note 21. See also Bolino, Klotz, Tunley, & Harvey, supra note 39 (exploring the hidden costs of excessive collaboration).

[42] Cross, Rebele, & Grant, supra note 21.

[43] Email from Eric F. Grossman to the author (July 16, 2018), on file with the author.

[44] Networking is listed as one of the 26 effectiveness factors in the classical empirical study by Professors Marjorie M. Shultz and Sheldon Zedeck. See Shultz & Zedeck, supra note 25, at 630.

[45] Desiree Jaeger-Fine, A Short & Happy Guide to Networking (2016).

- Networking is nothing more than building relationships, and we should approach networking in the same way as we do all other kinds of relationships we have in our lives.

- Networking, like building other relationships, takes time. Do not expect to see a direct or immediate benefit from networking.

- Networking is always for mutual benefit. Do not ask things of your networking partner or you will burden the organic development of that relationship.

- Networking works when networking partners build trust.

- Begin networking with those with whom you have some commonalities—those with whom you share *homophily*. Your network will spread from there.

- Networking requires active and engaged listening. When you give others space to shine, they will remember you fondly.

- Networking by action—doing things that demonstrate your professional persona—is much more effective that networking by mere presence or words. Become active in organizations and projects as a way of establishing your true value as a professional.

- Networking should not be a burden or unpleasant— it should be fun. Find a way to network that fits your own style. When you are unhappy networking, your mood speaks for you. When you like meeting and working with others, your enjoyment will be obvious and appealing.

B. WORKING ACROSS BOUNDARIES

In any of the myriad contexts in which we will be called upon to work, we will come across many, many people who are different from us along a range of characteristics. This is something that we should embrace and learn to deal with effectively. This includes developing cross-cultural competence, understanding generational issues, being aware of the significance of race and gender, appreciating other differences, and recognizing our implicit biases and thinking inclusively.

1. Cross-Cultural Competencies

The changing nature of our world, including the profession, demands that we have a level of inter-cultural sensitivity towards those who are different from us along any number of characteristics—social or economic backgrounds, gender and sex-based, race and ethnicity, age, cultural background, and other differences. Cross-cultural competence refers to our ability to develop knowledge and skills to work effectively with those different from us. Cross-cultural sensitivity is the key to attaining cross-cultural competence. Cross-cultural sensitivity is achieved through respectful curiosity, humility, inquisitiveness, and openness.

Achieving cross-cultural fluency is important because inaccurate attributions to cultural factors can cause significant errors in the work of an attorney. For instance, concepts of credibility and body language have important cultural undertones,[46] as do one's beliefs about what information is relevant[47] and our respective notions of individualism and competition.[48] In order to achieve cross-cultural competence, lawyers must be aware of the issues of difference among the range of constituencies with which we work, of the power of privilege, and of any implicit biases with which we may operate.

Professor Susan Bryant, in what remains a definitive piece about cross-cultural competency for attorneys, likens culture to the air we breathe—largely invisible but something on which we are deeply dependent.[49] She offers five habits that lawyers can use to make culture more visible[50] and to avoid and recover from

---

[46] Susan Bryant, The Five Habits: Building Cross-Cultural Competence in Lawyers, 8 Clinical L. Rev. 33, 43 (2001), available at https://academicworks.cuny.edu/cgi/viewcontent.cgi?article=1257&context=cl_pubs.

[47] Id. at 44.

[48] Id. at 45–46.

[49] Id. at 40.

[50] Id. at 43.

"cultural blunders."[51] Specifically, each of us should explore similarities and differences between ourselves and others;[52] identify and analyze the possible impact of those differences on our interactions with others;[53] explore alternative explanations for the behavior of others beyond those that come to mind based on our own cultural backgrounds;[54] pay "conscious attention to the process of communication" in the hope of averting cross-cultural misunderstanding;[55] and explore and reflect upon ourselves as cultural beings to identify and eliminate biases and stereotypes.[56] These tools should be consciously applied across the range of circumstances in which we find ourselves.

2. Generational Issues

While a common mantra that people always complain about the generations that follow them, it is a reality that older generations need to work with younger generations and *vice versa*.

Younger professionals need older people to act as mentors, sponsors, and role models. They also need more seasoned attorneys to provide them with opportunities that will facilitate their professional development. Most of the people in a position to hire or help younger professionals advance in their careers are older. Likewise, older generations need young talent. Firms that can harness the substantial energies and abilities of millennials and adapt to their style of working will thrive in the future. Those firms even may be able to attract the much sought-after business of start-ups and other companies run by millennials. Accordingly, it is important to understand the different perceptions and work habits of those in different generations. The following discussion is based on broad generalizations,[57] but offers useful points of reference.

---

[51] Id. at 35.

[52] Id. at 64–67.

[53] Id. at 68–70.

[54] Id. at 70–72.

[55] Id. at 72–76.

[56] Id. at 76–78; id. at 56 ("Effective cross-cultural interaction depends on the lawyer's capacity to self-monitor his or her interactions in order to compensate for bias or stereotypes thinking and to learn from mistakes.").

[57] Obviously, this discussion is in very broad strokes and does not suggest that everyone who falls into a particular generational class is the same. Nonetheless, there

Definitions

Although there is disagreement as to the exact years and characteristics that define different generations, common categorizations suggest the following:

The Silent Generation (Born 1925–1945)—The Silent Generation, also called the Traditionalists, grew up during the Great Depression and World War II. Many are children of service members. This generation tends to value conformity and discipline. Their career paths tend to be stable and predictable (many working for decades or an entire career for the same employer), and their work ethic is marked by loyalty and industry.[58]

The Boomer Generation (Born 1945–1963)—Baby boomers in the U.S. grew up in relative peace and prosperity and tend to be individualistic and hard working. They like to win and like to make an impact through their work.[59]

Generation X (Born 1964–1981)—Generation Xers are said to be skeptical of authority. They grew up in a time when divorce became more common and when large numbers of women entered the workforce. This generation was the first to grow up with computer and related technology and they are technologically sophisticated, resourceful, independent, and self-directed. They appreciate egalitarian environments and like having the opportunity to interact with more senior colleagues. They also like to have fun and look for work environments that are friendly and in which they can find personal meaning.[60]

Millennial Generation/Generation Y (Born 1981–1995)—Millennials, also known as Generation Y, thoroughly embrace digital communication and social media. They value time with family and friends and are less motivated by monetary rewards

---

are some generally applicable traits that tend to characterize those who fall into specific generations.

[58] See, e.g., http://extension.missouri.edu/extcouncil/documents/ecyl/meet-the-generations.pdf.

[59] Id.

[60] See generally Huichun Yu & Peter Miller, Leadership style: the X generation and baby boomers compared in different cultural contexts, 26 Leadership and Organization Development J. 35 (2015), available at https://epubs.scu.edu.au/cgi/viewcontent.cgi?article=1022&context=gcm_pubs.

and traditional career aspirations than preceding generations. Their collaborative skills are more refined than those of older professionals, and they enjoy and are good at teamwork. They were raised by so-called "helicopter parents" who are said to hover over their children, so they are confident and accustomed to frequent positive reinforcement and immediate feedback.[61] They crave excitement, personal meaning, versatility, and flexibility at work, and they seek work-life integration. They tend to be informal in dress and manner. Members of this generation celebrate diversity, are self-inventive, and are suspicious of conventional institutions.[62]

Why We Need Cross-Generational Understanding

There is a significant generational span in the practice of law. Each generation has its unique characteristics that impact their performance, expectations, and professional norms. When groups of different generations work together toward a common goal, as they do and must do, these differences become apparent and potentially problematic.

It is the responsibility of more junior attorneys to conform their behavior and expectations accordingly—or to choose an employer who is accepting of these generational differences and preferences. The reality is that most of the lawyers who are in decision-making positions, who have the experience to serve as mentors, and who have the power to be sponsors will be from older generations.[63] It is thus incumbent upon those in younger generations to appreciate and engage with older generations of lawyers. This does not mean shunning authenticity,[64] but it does mean being aware of how certain behaviors and attitudes might appear to those of other generations. It behooves young professionals who want to enter traditional law practice to demonstrate that they can follow the lead of more senior attorneys and work within established conventions.

---

[61] Their parents "nurtured them, supported them, and gave them lots of direction and praise, and they grew up in an 'all have won; all must have trophies' early educational environment." Susan Daicoff, Working with Millennials in the Law, 50-JUN Ariz. Att'y 16, 18 (2014).

[62] Id.

[63] Mentors and sponsors are discussed in Section C.2., infra.

[64] See Chapter 4.C.6., supra.

But the converse is also true—older lawyers need to understand the mindset and perspective of younger attorneys. Some may not fully appreciate why this is the case. There, of course, is the human case for better understanding, but there is also a potent business reason to embrace generational differences: Simply put, millennial lawyers are the future of the profession,[65] and are a key asset for firms that want to remain viable. Thus, seasoned attorneys need them as much or even more than they need us.[66] An overwhelming percentage of associates are millennials,[67] and their happiness is closely tied to associate retention, productivity, and other indicators of firm health. As baby boomers begin to retire, it is important to prepare millennials for senior positions in firms to avert a leadership vacuum.

Older attorneys and law firms can embrace rising Generation Y professionals and harness their enormous potential or ignore them at their peril. The presence of Generation Y lawyers already has been tied to profitability.[68] For firms that want to leverage associates into partner profits, the millennial lawyer is an essential asset.[69] Competition for top talent is intense—and that competition comes not only from other law firms but also from tech firms led by other millennials. Law firms that embrace and work with millennial attorneys on their own terms will attract and retain young talent.[70] Finally,

---

[65] Data collected by ALM intelligence shows that millennials outnumber lawyers from Generation X at firms in the AM Law 200 and the National Law Journal's NLJ 500. And they "far outnumber" lawyers in the baby boomer generation. See Lizzy McLellan, Millennials Won't Destroy Your Law Firm. Can They Save it?, The American Lawyer (October 23, 2017), available at https://www.law.com/americanlawyer/sites/americanlawyer/2017/10/23/millennials-wont-destroy-your-law-firm-can-they-save-it/.

[66] Id. ("Whatever new law is going to look like, it's going to be the millennials leading it.").

[67] Data reported in November 2017 indicates that millennials comprise nearly 88% of associates. See Lizzy McLellan, Where the Millennials Are: Tracking the Generations in Big Law (November 6, 2017), available at https://www.law.com/americanlawyer/sites/americanlawyer/2017/11/06/where-the-millennials-are-tracking-the-generations-in-big-law/.

[68] See Debra Cassens Weiss, This generational group is the largest in BigLaw, ABA Journal (November 8, 2017), available at http://www.abajournal.com/news/article/this_generational_group_is_the_largest_in_biglaw.

[69] McLellan, supra note 65.

[70] "The war for talent . . . requires us to be more thoughtful about adapting our firms to the workplace they would find engaging." Orrick chairman Mitch Zuklie, quoted in McLellan, id.

millennial attorneys armed with the right incentives and given the flexibility to do so, can attract and retain much sought-after tech industry and other clients led by younger entrepreneurs. These businesses will be more attracted to firms with attorneys that can speak the language of their generation.

Impact of Generational Issues in the Workplace

Millennials diverge significantly from their older counterparts along a number of variables that impact more seasoned professionals' view of them, among them work-life integration, information and communication, and working within hierarchical organizations.

Work-Life Integration—Baby boomers are accustomed to working hard and do not expect immediate rewards. Millennials want a more balanced work schedule, expect that their work will be consistently meaningful from the outset, and get easily frustrated with much of the drudgery of law firm work.[71] The millennial view toward work-life integration may appear to more experienced professionals to reflect a lack of ambition or passion, but that is not necessarily the case.

Information and Communication—Those of Generation Y are exceptionally skilled in and reliant upon new technologies and social media—far more so than their older counterparts. They are roundly criticized for their lack of in-person social and communication skills.

Hierarchy—Younger generations are often said to have a lack of regard for authority and an unrealistic sense of entitlement. Their coddled upbringing has left them accustomed to voicing their opinions, and with a sense that they have things to contribute, even when they lack experience in or knowledge of the matter at hand. They often are perceived as being too needy of validation. They also may exhibit a lack of respect and deference for those more senior and experienced. They seem too blunt and too fast to criticize others who are higher in the organizational food chain.[72] The relative informality of

---

[71] See Deborah L. Rhode, Foreword: Personal Satisfaction in Professional Practice, 58 Syracuse L. Rev. 217, 223–24, 228 (2008).

[72] See Jean M. Twenge, Generation Me: Why Today's Young Americans are More Confident, Assertive, Entitled—and More Miserable Than Ever Before 39 (2006).

millennials may also appear unprofessional, but it does not necessarily signal a more casual approach to work.

So what do these differences mean and how can an understanding of generational differences help in the workplace?

Advice for Millennials—Because Generation Y professionals still need the guidance, support, and help of more senior professionals, it is important that millennials actively consider how their behaviors and attitudes may appear to those of older generations.

Millennial attorneys should be sure that they are content with the work-life balance that is expected at a particular job so that there are no misunderstandings. Millennials also should appreciate that older lawyers are not as adept with technology as they are, and that texting and other forms of multi-tasking during a meeting appears impolite and unprofessional. If using your phone to take notes, millennials are advised to let others know that they are using the phone for that purpose. A piece in *The New York Times* describes a situation in which a young, new member of a team was on his phone for the duration of a meeting. It turns out that he was taking notes, but that was not known or understood by the older colleagues in the room. Upon learning that the young colleague in fact was taking notes with his phone, a thoughtful more senior colleague sent those notes to the group as a way of letting everyone in attendance know that the junior indeed was focused on the meeting.[73]

Even while you are waiting for more senior attorneys to prove that they are deserving of your respect, demonstrate a level of deference for those who hold more senior roles and positions. Understand that older lawyers may not be willing or able to provide real-time feedback (although they should).[74]

Advice for More Senior Professionals—More experienced professionals should remember that each generation complains about the next, so all of us once were subject to "young people

---

[73] Jonah Stillman, I'm Not Texting. I'm Taking Notes, Preoccupations, The New York Times (April 7, 2017), available at https://www.nytimes.com/2017/04/07/jobs/texting-work-meetings-social-media.html.

[74] See Chapter 8.B.13., infra.

today" criticism. To be sure, there will be elements of how younger professionals behave that will irritate older lawyers and seem unprofessional. Seasoned professionals should keep an open mind and be as flexible as possible, within whatever legitimate constraints exist, to work with the younger generation of lawyers. They should value millennial attempts to integrate their work lives with their personal lives as a healthy and sustainable antidote to the very unhealthy lifestyles that led so many older generation of lawyers to suffer from mental illness, drug addiction, alcoholism, and other maladies.[75] If millennial lawyers can avoid those traps, they will be far more effective lawyers[76] who are retainable.[77] They should recognize millennials as individuals rather than fungible assets; treat them as respected peers; and be transparent in explaining why things are done a certain way. They should recognize that millennials' lack of formality is not meant to be disrespectful or casual.

Firms should also adopt millennial friendly policies and programs. Firms that allow Generation Y lawyers the flexibility and space to use their skills creatively will find that millennials can add enormous value. In addition, older attorneys should welcome the highly sophisticated technology skills of younger-generation lawyers. Their ability to use technology effectively and creatively renders them extremely efficient. Some firms offer associates the ability to choose their technology[78]—a low-cost measure to demonstrate generational sensitivity, respect, and openness. Millennials seek flexibility in working arrangements, so flex time and remote work arrangements should be implemented when consistent with client and institutional needs.[79]

---

[75] See Chapter 6.B.1., supra.

[76] See Chapter 6.A.2., supra.

[77] See id.

[78] For instance, Cozen & O'Connor allow attorneys to choose the devices and operating systems of their choice for their office and home technology needs. See Alison Diana, Cozen O'Connor CIO: Delivering Freedom of Choice to Attorneys (April 8, 2015), available at https://biglawbusiness.com/cozen-oconnor-cio-delivering-freedom-of-choice-to-attorneys/.

[79] Morgan Lewis & Bockius has adopted a remote working program. This initiative is designed in large part with an eye toward attorney retention. See https://www.morganlewis.com/news/remote-working-program-pr-med-tile-redirect; millennials "thrive on . . . workplace flexibility. . . . [Law firms] will maintain a young talent pool by

Finally, more senior attorneys should remember that millennials offer unparalleled access to coveted clients and should leverage them to help attract and retain start-up and other clients who speak the language of Generation Y and are more comfortable with their counterparts than they may be with more conventional attorneys of a certain age. Encourage and support associates in their efforts to develop a book of business.

Finally, include millennial attorneys in senior management. Begin to develop their leadership capabilities and send a signal to other young attorneys that the firm is invested in their success and prepared to give them a place at the table. Such attorneys can also provide a valuable liaison to more junior associates.

3. The Continuing and Conspicuous Impact of Race and Gender

Race and gender, of course, are enormous drivers in how we relate to others, and these factors have significant implications for the hiring, retention, and promotion of attorneys.

Women are underrepresented in top-level jobs within the legal profession, such as law firm partner (equity and otherwise). Minority women are particularly underrepresented, making up a mere 2.6 percent of law firm partners. Even this figure is said to be skewed upward due to a number of standout markets. In some cities, the figure is less than 2 percent. Representation among judges has dropped in recent years, as has female representation among J.D. students and entry into private practice.[80]

Racial and ethnic diversity in the profession are sorely lacking. Aggregate minority representation in the profession stood at 14.5 percent in 2015, a drop from earlier data, with African-American representation the lowest among the groups

---

better aligning their incentives with what the Millennials seek in the workplace." Lauren Stiller Rikleen, Law Firms Need to Take Care of Their Talent, Harvard Business Review (July 10, 2012), available at https://hbr.org/2012/07/law-firms-need-to-take-care-of.

[80] Institute for Inclusion in the Legal Profession (IILP), IILP Review 2017: The State of Diversity and Inclusion in the Legal Profession 13–14 (2017), available at https://www.alanet.org/docs/default-source/diversity/iilp_2016_final_lowres.pdf?sfvrsn=2. See also National Association for Law Placement, 2017 Report on Diversity in U.S. Law Firms (December 2017), available at https://www.nalp.org/uploads/2017NALPReporton DiversityinUSLawFirms.pdf.

studied (which includes Asian Americans and Hispanics). African Americans are significantly less likely than other minority group members to start off in private practice. In 2015, African Americans made up only 4 percent of associates in U.S. law firms, a drop from earlier years. Minority representation among the ranks of law firm partners "remains stubbornly low."[81]

Clearly there is no easy solution to this unfortunate state of affairs. But on an individual level, each of us can be attuned to assumptions that we make and actions we take that may inadvertently undermine the role of minorities and women in the workplace. We should be attentive to opportunities to enhance the experience of our colleagues who may be the subject of implicit biases (discussed below[82]). When we mentor and sponsor junior talent,[83] we should consciously dedicate ourselves to ensuring that everyone gets equivalent opportunities, regardless of race/ethnicity or gender. When we mentor someone of a different gender or ethnic/racial makeup, humility is particularly important; we should demonstrate "genuine curiosity about her unique experiences," be transparent about the limits of our own understanding of those experiences, and demonstrate empathy for the challenges she faces.[84]

4. Appreciating Other Differences

People may come into our lives that have a range of characteristics and experiences different from us. Each of us should be prepared to meet such individuals and to deal with them in an intelligent fashion, again through openness and curiosity.

One interesting example brings this home: A colleague recently introduced me to a friend who has been deaf since birth. This friend became an attorney and, quite remarkably, chose litigation as her field of practice. She is adept at reading lips but does not use sign language. Yet virtually every judge and court

---

[81]   Id.

[82]   See Section B.5., infra.

[83]   See Section C.2., infra.

[84]   W. Brad Johnson & David G. Smith, The Best Mentors Think Like Michelangelo, Harvard Business Review (January 23, 2018), available at https://hbr.org/2018/01/the-best-mentors-think-like-michelangelo.

officer with whom this attorney comes into contact automatically assigns a sign interpreter to accommodate her. While the gesture is appreciated, this failure to fully understand counsel's needs is an example of how greater depth of appreciation for differences could give us a more complete understanding of the perspectives of others.

5.   Recognizing Our Implicit Biases and Thinking Inclusively

Implicit Biases

Most of us think that we are eminently open-minded and fair in our dealings with others, including those who may be very different from us. Yet it turns out that we are all plagued by implicit biases and other failures in our ability to see things as evenhandedly and objectively as we would hope. The whole trouble with implicit biases is their hidden quality; they are dangerous precisely because they are by their very nature unknown to us, which makes them much harder to recognize or manage.

Understanding that our thoughts and actions are in part motivated by unconscious biases and other factors may allow us to overcome them. Hand-in-hand with trying to recognize and defeat our implicit biases is the need to think inclusively.

Science confirms that implicit biases influence our behaviors and judgment in many ways, and they have proven to be quite intractable. Human reasoning occurs via two cognitive systems. The first is a system that is "rapid, intuitive, and error-prone." The second is "more deliberative, calculative, slower, and often more likely to be error-free."[85] It is the first, the unconscious cognitive system, that gives rise to our implicit biases. Although the second system is more conscious and thoughtful, our minds tend to rationalize ideas and feelings generated by our more automatic beliefs. Put simply, our minds are predisposed to associate items that, based on our own personal experiences, we logically expect to go together. These

---

[85] Christine Jolls & Cass R. Sunstein, The Law of Implicit Bias, 94 Calif. L. Rev. 969, 974 (2006), available at https://scholarship.law.berkeley.edu/californialawreview/vol94/iss4/2/. See also Daniel Kahneman, Thinking Fast and Slow 20–22 (2011).

"mental blueprints"[86] are "cognitive shortcuts" that allow us to make sense of the world.[87] In this way, our worldview is "dangerously fashioned by our own class, race, ethnicity/culture, gender and sexual background."[88]

The science of first impressions helps us to recognize that we indeed are affected by implicit biases. Science has demonstrated our natural tendency to make decisions about someone's character within a millisecond of seeing them. These impressions are extremely powerful and consequential,[89] they are effortless, and they have biasing effects on our decisions.[90] Perniciously, these first impressions are generally misinformed.[91]

Studies have shown a disturbing correlation between the results of the Implicit Assumption Test (IAT), which measures unconscious assessments or biases,[92] and discriminatory behavior across a range of settings.[93] One study found that lawyers reviewing a memo rated it as far better when they believed that a white associate had written it than when they believed the author was a black associate with identical credentials.[94]

---

[86] Richard K. Sherwin, The Narrative Construction of Legal Reality, 6 J. Ass'n Legal Writing Directors 88 (2009), available at https://digitalcommons.nyls.edu/cgi/ viewcontent.cgi?referer=https://www.google.com/&httpsredir=1&article=1260&context =fac_articles_chapters.

[87] Nicole E. Negowetti, Implicit Bias and the Legal Profession's "Diversity Crisis": A Call for Self-Reflection, 15 Nev. L. J. 930, 937 (2015), available at http://scholars.law. unlv.edu/nlj/vol15/iss2/19/.

[88] Bill Ong Hing, Raising Personal Identification Issues of Class, Race, Ethnicity, Gender, Sexual Orientation, Physical Disability, and Age in Lawyering Courses, 45 Stan. L. Rev. 1807, 1810 (1993), https://www.jstor.org/stable/1229128?seq=1#page_scan_tab _contents.

[89] See Alexander Todorov on the science of first impressions (May 2, 2017), available at http://blog.press.princeton.edu/2017/05/02/alexander-todorov-on-the-science -of-first-impressions/.

[90] Id.

[91] Id.

[92] For an overview of the IAT, see Understanding and Using the Implicit Association Test: I. An Improved Scoring Algorithm. 85 J. of Personality & Soc. Psychol. 197 (2003).

[93] See Mahazarin R. Banaji & Anthony G. Greenwald, Blindspot: Hidden Biases of Good People 47–50 (2013)

[94] See Arin N. Reeves, Nextions, Written in Black and White: Exploring Confirmation Bias in Racialized Perceptions of Writing Skills (2014), available at https:// nextions.com/portfolio-posts/written-in-black-and-white-yellow-paper-series/.

Here is a simple test to determine whether you may suffer from implicit bias or make unwarranted first impressions. If you are lost and need directions, do you ever ask for help of the first person you come across? My guess is no; and the reason why we do not ask the first person to come our way is because we are animated by some implicit bias, some first impression, however error-prone it may be and however open-minded we may think that we are.

Inclusive Thinking

Implicit biases are barriers to inclusive thinking, which is the "skill involved in using [diverse perspectives] to create a collective intelligence that is greater than any one individual's intelligence."[95] This includes leveraging diversity of backgrounds, cultures, experiences, strengths, and work styles, among other differences. The underlying premise of inclusive thinking is that our judgment and problem-solving abilities are enhanced when we embrace differing perspectives and approaches. When individuals and firms achieve inclusive thinking, they enjoy a significant competitive advantage.

How do we achieve inclusive thinking? An initial, crucial step is acknowledging and recognizing our own tendency toward cognitive bias.[96] Here are some additional steps we can take toward thinking inclusively:[97]

Diversify Your Networks—Identify how much diversity of identity, experience, perspective, and personality you have in your personal and professional networks. Develop your networks in areas in which you lack appropriate diversity. Make it a point to meet new people who can add diversity to your circle and, by extension, your perspectives.

Consider Other Perspectives—Bring inclusive thinking into your problem-solving style by deliberately identifying and considering perspectives that you might not naturally embrace in your decision-making. In doing so, it is important to

---

[95]   Arin N. Reeves, Inclusive Thinking, in The Essential Qualities of Professional Lawyers 79 (2013).

[96]   "Actively recognizing and interrupting these cognitive biases. . . is the key to becoming a more inclusive thinker." Id. at 85.

[97]   Id. at 87–88.

acknowledge and try to manage any implicit biases that you may have.

Be Your Own Devil's Advocate—Create "productive conflict" in your thought processes by challenging your own beliefs and trying to defend your decisions from a range of perspectives.

Evaluate Past Failures—Think about a time when you did not achieve a goal and consider how different perspectives could have been accessed that might have helped you reach that goal.

Be Alert to Surprises—Surprises often signal a lack of inclusive thinking and reflect our biases. Surprises have been described as "the brain's way to remind you that there is a gap between what you thought would be reality and actual reality. . . . The more you identify the sources of surprise, the better you get at recognizing and eventually interrupting your implicit biases."[98] When we experience a surprise, think about what caused the surprise and what it tells us about limits in our thinking.

C. WITHIN THE FIRM/ORGANIZATION

Each of us will have colleagues and supervisors with whom we must learn to work effectively. This includes working collaboratively with colleagues (as discussed above)[99] and being supervised gracefully by more senior attorneys. Each of us should also be mentors and mentored, which, along with sponsorships, are important to career development.

1. The Art of Being Supervised: Learning on the Job

> "Junior people need to think through a problem completely—and using all resources available to them, particularly their colleagues—before they give me a memorandum or draft brief. Junior lawyers should give senior lawyers solutions, not problems, and they should only give senior people their best work." Grant Hanessian, Partner, Baker & McKenzie LLP[100]

---

[98] Reeves, supra note 95, at 88.

[99] See Section A.3., supra.

[100] Email from Grant Hanessian to the author (July 13, 2018), on file with the author.

"A junior attorney should always bear in mind that for purposes of his or her work, the 'client' is the partner or other more senior person who will receive and review the junior's work product. This means that nothing should be passed up the chain that is not as thorough, accurate and well-written as the junior person can make it. Carefully re-reading (and proofreading) documents before passing them along is thus essential. When I review internal drafts as the partner on the case, just as when I read the parties' briefs as arbitrator, a typographical or other obvious error immediately undermines my confidence in the document: If the author didn't catch that, I wonder, what else did he or she get wrong? Younger lawyers should also be aware that they are likely to receive little sympathy in regard to such errors from older practitioners, who grew up using the dictionary in the days before Microsoft Word, in its infinite wisdom, started pointing out the spelling and grammar mistakes for you." Brian D. King, Partner, Freshfields Bruckhaus Deringer LLP[101]

"Make it easy for your seniors. Do not do the minimum. . . . . Be a grownup. Don't whine. Don't complain. You aren't entitled to a job—you have to earn it. . . ." Honorable Loretta A. Preska, United States District Court for the Southern District of New York[102]

With the exception of the relatively few of us of who own our own businesses, we spend much or most of our working lives being supervised by others. We have bosses, and those bosses have expectations about what we do and how we do it. When working with supervisors, keep in mind the following objectives:

Preserve Your Supervisor's Time and Energy

Always think about how to save your supervisor's time and energy so that she can focus on things that only she can do. Junior professionals should think of themselves as defenders in a soccer match: The job of the defense is to keep the ball away from the goal box and the goalkeeper. Likewise, a junior

---

[101] Email from Brian D. King to the author (July 18, 2018), on file with the author.
[102] Email from Judge Preska to the author (July 15, 2018), on file with the author.

associate should shield his supervisor from as many details as possible and minimize her involvement in matters that do not truly require her engagement. Your reliability and resourcefulness directly correlate to the supervisor's ability to release "psychological ownership" over projects.[103]

Before you go to your supervisor, be sure that you have used all resources at your disposal. And when you do go to your supervisor, have your questions and thoughts well-organized so that the supervisor's time and energies can be focused and efficient. This would be a good time to revisit the Doctrine of Completed Staff Work discussed earlier.[104]

Make Your Supervisor Look Good

Always make your superior look good. Never undermine or publicly challenge the authority of your supervisor. Instead, be thoroughly dedicated to advancing her goals and enhancing her image. Absolute loyalty is required. This does not mean that you cannot have a discussion with your boss when there is a difference of opinion. You should express your views, but this should be done at a time and in a place that preserves her dignity and in a way that does not compromise her authority.

Understand Your Level of Discretion

Closely connected to preserving your supervisor's time and energy for things in which she truly needs to be involved is understanding how much discretion you have and where your level of judgment ends. This may take some time to fully appreciate but you will get more comfortable with the limits of your judgment as time goes on. As you prove yourself to be a person of good judgment and responsibility, you will inevitably be given more and more latitude to make decisions alone or with minimal supervision.

Adapt Your Working Style to That of Your Boss

As you work with different people, you will learn quickly that they have unique styles and preferences. Try to channel

---

[103] See Chapter 4.B.4., supra.

[104] See http://www.dolan-heitlinger.com/quote/stafwork.htm. See also Chapter 4.B.1., supra.

your supervisor and adapt your own approach to hers. For instance, some supervisors prefer in-person meetings while others prefer email or phone calls; some supervisors want to be informed in real-time as developments occur, while others prefer to wait until the next scheduled meeting (except, of course, in urgent situations); some prefer more detail while others want only information that they need to make informed decisions; some supervisors prefer to communicate early in the morning while others prefer afternoons or evenings; some do not like to be interrupted without an appointment while others readily accommodate unannounced visits or calls. Do your best to understand and accommodate your supervisor's style.

Follow Up

Follow up with your supervisor and help keep her on track. Of course, every professional is responsible for her own schedule and other commitments, but a truly outstanding subordinate will help keep his boss on track and focus her when necessary.

Imagine that you are a junior associate who has submitted a draft memorandum to the partner well in advance of the deadline. But the date on which the partner promised the memo to the client is rapidly approaching and you have not received any feedback or other communication from the partner. Rather than just waiting to hear from the partner, be proactive. Reach out and remind him of the deadline and ask how you can help. Give advance and repeated reminders to your supervisor when he needs them.

Keep Your Supervisor Informed of Your Availability

Be sure that your supervisor knows when you will be unavailable for both short and more extended periods. When appropriate, send a reminder as the date approaches. For instance, if in January you tell your boss that you will be on vacation from April 1–15, do not expect that she will remember. Remind her as the date gets closer and be sure that you ask with sufficient advance time what projects and tasks you should do in anticipation of your departure. The same is true as for shorter absences (conferences, meetings, doctor appointments, family commitments, etc.).

Keep Your Supervisor Informed of the Status of Pending Projects

Keep your supervisor informed of the status of projects and your progress toward completion without having to be asked. If you will not make a deadline, difficult news as that is to deliver, be sure that your supervisor knows well in advance so that she can make alternate arrangements, plan her time accordingly, and adjust any client expectations.

Be Responsive

Be exceptionally responsive to your supervisor. Your supervisor should know that she can trust and depend on you.[105]

Understand Expectations

Take responsibility for understanding and meeting expectations. Be sure that you have the background information you need to complete an assignment and that you know when the project is due, the number of hours you should spend on it, and what the deliverable is to be. Ask clarifying questions whenever expectations are unclear.

Accept Feedback as an Opportunity

"Solicit, accept, and act on feedback." Eric F. Grossman, Executive Vice President and Chief Legal Officer, Morgan Stanley[106]

Being on the receiving end of negative feedback is never fun, but if you think of feedback as a means to self-improvement it will seem far more palatable.[107] (This sounds a lot like the advice given to young litigators that they should welcome questions

---

[105] See Jacquelyn Smith, Say these 3 simple words if you want your boss to trust you, Business Insider (October 9, 2015), available at http://www.businessinsider.com/phrase-to-earn-trust-at-work-2015-10. Honoring commitments is one of the top ten capabilities most important for starting lawyers based on the results of a study of 24,000 practicing attorneys around the country. See Foundations for Practice: The Whole Lawyer Character Quotient, supra note 3, at 26.

[106] Email from Eric F. Grossman to the author (July 16, 2018), on file with the author.

[107] "The most effective strategy to foster self-development in professional formation is to internalize the habit of actively seeking feedback and reflecting on it." Neil W. Hamilton, The Qualities of the Professional Lawyer, in Essential Qualities of the Professional Lawyer 14 (2013).

from the bench during hearings and oral arguments as an opportunity to help the judge answer questions she may have— difficult to accept, but true!) Accept feedback with grace, acknowledge criticism, and take responsibility for any shortcomings. Internalize and be proactive in your approach to feedback. Think about how feedback can be used to improve your work more broadly.

2. The Importance of Mentors and Sponsors

"Take advantage of mentors and opportunities to be mentored, including from those who do not look or think like you. The best advice can come from the most unexpected sources. When someone asks me for advice, I feel honored to be asked; it is never a bother. Seek advice from whoever is in your life. Just ask." P. Anthony Sammi, Partner, Skadden, Arps, Slate, Meagher & Flom LLP[108]

"Juniors who have mentors that are willing to invest in their development reap the rewards. Mentors are everywhere but it is up to young lawyers to seek out their guidance." Ken Schwartz, Partner, Skadden, Arps, Slate, Meagher & Flom LLP[109]

Mentors and sponsors are crucial to professional development.[110] Everyone should have at least one mentor— someone to help guide you and help you develop your career. Most successful professionals have had the benefit of guidance from and the support of mentors.[111] Professionals who show the

---

[108] Email from P. Anthony Sammi to the author (August 6, 2018), on file with the author.

[109] Email from Ken Schwartz to the author (August 7, 2018), on file with the author.

[110] The placement of this section was tricky. Because sponsor and many mentor relationships come from within one's own organization, it was placed in the section on working within the firm or company. Readers should note that mentors often come from outside their organizations, which carries numerous benefits.

[111] Louis D. Bilionis, Professional Formation And The Political Economy of the American Law School, 83 Tenn. L. Rev. 895, 910 (2016) available at https://scholarship. law.uc.edu/fac_pubs/284/ ("High-functioning professionals will tell you that mentors and role models were integral to their development and achievement and that they continue to accumulate mentors and role models as the years pass. No one does it alone."). See also New York City Bar Association Task Force on New Lawyers in a Changing Profession, Developing Legal Careers and Delivering Justice in the 21st Century 63 (Fall 2013), available at http://www2.nycbar.org/pdf/developing-legal-careers-and-delivering-justice-in-the-21st-century.pdf ("[N]ew lawyers must . . . receive formal and informal

most promise may also land a sponsor—someone who is willing to be an advocate for that person within the organization and help provide meaningful opportunities for development. One is more likely to have several mentors whereas sponsors will be harder to come by. Mentors over time can become sponsors. Sponsors are said to be one of the most valuable types of relationship that a rising young professional can have.

Mentors and sponsors have overlapping roles and responsibilities. Being a mentor or a sponsor requires a commitment of time and energy and there are reputational considerations associated with both roles.

There is an important subtext to the process of mentoring and sponsoring junior attorneys that must be recognized: The fact that we often mentor those with whom we have the most in common.[112] This reality reinforces the white-male-centric nature of many legal organizations—large law firms in particular—and the profession more broadly. Organizations and individuals should be intentional about ensuring that there are equivalent mentoring and sponsorship opportunities for all.

Mentors

The Decline of Mentorship—Despite its importance to professional development, the role of mentors has declined in recent years, a casualty of the intense pressure on billable hours and the unwillingness of clients to pay for the training of junior associates.[113]

---

mentoring by experienced attorneys who can provide guidance about how best to handle specific legal issues and about overall career development and planning."); Eli Wald & Russell G. Pearce, Making Good Lawyers, 9 U. St. Thomas L. J. 403, 425 (2012) (citation omitted) ("A growing body of literature identifies mentorship as a fundamental aspect of the formation of professional identity."); id. at 438 (identifying mentorships as "relationships that are central to developing professional identity.").

[112] See, e.g., Alexandra E. Petri, When Potential Mentors Are Mostly White and Male, The Atlantic (July 7, 2017), available at https://www.theatlantic.com/business/archive/2017/07/mentorship-implicit-bias/532953/.

[113] See Chapter 2.A.3., supra. See Thomas J. DeLong, John J. Gabarro, & Robert J. Lees, Why Mentoring Matters in a Hypercompetitive World, Harvard Business Review (January 2008), available at https://hbr.org/2008/01/why-mentoring-matters-in-a-hypercompetitive-world; Susan Saab Fortney, Soul for Sale: An Empirical Study of Associate Satisfaction, Law Firm Culture, and the Effects of Billable Hour Requirements, 69 UMKC L. Rev. 239, 281 & n. 257, 258 (2000), available at https://papers.ssrn.com/sol3/papers.cfm?abstract_id=1505619.

Why Mentors Matter—Mentors can be thought of as comprising a "personal advisory board"[114] who can help their mentees understand and navigate the larger profession, specific practice areas and specific organizations, and advance their careers and help them achieve their professional goals more generally.

Mentor advice can range from more granular issues such as helping manage specific professional situations (such as managing office politics or dealing with a particular individual) to larger development issues (such as introducing you to a network of professionals, giving career advice, and getting you involved in bar and trade associations). They can be a sounding board for challenging issues and may even be able to talk through substantive and procedural points of law. They can offer tough love and help instill confidence. They can share lessons from their own experiences and can be a source of comfort when you feel isolated or overwhelmed. They can be trusted counselors and guides. Mentors can help bridge generational divides by offering insights into the practice of law and the politics of the practice of law. They can introduce the language and cultural nuances of the profession. Mentors act as models of a professional persona. If we admire our mentors, as we should, it is easier to incorporate the ideals they represent into our own professional persona.[115]

It is common and advisable to have several mentors. Multiple mentors, each with different experiences, perspectives, and strengths, can be beneficial as each of us strives to develop and embrace our own professional persona. All told, mentors can have a profound impact on a younger attorney's development by influencing their professional persona at a formative stage of development.

---

[114] DeLong, Gabarro, & Lees, supra note 113.

[115] Mentorships from practice "provide students with an experiential window through which to view the professional world and exposure to the diverse spectrum of work that lawyers and judges do." Neil Hamilton & Lisa Montpetit Brabbit, Fostering Professionalism through Mentoring, 57 J. Legal Ed. 102, 123 (2007), available at http://coloradomentoring.org/wp-content/uploads/2013/09/Hamilton-N-Fostering-Professionalism-through-Mentoring-Journal-of-Legal-Education-Vol.-57-No.-1-March-2007.pdf.

Why Mentor?—Being a mentor is a time and energy commitment, and mentorship roles should not be taken on lightly. However, mentoring is an incontrovertible service to the profession and to the individuals on the receiving end.

Being a mentor also offers numerous benefits to the mentor herself. First, mentors will learn things about themselves and will learn things directly from their protégés. Second, mentoring demonstrates to juniors that the firm and its more senior attorneys care about the wellbeing and development of the more junior members of the team. Finally, sharing your experiences with others and helping to guide others is a way to secure your own legacy and achieve some measure of immortality. By sharing your wisdom in helping to shape more junior attorneys, elements of your own professional persona can live on in others.

How to Secure and Work with a Mentor—

"If you want a mentor, start acting like you do. . . ."
Thomas J. DeLong, John J. Gabarro, & Robert J. Lees[116]

There are numerous ways to secure mentors.

Some law schools, bar associations, and law firms and other legal employers offer formal mentoring programs. Take advantage of these opportunities to meet professionals with whom you might otherwise not come into contact. Some of these opportunities are affinity-based, pairing young lawyers with others from the same racial, ethnic, or other group.

The best mentoring relationships, however, generally arise more organically. Young attorneys who put themselves in situations in which they can meet and impress more seasoned lawyers will have excellent opportunities to build mentoring relationships. Become active in bar and other trade associations, which offer the opportunity to leverage large numbers of affiliations with professionals who share common interests; volunteer to help at conferences and other events, which gives you access to organizers and participants; and reach out to people who you admire and would like to meet.

---

[116] DeLong, Gabarro, & Lees, *supra* note 113.

Finally, do not overlook your peers as potential mentors. And contrary to conventional wisdom, even those younger can be valuable mentors.

How you approach potential mentors is important. Generally, you do not ask someone to be your mentor in the same way you might ask someone you are dating to make the relationship exclusive. A few times I have been asked by younger colleagues or students to be their mentor. These requests seemed both odd and imposing—what an awesome responsibility it would be to accept! Mentoring relationships develop more naturally and over time. The words mentor or mentee are rarely used explicitly in the context of a relationship, but when such a connection emerges it is understood and valued by both parties.

Once you have a mentor, there are a few basic rules to keep in mind:

- *Show Gratitude*—Always show gratitude toward your mentor for actions both large and small. It is the small gestures that often get overlooked. If a mentor has taken even a few minutes from his schedule to guide you, if he has written a short email to introduce you to someone in his network, these efforts must be acknowledged and appreciated—and that is true regardless of the outcome.

- *Never Have Expectations of a Mentor*—Whatever time and energy a mentor spends is a reflection of her generosity and kindness. A mentor's role is voluntary and a matter of grace. The mentor owes nothing to the protégé and the mentee should feel no sense of entitlement. The mentee must remember that the mentor has his own life full of pressures and commitments and challenges. Respect whatever limits the mentor places on the relationship, expressly or by implication. In particular, a mentee should never expect a mentor to do for her what she can do for herself. Imagine that your mentor tells you to reach out to his former colleague, Fran Moring. Do not ask your mentor how you can reach Moring or whether Moring is male or female. In most cases, these are things that can easily be learned using the Internet. In a similar vein, always be prepared for conversations with your mentor. Do research on latest developments in the field, etc. It is to your great benefit to show your mentor that you are prepared, engaged, and proactive.

- *Ask the Right Questions*—Closely related to the point above, ask your mentor the right kinds of questions—questions that are manageable. Questions that are too big may be intimidating and may trigger a fear response that shuts down the brain.[117] The mind can readily absorb and handle more modest questions. For instance, this kind of question is likely to overwhelm: "How can I become the managing partner of the biggest law firm in the United States?" Ask instead, "What kinds of behaviors and experiences are most important for me to develop on my track to partnership?"

- *Mentoring Relationships Must Be Reciprocal*— Mentoring relationships must involve a give-and-take by both parties. Even law students and very inexperienced attorneys can bring tangible value to more experienced attorneys—and should seize every opportunity to do so. The mentoring relationship should be engaging and beneficial to both parties and should never feel to the mentor like a one-way street.

- *The Burden Is Always on the One Seeking Advice*— The burden of keeping in touch and following up is always on the mentee, never on the mentor. Stay in touch with people who mentor and assist you—not only is it an appropriate demonstration of gratitude but it is a way to continue to maximize the potential of the relationship.

---

[117] See, e.g., Robert Maurer, "Thinking Big" Could Make You FAIL, Talent Development Resources, available at http://talentdevelop.com/articles/TBCBMYF.html.

- *Treasure Your Mentors*—Hold your mentors near and dear. In addition to showing gratitude for acts done, show them how you value the relationship in other ways. Find ways to help them when you can. Keep them posted on developments in your life and keep in touch with them even when there is no special news to share. An occasional note or email is an easy way to let the person know you appreciate her time and advice. A mentor will be put off by hearing from you only when you need a favor.

Sponsors

What Is a Sponsor?—A sponsor, rather than being a personal advisor, is more like an advocate. Sponsors typically hold powerful and influential roles in the law firm or organization in which you work. A sponsor will openly promote and publicly endorse you. This may include recommending you for particular types of assignments that will allow you to develop certain skills and other career opportunities (for instance speaking engagements or roles on bar committees), ensuring that you get to work with certain high-profile partners, helping you achieve visibility within the organization, and serving as your champion at critical junctures in the promotion process.[118] Unlike the more nurturing and advising role of mentors, the role of sponsors is more transactional. Sponsors serve a critical, high-level marketing function for their protégés.

How to Get a Sponsor—Sponsors are not easy to come by, and many people go through their professional careers—and do quite well—without a sponsor. A sponsor, however, can dramatically enhance your career trajectory.

The best way to get a sponsor is to consistently do excellent work and to adhere to the behaviors discussed in this book. Stand out as exceptional. Go the extra mile. Inspire confidence at every step; do not expose vulnerabilities to a sponsor or

---

[118] Sponsors "have the power and influence to advocate on one's behalf and champion one's career at critical junctures. Sponsors go beyond the mentor role of providing feedback, friendship, and advice. Sponsors occupy a seat at the table, and their clout is indispensable. . . ." Roberta D. Liebenberg, Women in the Law, in Essential Qualities of the Professional Lawyer 95–96 (2013).

prospective sponsor (although you can to a mentor, depending on the nature of the relationship).[119]

Trust and dependability are probably the most important elements in cultivating a sponsor. You must demonstrate an absolute sense of loyalty to your sponsor/potential sponsor and she must have complete confidence in your continuous commitment to excellence. As Kerrie Peraino, global head of talent at American Express, explains, "[w]hen I put my faith in up-and-coming talent and become their sponsor, I need to know I can totally depend on them—because they are, after all, walking around with my brand on."[120] These are words to live by.

D. EXTERNAL CONSTITUENCIES

Attorneys work with a range of constituencies in their everyday lives. These include clients and prospective clients, counterparties and collaborators, judges and court personnel, adversaries, and the public at large. Here are some tips for working across these groups.

1. Business Development and Client Management

"I talk with lawyers from around the country to see how we as legal educators can better prepare students for the practice of law. What they want is young associates who better understand what clients need. I think of this as the transition from being a student to being a professional—from primarily worrying about yourself to having a service orientation." Matthew Diller, Dean and Paul Fuller Professor of Law, Fordham University School of Law[121]

Attorneys are in a service business, and for private practitioners, client development and management is where the

---

[119] Sylvia Ann Hewlett, Mentors Are Good. Sponsors Are Better, The New York Times (April 13, 2013), available at https://www.nytimes.com/2013/04/14/jobs/sponsors-seen-as-crucial-for-womens-career-advancement.html.

[120] Id., quoting Kerrie Peraino, global head of talent at American Express.

[121] Email from Matthew Diller to the author (July 14, 2018), on file with the author.

rubber hits the road.[122] Increasingly, attorneys are expected to develop a book of business as an important element of the value they bring to their firms. Competition for clients is more intense than ever, making client stewardship critical. Client loyalty has become subordinate to the realities of today's competitive marketplace and clients accordingly are making increasing demands for efficiency and cost effectiveness.[123] The 2017 Clio Legal Trends Report finds that 33% of lawyers' non-billable time is dedicated to business development, demonstrating that "earning new clients is a constant concern for most law firms."[124]

Client development is only the first challenge: Retaining clients is also of critical importance. Many law firms tend to focus on client development at the expense of client retention. "The client life cycle does not stop once the client engages the firm."[125] Client retention is much less expensive than client development and, when done right, has the potential to exponentially increase profits.[126]

What follows are some basic tools to help in these essential skills of client development and management.

Learn About Your Client/Prospective Client—Each client is unique. In preparing to represent a client or to seek business from a prospective client, learn as much about the client as possible—its business, its internal dynamics, its values, and its goals. Attorneys sometimes make the mistake of focusing too narrowly on the specific legal matter brought to the representation. Read the client's 10-Ks and Qs. Read the news

---

[122] Business development and building relationships with clients are listed as among the 26 effectiveness factors in the classical empirical study by Professors Marjorie M. Shultz and Sheldon Zedeck. See Shultz & Zedeck, supra note 25.

[123] See Chapter 2.B.1., supra.

[124] Clio 2017 Legal Trends Report, Executive summary 3 (2017), available at https://files.goclio.com/marketo/ebooks/2017-Legal-Trends-Report-Executive-Summary.pdf. See also Clio 2017 Legal Trends Report 13 (2017), available at https://www.clio.com/resources/legal-trends/2017-report/. The report also indicates that 41% of respondents would spend more time on client development if they could. Executive summary at 4. See also Legal Trends Report 15.

[125] Kathryn B. Whitaker, Focusing on Client Retention May Mean Restructuring the Firm, The American Lawyer (April 4, 2018), available at https://www.law.com/americanlawyer/2018/04/04/focusing-on-client-retention-may-mean-restructuring-the-firm/.

[126] Id., citing research by Fred Reichheld of Bain & Co. indicating that by increasing customer retention by 5% a firm can increase profits by 25–95%.

to anticipate issues that may affect a client. Always think of the context in which the client does business and the broader implications of the matter and how it may impact the client's overarching business goals.[127] Also learn about the client's industry by reading trade publications and seeking other sources of news that afford a better understanding of the larger business context in which the client operates.

Make Sure Your Client Feels Like Your Highest Priority— Each client and prospective client should feel like a veritable king or queen. A lawyer generally should not speak about other matters or clients—and this goes well beyond the ethical requirement of confidentiality[128]—so that the client does not feel that you are torn by competing priorities. Go the extra mile and make a personal visit to the client's office, a gesture that clients seem to prize.[129]

It turns out that such visits can provide tangible benefits beyond client gratitude. A former student who is now a tax lawyer told me that after a visit to a client's factory and discussions with the foreman and others involved in the manufacture of the product, he was able to make a change to the way the client reports its income, leading to a savings of one million dollars per year. That visit went a long way toward solidifying the attorney's relationship with the client.

Guide the Client Toward Best Solutions, Even if It Means Less Business—There may be times when the lawyer's immediate interests are in tension with the interests of the client. These conflicts always must be resolved in the client's

---

[127] See Gina Passarella Cipriani, For Love of Client, GCs Say Law Firms Need to Be More Proactive, The American Lawyer (October 30, 2017), available at https://www. law.com/americanlawyer/sites/americanlawyer/2017/10/30/for-love-of-client-gcs-say-law -firms-need-to-be-more-proactive/. See also What 10 Legal Department Luminaries Have Said About Outside Firms, ALM Media (April 16, 2018) (quoting the general counsel and chief compliance office of DHL Supply Chain Americas as saying "Don't take [your clients] to golf. Go visit them."), available at https://finance.yahoo.com/news/10-legal-department-luminaries-said-155650368.html.

[128] See, e.g., Rule 1.6, Model Rules of Professional Conduct, available at https:// www.americanbar.org/groups/professional_responsibility/publications/model_rules_of_ professional_conduct/rule_1_6_confidentiality_of_information.html.

[129] See David H. Freeman, Keep Your Friends Close and Your Prospects Closer, Legal Management (September 12, 2016), available at http://www.davidfreeman consulting.com/wp-content/uploads/2016/09/Keep-Your-Friends-Close-and-Your-Prospects-Closer-_-Legal-Management.pdf.

favor. These matters sometimes are addressed by rules of professional responsibility, but there are times where the tension is more nuanced. For instance, outstanding client service may mean allowing others—within or outside the firm—to bill the work in question because that other attorney can do the work more effectively or efficiently. Attorneys who can think beyond their own silos and share work, regardless of billable hour or origination credit, perform a great service to their clients and to the firm. Such sharing is surely to be appreciated by the client and by the receiving attorney and returned in client loyalty and cross referrals.

Be Proactive and Creative—An article in the *American Lawyer* outlines suggestions by general counsel of a range of companies for securing and retaining business. A common theme is the "desire for . . . outside firms to be more proactive.[130] Examples of successful pitches and retention efforts reported are law firms that provided some free service when they knew that a client was undergoing a difficult situation; that proactively embrace technological changes that would make the relationship more efficient and more user-friendly; that send associates to the company for secondments; and that deliver business pitches based on meaningful background research and a proposed strategy rather than just glossy brochures.[131]

Be Compulsively Responsive—An essential element of client satisfaction, it turns out, is one of the simplest things to do: Be fully responsive to the client. The 2017 Clio Legal Trends report finds that the single biggest factor used by consumers in deciding whether to retain a lawyer is whether the attorney responded immediately to a phone call or email.[132] Clients expect real-time responses from their attorneys, even if that response is simply to acknowledge receipt of a message, indicating when a more thorough reply will be forthcoming.

Be Clear and Keep the Client Informed About Expectations, Fees, and Other Features of the Representation—Hand-in-hand with responsiveness is the need to be transparent with clients

---

[130] Passarella Cipriani, supra note 127.

[131] Id.

[132] Clio 2017 Legal Trends Report, supra note 124, Executive summary at 4.

about fees, timing, availability, turnaround time, likely risks and benefits of certain actions, and other sensitive matters.

The attorney should stay in touch with the client and provide regular status reports and updates. Working effectively with the client requires advance planning on the part of the attorney. Communicate key dates and give the client ample time to provide necessary information and to review drafts and make decisions.

One of the most delicate client issues is billing. Attorneys should be completely transparent when it comes to fees, including total projected costs, any contingencies associated with fees, how bills are calculated, billing procedures, what expenses will be the responsibility of the client, and any other financial implications associated with the representation.

Clients are also very sensitive to staffing decisions and should be kept informed of staffing assignments and any changes that need to be made to the team. Clients do not want to find out incidentally about partners or associates that have been added to or removed from a pending matter.[133]

Communicate with the Client in the Way the Client Prefers— As discussed below,[134] lawyers should communicate with others in the manner most appropriate to the situation. Whenever possible, use the means of communication that the client prefers.

With clients who are not attorneys, be especially careful to keep your language clear and understandable to the person with whom you are communicating. Doing so ensures that the client has a full appreciation for what you are saying, including her options, the benefits and risks associated with each option, and all other relevant information.

Recently I had the chance to be on the receiving end of a communication that was completely foreign to me: I attended my first CrossFit class. Here are the instructions provided by the instructor:

> Welcome to the Box! Here is the WOD: Warm-up on the
> C2 for 200 meters; AMRAP for 20 minutes of 10 reps

---

[133] See Chapter 6.A.2., supra.
[134] See Chapter 9.A.1., infra.

DHP; 10 reps TTB; 15 calories on the assault bike; 5 clean and jerk using PR weight. Take a rest. Now do EMOM front squats, ATG, using BW.

This is what I understood:

Welcome to the *what*? Here is the *what*? Warm up doing 200 meters of *what*? *What for 20 minutes*? 10 reps of *what*? 10 more reps of *what*? 15 calories on the *what*? 5 *what* using *what* weight? Take a rest. Do *what* with a front squat *how*?

This experience gave me a firsthand experience with how confounding it can be to hear a vocabulary that is wholly unfamiliar, and a stark reminder of the importance of using language that is clear and accessible to any specific listener.

Demonstrate Generosity Toward Others—Do favors for others. When another attorney asks you to help on a matter within your expertise, oblige whenever possible. If a client or prospect has a question that you can answer easily, do so without billing (when consistent with firm policy). Direct business to colleagues when you are not the best person for a representation. At the end of the day, it is old-fashioned values like these that will help you land and retain clients, directly or through referrals from other lawyers.

Ask the Client for Feedback—Despite the primacy of feedback systems in many fields, lawyers have been reluctant to ask clients for feedback.[135] Lawyers who ask their clients for feedback can differentiate themselves as offering a more "client-centric experience."[136] Some clients are now using sophisticated systems to measure and track performance.[137]

Guard Your Reputation—There are of course many reasons to develop and maintain a stellar reputation, and client development is among them. The 2017 Clio Legal Trends Report indicates that consumers of legal services predominantly use

---

[135] Whitaker, supra note 125.

[136] Id.

[137] See Passarella Cipriani, supra note 127, describing Qualmet, a software system devised in part by Mark Smolik, general counsel of DHL Supply Chain Americas. See http://www.qualmetlegal.com/.

referrals by others in selecting an attorney.[138] Protect your reputation as the valuable asset it is.

2.   Counterparties and Collaborators

It may be easy to neglect relationships with counterparties and collaborators as not offering true value to our professional lives. This would be a mistake. In many practice areas, especially in transactional fields of law, counterparties and collaborators make up an important element of an attorney's professional network. In many practice areas, one can expect to work with repeat players—both on the same and the opposing side. Both can be potential sources of business, but more importantly, developing constructive working relationships with these individuals can lead to smoother dealings in the current and subsequent deals.

A friend who works in-house doing real estate deals recently told me that she often works with many of the same attorneys, both as collaborators and counterparties. She mentioned one lawyer who is often on the other side of the table who she respects enormously. Whenever that attorney is involved in a negotiation, she knows—and tells her colleagues—that the matter will be dealt with professionally and expeditiously. She has even directed business to this attorney on several occasions.

3.   Judges and Court Personnel

Courts are uniquely treasured institutions in our legal system. Judges wield tremendous power, and as singular representations of the rule of law, they command the highest level of respect and deference. Many of the elements discussed below regarding dealings with the court seem so obvious as to not require exposition. But the fact that many judges have written about standard behavior before the court[139] suggests

---

[138] Clio 2017 Legal Trends Report, Executive summary, supra note 124, at 4 (showing that 62% of respondents get referrals from friends or family and 31% seek referrals from other lawyers).

[139] See, e.g., Warren E. Burger, The Decline of Professionalism, 63 Fordham L. Rev. 949 (1995), available at https://ir.lawnet.fordham.edu/cgi/viewcontent.cgi?article=3181& context=flr; Gerald Lebovits, Alifya V. Curtin, & Lisa Solomon, Ethical Judicial Opinion Writing, 21 Geo. J. Legal Ethics 237 (2008), available at https://core.ac.uk/download/pdf/ 76623413.pdf; and Randall T. Shepard, Judicial Professionalism and the Relations between Judges and Lawyers, 14 Notre Dame J. Law, Ethics & Public Policy (February

that many attorneys do not fully appreciate basic rules of conduct to which advocates should adhere.[140]

The following advice is borrowed liberally from an article co-written by my friend and colleague Judge Mimi Tsankov of the United States Immigration Court.[141] That article, in turn, was based on a lecture delivered by United States Magistrate Judge Kristen L. Mix.[142] Their suggestions include the following:

Maintain   Courtroom   Decorum—Attorneys   must   be "courteous, prompt, and prepared" and formality should be every attorney's default position.[143] Attorneys should refer to the judge as "your honor" rather than the more informal term "judge";[144] stand when the judge enters or leaves the courtroom and when addressing the judge;[145] direct all comments to the court;[146] and avoid interrupting the judge or repeating oneself.[147]

Chief Justice Warren Burger spoke of "truly great advocates" who exemplified civility by abiding by norms of decorum in the courtroom:

> [T]hey were all intensely individualistic, but each was a lawyer for whom courtroom manners were a key weapon in his arsenal. Whether engaged in the destruction of adverse witnesses or undermining damaging evidence or final argument, the performance was characterized by coolness, poise and graphic clarity, without shouting or ranting, and without baiting witnesses, opponents or the judge.[148]

2014), available at https://scholarship.law.nd.edu/cgi/viewcontent.cgi?referer=https://www.google.com/&httpsredir=1&article=1333&context=ndjlepp.

[140] See Mimi E. Tsankov & Jessica L. Grimes, A new take on the top ten rules for court and professional life, 89 Denv. U. L. Rev. 369, 370 (2012), available at https://www.researchgate.net/publication/292485079_A_new_take_on_the_top_ten_rules_for_court_and_professional_life.

[141] Id.

[142] See id. at 370.

[143] See id. at 372.

[144] Id.

[145] Id.

[146] Id.

[147] Id.

[148] Warren E. Burger, The Special Skills of Advocacy: Are Specialized Training and Certification of Advocates Essential to Our System of Justice?, 42 Fordham L. Rev. 227,

Follow Court Rules and Procedures—Following rules of the court promotes respect for the rule of law[149] and saves the time and resources of the court and the parties.[150] It is important to "know your judge" and "know your court."[151] These rules include formal codifications but also more informal, unwritten rules of appropriate dress, demeanor, and etiquette that often have local nuances.[152] Courtroom observation is a great way to develop a sense of local practice.[153]

When I was a law student I had an externship in a small law office located in Durham, North Carolina. During my first visit to court, I was struck by the fact that attorneys did not rise to address the court. My supervising attorney told me that this local practice was a holdover from many, many years earlier when there was a well-respected litigator in Durham who was wheelchair-bound. Out of respect for him, a practice of not rising to address the court was cultivated, and it stuck in reverence for this much-admired attorney. This practice is something I would never had known had I not visited the court to observe proceedings.

Do Not Question the Judge's Authority—Never allow zealous advocacy to undermine the authority of the court. Any showings of "displeasure, disgust, or anger at a judge's ruling or at a case outcome is both childish and unprofessional" and may compromise your client's chances of success.[154]

Consider "What Will the Judge Think?"—Think about how your actions and words, and the way that they are delivered, will be perceived by the court, and "use sound judgment and discretion" in determining which issues to pursue and which to simply let go of.[155]

---

236 (1973), available at https://ir.lawnet.fordham.edu/cgi/viewcontent.cgi?referer=https://www.google.com/&httpsredir=1&article=4570&context=flr.

[149] Tsankov & Grimes, supra note 140, at 376.

[150] Id.

[151] Id.

[152] Id. at 376–83.

[153] Id. at 382.

[154] Id. at 382–83.

[155] Id. at 384.

Write with Precision and Clarity—As discussed more thoroughly elsewhere,[156] legal writing is most effective when it is "formal, clear, precise, and sensitive to nuance."[157] Obfuscating takes up time and energy of the court and threatens to muddle the issues at stake.

Confer in Good Faith with Opposing Counsel—Before a court appearance, attorneys should undertake "meaningful efforts to confer with opposing counsel" in order to save resources of both the court and the parties and to foster civility.[158] Among other things, this can take the shape of joint motions, joint stipulations, and other less formal methods that have the potential to narrow the issues to be brought to the court.[159]

Deal with the Court in Complete Candor—Complete candor in dealings with the court is an essential element of professionalism, "perhaps one of the most important roles of a practicing attorney."[160]

Treat Court Staff with Respect—Attorneys should be thoughtful about and restrained in making requests of members of the court staff. Anticipate your needs and come prepared.[161] Avoid filings made minutes before the court clerk's closing time.[162]

Expect Delays—Expect delays in court and manage your affairs accordingly. Do not schedule meetings too close in time to court appearances, bring a snack, and, if the client is attending the proceedings, manage your client's expectations about the time she may need to spend in court.[163]

Guard Your Reputation—As noted above, an attorney's reputation is one of her most valuable assets, and it should be scrupulously protected through "careful and thorough

---

[156] See Chapter 9.A. and B., infra.

[157] See Tsankov & Grimes, supra note 140, at 385.

[158] Id. at 387, 388.

[159] Id. at 388.

[160] Id. at 389.

[161] Id. at 389–90.

[162] Id. at 392. This echoes the need to manage your time, as discussed in Chapter 5.A., supra. There is simply no good reason to wait until the very last minute to submit a filing. There is always a risk that something goes wrong, resulting in a missed deadline.

[163] Id. at 390–92.

preparation, including the preparation of thoughtful, concise, well-organized, well-edited, and proofread written materials."[164]

4. Adversaries

Working with adversaries is largely about civility, as discussed earlier.[165] It is when we interact with adversaries that our patience may be particularly strained, so it is particularly important to exercise civility when dealing with adversaries. Allow an extension of time when it does not disadvantage your client. Resist the temptation to respond vindictively to unkind words. Exercise restraint even when under pressure. How you deal with adversaries will be the true mark of your ability to act civilly.

5. The Public At-Large

As attorneys we must always remember that we hold positions of public trust, privilege, and responsibility. In all of our dealings—public and private—we must do our best to advance the goals of society and uphold the honor of the profession, gain the public trust, enhance the rule of law, and serve the needs of the pubic.

E. QUESTIONS FOR REFLECTION

1. Think of three classmates or colleagues who are in some ways different from you (e.g., gender, race, ethnicity, religion, sexual preference, sexual identity, generational). Have you noticed ways in which their thinking, attitudes, and/or mannerisms differ from yours? Have you experienced any conflict as a result of these differences? How have you managed to bridge the gap?

2. Think of a time in which you had tension with a classmate, colleague, or supervisor. How did that affect the work you were engaging in? What efforts did you undertake to manage the conflict?

3. Do you have or have you been a mentor? If so, how did you develop those relationships? Name three

---

[164] Id. at 393.

[165] See Section A.1., supra.

benefits of that relationship. If not, do you wish to have or to be a mentor? If so, how do you think you can achieve that? If not, why not?

4. Have you ever worked as part of a team, at a job or in school? If so, did you enjoy it and find it productive? If so, why? If not, why not? Discuss some challenges associated with teamwork that you have experienced and how you managed to advance the team goals.

CHAPTER 8

TALENT MANAGEMENT

This chapter addresses the importance of talent management in law firms and other organizations and some characteristics of great managers.

As professionals, we are never too young or inexperienced to share and teach others. Lawyers begin to supervise on their very first day on the job. This early supervision, generally of non-legal support staff, extends to summer associates and more junior associates quickly, and accelerates with each passing year.

If you are relatively junior, keep these tips in mind as you begin to take on supervisory roles of greater responsibility. If you are more senior and have been supervising others for some time, this chapter provides a set of practical tools to enable each of us to improve our management style.

Note that talent management and supervision of others is not the same thing as leadership, although there is inevitably some overlap in concepts. Leadership, as explored earlier,[1] is about a mindset and general orientation. Talent management is more about position and concrete actions that should be taken in managing others.

A. THE IMPORTANCE OF TALENT MANAGEMENT

Talent management should be integral to the strategy of every organization and of each individual supervisor. This is particularly important in professional services firms, which "live and die by their intellectual capital."[2] Significant resources are used in recruiting this talent, and a concomitant level of commitment should be applied to nurturing it.[3] Talent is an

---

[1]   See Chapter 3.D., supra.

[2]   Thomas J. DeLong, John J. Gabarro, & Robert J. Lees, Why Mentoring Matters in a Hypercompetitive World, Harvard Business Review (January 2008), available at https://hbr.org/2008/01/why-mentoring-matters-in-a-hypercompetitive-world.

[3]   "When people are your product, your business principles must be singularly focused on talent management. If law firms want to prosper from defining themselves in business terms, they must also commit to stable and sustainable business practices when

important asset and its management is especially critical in the current environment in which employees are "more powerful and less loyal" than ever.[4] The trend of many large law firms to hire chief talent officers reflects the institutional importance of talent management.[5]

As discussed earlier,[6] clients also care about talent management, which enhances the efficiency and effectiveness of service. Turnover, often a result of poor talent management, disrupts workflow and is frustrating to clients. The development of talent is also crucial for the sustainability of law firms and other organizations as younger generations increasingly will be called upon to assume managerial roles.

B. WHAT GREAT SUPERVISORS DO

Proper supervision is an essential element of talent management. Here are some of the ways in which supervisors can protect their firms' investment in talent. Among other things, great managers ensure that associates get the right kind of assignments and opportunities to observe more senior practitioners; involve subordinates genuinely in their work; model appropriate behavior; take responsibility for anything that goes wrong; are eminently human; embrace a culture of teamwork; have patience as juniors go through the process of learning; are reasonable and clear about expectations; make themselves available; provide effective feedback; take wellbeing seriously; manage conflict swiftly and fairly; and are flexible to the extent permitted by the circumstances.

---

it comes to managing and developing an engaged workforce." Lauren Stiller Rikleen, Law Firms Need to Take Care of Their Talent, Harvard Business Review (July 10, 2012), available at https://hbr.org/2012/07/law-firms-need-to-take-care-of.

[4]   Deloitte Center for the Edge, Unlocking the Passion of the Explorer 5 (September 17, 2013), available at https://www2.deloitte.com/insights/us/en/topics/talent/unlocking-the-passion-of-the-explorer.html.

[5]   See Lizzy McLellan, Law Firm Talent Execs Get a Seat at the Table, The Legal Intelligencer (June 19, 2017), available at https://www.law.com/thelegalintelligencer/almID/1202790526500/Law-Firm-Talent-Execs-Get-a-Seat-at-the-Table/.

[6]   See Chapter 6.B.2., supra.

1. Use Fair and Meaningful System of Work Assignments: Play Chess, Not Checkers

Work should be assigned with an eye toward advancing junior talent. Associates should receive comparable opportunities to develop and demonstrate their skills. Each associate should be provided with challenging work that allows her to mature and demonstrate the full range of her capabilities. The system of assignments also should ensure that junior associates have access to more senior attorneys with similar levels of influence. Consistent with the firm needs, assignments should also take account of associate interest.

Great managers recognize and help maximize the skills of each member of the team. The difference between managers who capitalize on individual strengths and those who do not can be likened to the difference between those who play chess and those who play checkers:

> Average managers play checkers, while great managers play chess. The difference? In checkers, all the pieces are uniform and move in the same way; they are interchangeable. You need to plan and coordinate their movements, certainly, but they all move at the same pace, on parallel paths. In chess, each type of piece moves in a different way, and you can't play if you don't know how each piece moves. More important, you won't win if you don't think carefully about how you move the pieces. Great managers know and value the unique abilities and even the eccentricities of their employees, and they learn how best to integrate them into a coordinated plan of attack.[7]

Great managers understand and accommodate the individual learning styles of those on the team. Some team members may be *analyzers*—they do research, can act only when they have complete information, and are very risk averse and perfectionist; some may be *doers*—those who are willing to learn through experience and trial and error; others may be *watchers*—those that learn by observing more experienced

---

[7] Marcus Buckingham, What Great Managers Do, Harvard Business Review (March 2005), available at https://hbr.org/2005/03/what-great-managers-do.

practitioners. Watchers rely heavily on modeling. Work assignments to the extent possible should take account of the learning style of each associate.[8]

2. Provide Opportunities to Observe

Associates should be given the chance to shadow more senior practitioners and see them in action. Junior attorneys should observe client interactions, meetings with government officials, depositions, hearings, and other activities relevant to the firm's practice.

3. Involve Subordinates Genuinely

Supervisors should engage juniors deeply in the work of the organization. Encourage subordinates to take ownership over projects. Ask them to brainstorm and help develop solutions. Ask junior associates to share their views, which helps them develop their problem-solving skills and has the added benefit of bringing broad perspectives to pending issues.

4. Allow Juniors a Sense of Control and Autonomy

Subordinates should be given a sense of control and autonomy consistent with their ability. Research has shown that work environments that enable control and autonomy facilitate "optimal functioning and well-being"[9] and that, conversely, when managers do not empower individuals, workers are more likely to suffer a range of psychological disorders.[10] Where

---

[8] Id.

[9] American Bar Association, National Task Force on Lawyer Well-Being, The Path to Lawyer Well-Being: Practical Recommendations for Positive Change 17 (August 14, 2017) (citation omitted), available at https://www.americanbar.org/groups/lawyer_assistance/task_force_report.html. See also id. at 54 (internal citations omitted) ("[F]eeling a lack of control over work is a well-established contributor to poor mental health, including depression and burnout. A sense of autonomy is considered to be a basic psychological need that is foundational to well-being and optimal functioning. . . . . [L]eaders can be trained to be more autonomy-supportive. Other organizational practices that can enhance a sense of autonomy include, for example, structuring work to allow for more discretion and autonomy and encouraging lawyers to craft aspects of their jobs to the extent possible to best suit their strengths and interests.").

[10] See, e.g., Jong-Min Woo & Teodor T. Postolache, The impact of work environment on mood disorders and suicide: Evidence and implications, 7 Int'l J. Disability & Human Dev. 185 (2008), available at https://www.ncbi.nlm.nih.gov/pubmed/18836547; Joan M. Griffin, Rebecca Fuhrer, Stephen A. Stansfeld, & Michael Marmot, The importance of low control at work and home on depression and anxiety: do these effects vary by gender

possible, legal employers should enable their juniors to exercise discretion and independence.

5. Model Appropriate Behavior

Managers who expect others to "do as I say, not as I do" do not inspire confidence, respect, or trust. Supervisors must embody characteristics and demonstrate behaviors that are worthy of respect and imitation. If you expect a lot from your subordinates, expect a lot from yourself. If you demand perfection from others, demand it of yourself. If you expect others to work hard, set the tone with your own work ethic. A friend recently made a quip about obese physicians whose weight loss practices fail miserably. I do not know whether this is a true story, but it provides a powerful metaphor for why we need to model appropriate behavior.

6. Take Responsibility for the Mistakes of the Team

A supervisor is always accountable and takes responsibility for the failures of his subordinates. A good boss never throws a member of her team under the proverbial bus. When something goes wrong, the team leader should shoulder the responsibility for the shortcomings and absorb any criticism that comes with it.

7. Be Human

Being a professional or a supervisor does not mean giving up one's humanity. Be excited, disappointed, empathetic, and frustrated when circumstances warrant. Above all, show genuine pride and joy in the achievements of others. Small gestures of appreciation are valued, and their significance far exceeds the cost. Such acts need not be remunerative—a simple note or call to acknowledge a job well done makes a difference. Public expressions of appreciation or recognition for excellent work are deeply meaningful. Good bosses fully embrace the notion that when their team members look good, they look good.

---

and social class?, 54 Soc. Sci. & Med. 783 (2002), available at https://www.ncbi.nlm.nih.gov/pubmed/11999493.

Alternatively, shouting and ranting have deleterious effects that are completely counterproductive.[11]

8. Encourage "Explorer Passion"

As discussed earlier,[12] "Explorer passion" has been identified as a key metric of success. The same research shows that explorers tend to switch jobs frequently—especially when their current positions do not allow them to undertake the challenges they crave.[13] Passion can flourish or languish depending on the environment.[14] Managers have a role in encouraging and inspiring explorer passion and in creating an environment that maximizes the potential of all.[15]

9. Embrace a Culture of Teamwork

It is important to develop an institutional culture of teamwork. Collaborative efforts must be recognized as important and rewarded.[16]

10. Have Patience

Recall the Dunning-Kruger effect discussed earlier.[17] There is a complementary deficit to our tendency to overestimate our own competence when we are incompetent: We may mistakenly believe that the tasks that are easy for us are universally so and that others can perform them with the same level of

---

[11] Daniel Goleman, Social Intelligence: The New Science of Human Relationships 13 (2006).

[12] See Chapter 4.A.3., supra.

[13] See Deloitte Center for the Edge, Passion at work: Cultivating worker passion as a cornerstone of talent development 10, Deloitte Center for the Edge (October 7, 2014), available at https://www2.deloitte.com/insights/us/en/topics/talent/worker-passion-employee-behavior.html.

[14] Id. at 19. Managers should encourage Explorer passion by identifying and removing elements in the work setting that may discourage passion. Managers should also identify those with Explorer potential and help cultivate their passion. Organizations should "ignite, amplify, and draw out worker passion within all of their workers" without regard to status or position. Deloitte Center for the Edge, supra note 4, at 23.

[15] "Work environment and management practices that cultivate the passionate disposition will not only help stimulate and engage workers who are already passionate but also allow those who do not demonstrate all the attributes of a passionate worker to cultivate the missing ones." Deloitte Center for the Edge, supra note 13, at 22.

[16] See Chapter 7.A.3., supra.

[17] See Chapter 3.A.1., supra.

competence.[18] For this reason, those who are competent in a skill or behavior often overestimate the capabilities of others.

Supervisors who have reached a certain level of competence with regard to specific tasks may be frustrated by the relative incompetence of more junior attorneys. The Dunning-Kruger effect reminds us that our competence was learned and that we should have patience with those who still need to move through the levels of competence.

11. Be Reasonable and Clear About Expectations

Expectations for work by subordinates should be reasonable and they should be clear. Unreasonable expectations for juniors given individual levels of experience and ability are likely to frustrate both parties. At the same time, supervisors should challenge their charges to be sure that everyone on the team is fully engaged.

Assignments should be given sufficiently in advance whenever circumstances permit. The supervisor should never be a bottleneck that causes unnecessary delay, and she should never impose false deadlines to test an associate.

Supervisors should take the time to fully explain assignments and give the junior background so that she can more fully appreciate the larger context. This investment will pay off both in terms of the quality of work and subordinate satisfaction and loyalty. For legal research and other assignments where it would be useful, suggest possible starting points.

Communicate expectations for the project, including the client's goals, what the deliverable should be, a timeline for completion, any limits on the number of hours or other resources that may be used, and an action plan. Help the associate prioritize tasks and projects. For larger projects, it may be wise to establish interim deadlines and progress meetings or reports to be sure that the work is moving apace.

---

[18] Justin Kruger & David Dunning, Unskilled and Unaware of It: How Difficulties in Recognizing One's Own Incompetence Lead to Inflated Self-Assessments, 77 J. Personality & Soc. Psychol. 1121, 1131 (1999), available at https://www.avaresearch.com/files/UnskilledAndUnawareOfIt.pdf.

12. Be Accessible

Make clear to subordinates that questions are welcome and that you encourage their ideas and thoughts. Be supportive by listening to their concerns and help associates work through challenges they face in completing tasks.

13. Provide Effective Feedback

"Give a man a fish and you feed him for a day; teach a man to fish and you feed him for a lifetime."[19]

Feedback Must Be Meaningful and Continuous

Feedback is critical to attorney development. The common law firm tradition of very general, annual feedback is completely insufficient in today's world, especially for millennials that make up the majority of associates. Feedback needs to be very specific and delivered in real time.[20] Feedback should include direction regarding a junior's career advancement.

Feedback Must Be Designed to Improve Performance

Feedback should be delivered in a way that is intended to improve performance. It should never be punitive or *ad hominem.*

Feedback Must Be Fair and Balanced

Feedback should be balanced and fair and should consist of both positive and negative elements. Formal appraisals should be based on ascertainable criteria and should reflect the views of more than one evaluator.

Negative Feedback Should Be Delivered Openly and Honestly

Negative feedback is difficult to deliver. While it is acceptable to "sandwich" criticism between positives, it is important that the recipient hear the feedback and understand how to improve. Because the goal is always to improve

---

[19] Origin disputed. See https://quoteinvestigator.com/2015/08/28/fish/.

[20] Law firm feedback systems have long been subject to criticism for being merely perfunctory, with limited substance. Rikleen, supra note 3.

performance, criticism should be delivered in a way that allows the junior to maintain his self-esteem. The physical setting also should be considered. For instance, both parties should be standing or sitting. The vision of a supervisor hovering over a seated junior is one that seems intended to intimidate. I read of one partner who liked to discuss his associate's work while taking a walk around the block, which serves to diffuse some of the tension of delivery in a more formal office setting.

Feedback Systems Should Be Reciprocal

The evaluator should solicit feedback about her own performance and how she can improve as a supervisor. The supervisor should be open to ways in which she may have played a role in any shortcomings of the more junior team member.

Feedback Should Be Mindful of Implicit Bias

As discussed in the preceding chapter,[21] all of us should be mindful of any implicit biases we may have, and this is especially true when providing feedback on the work of our subordinates. The impact of implicit bias in feedback is real; research shows, for instance, that women get less constructive and less specific feedback than men.[22] In order to help neutralize any implicit biases, as suggested above, feedback should be based on objective, structured criteria[23] and assessment processes whenever possible should engage a range of people with diverse backgrounds and characteristics.[24]

Feedback Should Be Accompanied by Time for Reflection

Supervisors should encourage employees to take time and space for reflection to capture—understand, internalize, and react to—feedback.[25]

---

[21] See Chapter 7.B.5., supra.

[22] See Paola Cecchi-Dimeglio, How Gender Bias Corrupts Performance Reviews, and What to Do About It, Harvard Business Review (April 12, 2017), available at https://hbr.org/2017/04/how-gender-bias-corrupts-performance-reviews-and-what-to-do-about-it.

[23] Id.

[24] Id.

[25] See Deloitte Center for the Edge, supra note 13, at 22.

14. Use Power Sparingly

Supervisors should not flex their muscles to show their power. They should use powers of persuasion and exercise other leadership traits[26] to motivate others to act. Power should be utilized judiciously.

15. Make Wellbeing a Priority

How you manage people matters to their health and ability to work effectively:[27] Low quality supervision is a major contributor to stress, depression, burnout, and other mental and physical health disorders. Even seemingly low-level incivility by leaders can have an impact on workers' health and motivation. Research has found a range of harmful effects resulting from poor management, for example, playing favorites, criticizing unfairly, and failing to provide information, listen to problems, explain goals, praise good work, assist with professional development, and show that they care. On the other hand, positive management styles contribute to subordinates' mental health, work engagement, performance, and job satisfaction. Many studies confirm that positive supervisory behaviors can be trained and developed.[28]

Employers should demonstrate a personal and genuine commitment to wellbeing—their own personal wellbeing of course, but also that of their colleagues. This is not purely for benevolent reasons: As discussed earlier, there are demonstrable business benefits to a happy and healthy workforce.[29] An appropriate work-life balance is particularly important to millennial lawyers.[30] With the substantial and mounting evidence of lawyer unhappiness and the longstanding inattention to lawyer wellbeing, it is time for firms to consider a

---

[26] See Chapter 3.D., supra.

[27] See Chapter 6.A.2., supra.

[28] National Task Force on Lawyer Well-Being, supra note 9, at 4 (internal citations omitted).

[29] See Chapter 6.A.2., supra.

[30] See The 2016 Deloitte Millennial Survey: Winning over the next generation of leaders 16, 20, available at https://www2.deloitte.com/content/dam/Deloitte/global/Documents/About-Deloitte/gx-millenial-survey-2016-exec-summary.pdf.

significant culture shift and prioritize the wellbeing of the members of their community.

Law firm supervisors should put in place work-life balance and related policies and practices to promote wellness. Organizational culture should encourage vacation time, for instance, which often goes unused by attorneys, and firms should enable associates to truly disengage from their work as much as possible during vacations.[31]

Supervisors should be attuned to signs that colleagues may be struggling. Take a personal interest in team members and facilitate candid conversations. Encourage those who may need it to get outside help.[32] Engender an environment in which mental health and related issues are de-stigmatized. Take a cue from Joe Milowic, a partner at Quinn Emanuel Urquhart & Sullivan who, with the support of the senior leadership of his firm, publicly announced his decade-long battle with depression.[33] This announcement was roundly—and fittingly—applauded.[34]

16. Deal with Conflict Directly and Fairly

Conflict in the workplace is inevitable, especially in the high-pressured, competitive space of law practice, but how supervisors manage conflict can make a significant difference. Do not let conflict fester or infect the work environment. Manage conflicts directly and fairly by listening attentively to all sides of the issue. Help the conflicted parties find common ground. Remind them of the larger institutional goals to be pursued.

---

[31] National Task Force on Lawyer Well-Being, supra note 9, at 60.

[32] Visit https://www.americanbar.org/groups/lawyer_assistance/resources/lap_programs_by_state.html for a directory of lawyer assistance programs around the country.

[33] Joseph Milowic III, Quinn Emanuel Partner Suffers From Depression and He Wants Everyone to Know, New York Law Journal (March 28, 2018), available at https://www.law.com/newyorklawjournal/2018/03/28/quinn-emanuel-partner-suffers-from-depression-and-he-wants-everyone-to-know/.

[34] See, e.g., Hilarie Bass, ABA President Sees Call to Action in Quinn Emanuel Partner's Story of Depression, New York Law Journal (March 30, 2018), available at https://www.law.com/newyorklawjournal/2018/03/30/aba-president-sees-call-to-action-in-quinn-emanuel-partners-story-of-depression/.

17. Offer Flexible Work Arrangements When Possible

Associates, particularly millennials, want more flexibility in their work arrangements. This includes not only the ability to work remotely when possible but also flexible career paths.

Associates should have the flexibility to work reduced hours to accommodate family needs and other interests. Accommodating valuable associates when possible and done thoughtfully is generally better than losing them.

Firms also should be flexible when it comes to roles within the firm. Several large firms, including King & Spalding, Orrick, Ropes & Gray, Seyfarth Shaw, and Winston & Strawn[35] offer disaggregated roles for associates not interested in being on a partnership track.

C. A NOTE ABOUT SUPERVISING SUPPORT STAFF

Members of the firm's support staff are essential members of any team and should be treated as such. It is of course the right thing to do. Recall that most support staff members are not as highly compensated as the attorneys, and that they generally do not enjoy the same level of prestige within the organization as even the most junior lawyer. Beyond the human case, support staff are an excellent source of information, insight, and institutional knowledge. Their assistance can help advance your professional goals; failure to use support staff well and to treat them with the respect they deserve has the potential to undermine your work.

Keep your secretary/assistant, paralegals, and other support staff members informed about your projects, deadlines, and the bigger picture of projects on which you are working. Doing so will enable them to do their own work more effectively and give them a sense of involvement and ownership over their work. Be clear about expectations. Show that you respect the expertise and appreciate the efforts of your staff, give them

---

[35] See Chelsey Parrott-Sheffer, Best Practices for Hiring and Retaining Nontraditional-Track Attorneys, NALP Bulletin 18 (April 2018). See also https://www. orrick.com/Innovation/Talent-at-Orrick; https://www.ropesgray.com/en/legalhiring/The-Culture/Supporting-Your-Career.

autonomy when possible, provide appropriate feedback, ask how they like things done, and demonstrate your appreciation. I recently heard a partner at a leading law firm say that he treated an appointment with his secretary with the same level of commitment and seriousness as client meetings. This is something we would all do well to remember and embrace.

D. QUESTIONS FOR REFLECTION

1. Have you ever been in a supervisory position? If so name three things you did well and three areas in which you think you could improve.

2. Have you ever been supervised by someone else? If so, name three things you appreciated and admired about your supervisor and three things you thought he or she could improve upon.

CHAPTER 9

EFFECTIVE COMMUNICATION

A. COMMUNICATION SKILLS GENERALLY

Communication is the essence of what we as humans do, and the ability to communicate effectively and efficiently is at the heart of the work of any legal professional.[1] Others' perceptions of our competence are formed in large part by how effectively we communicate. This in turn is influenced by the words we use to communicate; the tone, style, and body language we use when communicating; and our ability to listen attentively and actively.

Happily, we have been developing communication skills over a lifetime. These skills are not new, but as professionals we have the opportunity to refine them to meet the demands of our chosen career. We should be particularly mindful of the need to transmit information in a way that is best understood by the recipient of the information; to do so in the most effective and efficient way possible; and to do so in a way that is civil and respectful.

1. Consider Your Audience

That the audience is paramount in how we communicate has become such a cliché that one might be tempted to ignore it. Platitudinous as it may seem, it is sound advice and should be taken into account with regard to any form of communication. Everything you communicate, and the way you communicate it, must be shaped by keeping in mind the intended recipient(s) of the message. Communicate what the receiver wants or needs to know in the manner she wants the information or can best appreciate it. Context matters—in some circumstances a formal

---

[1] Effective communication is listed as one of the 26 effectiveness factors in the classical empirical study by Professors Marjorie M. Shultz and Sheldon Zedeck. See Marjorie M. Shultz & Sheldon Zedeck, Predicting Lawyer Effectiveness: Broadening the Basis for Law School Admission Decisions, 36 L. & Soc. Inquiry 620, 630 (summer 2011), available at http://citeseerx.ist.psu.edu/viewdoc/download?doi=10.1.1.418.7400&rep=rep1&type=pdf.

memo may be required whereas at other times a quick email would be best.

2. "Say What You Are Going to Say, Say It, and Say That You Have Said It"

The best advice I ever got about writing was when I was a child (and which I have reheard numerous times since). The advice came from a family friend who was an attorney, and it is applicable to oral communication as well: "Say what you are going to say, say it, and say that you said it." Communication should be succinct and structured. It should have an introduction, a body, and a conclusion. This is a fairly straightforward and eminently achievable proposition.

3. Formality in Professional Communications

All communication in or relating to the workplace should be formal in tone, content, and style. This may be particularly challenging for those who came of age in an era of general informality. In particular, those for whom email and texting have been primary methods of communication for essentially their entire lives may not be accustomed to the more formal style of communication that is expected in professional circles.

It is always best to err on the side of formality with those with whom we work, in particular more senior professionals and clients. Do not confuse the seeming informality or friendliness of many of these individuals with an invitation to be casual, especially with respect to written communication.

4. Have Your Objective(s) Firmly in Mind

Make certain that your goals are clear and that your audience understands what you are trying to communicate. Whenever communicating, whether in writing, in conversation, or through a presentation, be thoughtful about how to communicate your goals in a way that maximizes the chances of accomplishing them. Keeping your objectives at the forefront of your mind will help you present what you want to convey in the most effective way.

5. Be Efficient and Direct

"In writing, less is more. Convey information in the most succinct way possible. Condense your writing to what matters most." Eric F. Grossman, Executive Vice President and Chief Legal Officer, Morgan Stanley[2]

"Knowing how to package and present communications . . . how to simplify complex issues and give business decisionmakers the information they need are crucial to success." Andrew Bonzani, Senior Vice President, General Counsel & Secretary, The Interpublic Group[3]

Be efficient and organized in communicating so that your message is clear. Avoid ambiguity (unless you make a deliberate decision that ambiguity is desirable in a particular context). Begin with a clear thesis—a statement of what you hope to achieve. This should relate to the central theme of your communication, and the rest of what you say should be structured and unified around that theme.[4] Keep in mind your audience—often clients or more senior attorneys, usually exceptionally busy—and consider using bullet points when appropriate.

6. Communicate Without Legalese

Minimizing the use of legalese helps us to communicate efficiently and directly. There are, of course, times when the language of the law is needed to communicate accurately. While it is appropriate to use terms of art, never use legal language to make your work seem sophisticated or to justify your billing rate. The general rule is that your writing should be as simple as possible—but no simpler than that. Both lawyers and judges have noted the evils of legalese.[5] Unless legal terms are necessary, choose plain language.

---

2   Email from Eric F. Grossman to the author (July 16, 2018), on file with the author.

3   Email from Andrew Bonzani to the author (June 27, 2018), on file with the author.

4   The need for clarity and succinctness in legal writing is discussed in greater detail in Section B.1., infra.

5   See, e.g., Albert M. Rosenblatt, Lawyers as Wordsmiths, 69 N.Y.St. B.J. 12, 12 (Nov. 1997) ("There is still a lot of 'legalese' in current usage, but the best writers have come to regard it as pretentious or bad writing."); Hollis T. Hurd, Writing for Lawyers

B. WRITTEN COMMUNICATION

1. Writing Generally

Lawyers often communicate in writing, and we must write with exacting precision and attention to detail. This section will focus on certain important attributes of writing in a legal context that bear reinforcing. In particular, the sections that follow discuss the need for writing that is clear, concise, convincing, complete, and candid; to understand the assignment; to follow applicable protocols; to produce an attractive document; to be mindful of style; to offer a helpful introduction; to properly attribute sources; and to carefully proofread and edit.

The Five Cs of Legal Writing

When I taught legal writing several years ago, I came up with these *Five Cs of Writing*: Writing should be clear, concise, convincing, complete, and candid.

Clear—Write in plain and clear English. Ask yourself whether each sentence is understandable and the best way to have written it. If not, rewrite it until it is. When writing for someone who is not trained in the law, your work must have even more clarity and purpose.

Use headings and subheadings to divide the text and guide the reader.

My friend and colleague Judge Gerald Lebovits teaches and writes extensively about legal writing and offers the following suggestions for achieving clarity:[6]

- "Put essential things first."

- "Introduce before you explain."

- State the rule first, *then* provide any exceptions in a separate sentence.

---

34 (1982) ("When legalese threatens to strangle your thought process, pretend you're saying it to a [non-lawyer] friend. Then write it down. Then clean it up."); George Rose Smith, A Primer of Opinion Writing, for Four New Judges, 21 Ark. L. Rev. 197, 209 (1967) (urging that we avoid words that we "would not use in conversation.").

   [6] Gerald Lebovits, Free at Last from Obscurity: Achieving Clarity, 16 Scribes Journal of Legal Writing 127–131 (2014–2015), available at https://papers.ssrn.com/sol3/papers.cfm?abstract_id=2654480.

- State a point or raise a question before giving details or providing the answer. Answer questions before justifying the answer.

- Focus on legal issues rather than on specific sources of authority. The issue should drive the discussion; authority is support for your conclusions, not conclusions in and of themselves.

- Tell the reader who or what a person or entity is before you discuss what the person or entity did or did not do.

- Related matters should be kept together.

Achieving clarity in writing is not always as easy as it may appear, but it is worth whatever effort is needed to accomplish it. As Former Chief Justice of the United States William Howard Taft said: "Don't write so that you can be understood; write so that you can't be misunderstood."[7]

Concise—Be as efficient as possible in your writing. Ask yourself whether every sentence adds value. Redundancies should be eliminated. Use short sentences rather than long, complex sentences that may seem lawyerly but which ultimately are difficult for the reader to process. Omit unnecessary words, phrases, and sentences. Ask yourself whether each word adds in some way to the reader's understanding or is necessary for some other reason. If not, edit appropriately. Never make a written product longer for fear that a shorter document looks like it should have been done more quickly; it is commonly recognized that communicating concisely is more difficult and time-consuming than saying the same thing with more words. Although writing concisely is hard work, it is well worth the effort.

Convincing—We usually think of the need to be convincing in an adversarial setting, but in any kind of writing, we should leave the reader convinced that our analysis is correct. Provide whatever support is needed to reach that goal.

---

[7] Original source unknown. See https://www.brainyquote.com/quotes/william_howard_taft_385396.

Complete—You must take the reader through each step in the analysis, A through Z. Do not skip steps in the thought process because they seem obvious to you, and do not force the reader to guess at what you are trying to communicate or the legal basis for it. Remember that although you have become the specialist in the subject about which you are writing, your reader should be thought of as a generalist and you must walk her methodically through the analysis. Assume that even the most sophisticated reader will not have the command of the specific law and facts that you will have acquired.

Candid—Never manipulate, misstate, or mischaracterize the law or the facts. Be honest or you will lose credibility. When writing internally, raise any weaknesses in the recommended course of action for consideration by your supervising attorney or client. Failing to do so means that the client may be making decisions based on incomplete facts or a distorted analysis.

Follow Applicable Protocols

Always follow law firm/organization protocols or templates and any applicable court rules regarding format and other stylistic issues. Although such conventions may seem quaint or unimportant, failing to follow them is an easily avoidable error that will mark you as someone who lacks attention to detail. In the case of court rules, such errors can be catastrophic. In other contexts, inattention to detail of this and other types will lead to losing credibility with the reader.

Produce an Attractive Document

Your document should be readable and attractive. Evaluate your font choices, margins, and other elements of your document for readability, consistency, and appearance. Meticulous attention to detail is important.

Style and Process Matters

There are several style and process elements to be attuned to when you write. Some things to pay attention to are set forth below.

Formality—Professional writing should always be formal, no matter how close the relationship you have with the intended reader. This means that there is no room for casualness in approach, tone, or style. Avoid contractions, exclamation points, and the overuse of underlining, boldface, or italics, which lend an air of informality. Also keep in mind that people other than the intended recipient may see your written work, which should help guide the formality of what you write.

Mimic the Style of Writers You Admire—It has been said that "imitation is the sincerest form of flattery."[8] If there is a lawyer or other professional whose style you admire, ask yourself why and try to mimic his style while remaining authentic to your own voice. You can try to adapt different styles to appeal to different readers.

Offer a Helpful Introduction—In all but the shortest written communication, begin with a clear introduction to the document. The introduction need not (and generally should not) be lengthy or complex but it should do the following: First, it should give the reader basic information she needs in order to understand the remainder of the document; second, it should get the reader's interest in reading on and in engaging genuinely in the document; and third, the introduction should let the reader know what to expect by providing her with a roadmap.

Write from an Outline—An outline is a helpful way to organize your thoughts and be sure that your document is structured in the most efficient and effective way possible. An outline allows the writer to note the major points she wants to address, as well as the sub-points for each matter. In this way, we can be sure that we have incorporated each of the issues we want to address, that we have organized them in the most logical way, that each of the sub-points is placed within the correct section, and that our written work proceeds from the most general to more specific points. For virtually any writing, no matter how brief, an outline can help us organize our thoughts and enable us to keep our eye on both the proverbial "forest" and the "trees." Write an outline—a very simple one will suffice—and keep it by your side as you write; update it as your thoughts clarify. Ask yourself periodically whether you are keeping on track and whether the outline needs to be revisited as you better

---

8   Charles Caleb Colton, https://www.brainyquote.com/quotes/charles_caleb_colton _203963.

understand the task at hand. For documents on the longer side, consider including the outline for the convenience of the reader.

Your Writing Should Be Well Structured—Your written work should be well-structured. This entails an overall structure, paragraph structure, and sentence structure. A document's overall organization should be straightforward and logical. Use headings and sub-headings to reflect your organization and to guide the reader.

Each paragraph should begin with a topical sentence, which consists of a conclusion supported by the rest of the paragraph. Paragraphs should not be too long, and you should use transitions so that the reader can move seamlessly from paragraph to paragraph. Sentences should be short enough to be clear to the reader.

Mix It up for Effect—Professional writing does not have to be boring. In fact, interesting writing will keep the reader engaged, and one way to keep your writing interesting is to vary the length of sentences and paragraphs. Although they should be short enough to be readily comprehensible, mixing up the length of sentences and paragraphs can make the read more interesting and is a good way to emphasize important points.

Consistency—Invariably, there will be style choices, such as those related to numeration, capitalization, italicization, and the like. Whatever choices you make, they must be consistently applied throughout the document.

Take Care with Commas, Apostrophes, and Plurals—Be careful with your use of commas, apostrophes, and plurals. Mistakes look sloppy and at times can dramatically change your meaning.[9]

Take Special Care with Attribution—Professional writing demands precision with respect to the citation of sources. This is true whenever you quote language, paraphrase language, or use an idea first expounded by someone else. Failure to do so will

---

[9] For a primer on the confounding use of apostrophes and plurals, see Gerald Lebovits, Apostrophe's and Plurals', 76 New York St. Bar J. 64 (February 2004), available at https://ssrn.com/abstract=1297331.

undermine your integrity and may even lead to charges of plagiarism.

Edit, Edit, and Edit Some More

"Make your work product as perfect as you can make it. Engage both your eyes and your brain, no matter how tired you are. . . ." Honorable Loretta A. Preska United States District Court for the Southern District of New York[10]

The importance of the proofreading and editing processes cannot be overstated; as Justice Louis Brandeis reportedly said, "[t]here is no such thing as good writing. There is only great rewriting."[11] You can never be too busy to proofread your work before finalizing it or underestimate the importance of this step in the writing process.

Never send a half-baked "draft" to your supervisor or a client, even if she asks for one. Any work that is sent to someone in a supervisory or senior position should be your very best work.[12]

As you approach your final proofreading stages, try to create some distance between the document and yourself. When possible, leave time before your penultimate and final draft so that you can approach the document with a fresh perspective. I also find it useful to read my final product in a place other than that in which I originally wrote it. Whatever approach you use, your final edit and proofread must command your full attention.

2.   The Special Case of Email

Introduction to Email

When I practiced law in the 1980s and early 1990s, there was no such thing as email. There was one partner at my firm who was relatively technologically advanced and who insisted that the future was in electronic mail. We thought that this was

---

[10] Email from Judge Loretta Preska to the author (July 13, 2018), on file with the author.

[11] Original source unknown. See https://www.goodreads.com/quotes/6772530-there -is-no-great-writing-only-great-rewriting.

[12] See the discussion of the Doctrine of Completed Staff Work, Chapter 4.B.1., supra.

preposterous, the musings of a somewhat peculiar futurist. At the time, our primary means of communication was face-to-face where possible and, when not, by telephone, post, or, beginning in the late 1980s, fax.

Needless to say, my curious colleague was right. Each of us can be expected to send dozens if not hundreds of business-related emails in a single day, and these messages are sent to a range of individuals, including supervisors and clients, so it is imperative that they bear the hallmarks of professionalism. It may be particularly important for millennial attorneys to keep this in mind, given that many of them have for virtually their entire lives used informal emails and texts as their primary form of written communication.

In any professional context, emails must have all of the attributes of proper, formal communication. Simply because we use a medium that allows us to communicate quickly and easily does not give us license to be informal or sloppy. It is also critical that we remain vigilant about striking the right tone in our emails.

The following sections explore numerous aspects of using email. One preliminary note of caution: Anytime you send an email, assume that it will be read by the person you would least want to see it. The nature of email makes it likely that others may see it, either through deliberate or accidental action. This reality should guide our email practices.

Is Email the Best Form of Communication?

Many of us send emails out of habit, and for good reason: Email is an extremely convenient and efficient way to communicate. We can write messages when we want and know that the messages will be received quickly. It is less intrusive to the recipient than other forms of communication and can be dealt with by the recipient at her convenience. And virtually everyone in our professional circle has access to email.

While email may indeed be a good default form of communication, it remains important that we consider in individual situations whether email is appropriate and the best way to communicate. Inevitably, there will be occasions when email may not be the appropriate medium of communication, so some restraint is required. Perhaps an issue is difficult to explain in writing and would be more easily discussed in person or on the phone. In some cases, striking the right tone will be challenging, and more easily accomplished orally than in writing. Sometimes, there has simply been too much back-and-forth without reaching a consensus or conclusion to the matter. If messages are getting confrontational, it is time to change the medium of communication. It may be that the subject of the communication is confidential or too sensitive for email. Criticism, for instance, is best reserved for an oral conversation. Do not use email to hide behind something that you would not say in person. Do not let email make you courageous; if you write something in an email that you would not say in person it should be a signal to exercise self-control and refrain from sending the message.

In still other situations, the recipient may be someone who does not work comfortably with email; this may be the case with older individuals, some of whom still prefer other forms of communication. It may be that the message is extremely time-sensitive, and you are not certain that the recipient checks emails on a regular basis, in which case email would not be the best way to communicate. Some from the younger generation may find this inconvenient, but there is a personal touch to a phone call or an in-person meeting that simply cannot be replicated by email.

There may be myriad other situations in which email is not the best way of communicating, so this should be the first question to consider when preparing to send an email.

Is Now the Right Time to Send This Email?

Once you have decided that email is the appropriate form of communication, consider the best time to send the email. There are at least two important factors to consider: First, whether you are in the right state of mind to send a message; and second, whether this is a suitable time for the recipient to receive the message.

Do Not Send Email When Angry, Tired, Rushed, or Stressed—It is conventional wisdom that we should never send emails written when we are angry or extremely tired, stressed, or rushed. Writing an email when angry might give us some momentary sense of satisfaction but will likely escalate a difficult situation and compromise our professionalism. Impulsive reactions to a situation can have unfortunate and unintended long-term consequences and reflect immaturity and poor judgment. Likewise, we should try not to write emails when we are especially stressed or tired or in a great hurry. Sending emails while we are in one of these states increases the likelihood of making errors, which undermines our credibility.

A recent example makes this clear: I wrote an email to the assistant of a law firm colleague who I was hoping to speak with that day. My message indicated that I was available at any time other than 9:00 a.m.–12:00 p.m. Yet in his haste to reply, the assistant offered me 9:30 a.m. as the time for a call. While I appreciated the fast reply, it took more of both our time to reiterate my unavailability at that hour. Take a few extra moments to clearly read and understand a message before replying.

Consider the Convenience of the Reader—Depending on the nature of the relationship the sender has with the recipient of the emails, you may consider not sending emails at a time that you believe would be inconvenient for the recipient, unless the message is particularly time sensitive. One of its great virtues, of course, is that you can send email whenever it is convenient for you and the recipient can respond whenever convenient for her. However, in hierarchical relationships such as those between partner and associate or client and attorney, the recipient may feel compelled to respond immediately on a 24-hour, 7-day basis. If the sender is thoughtful about this, and the matter is not urgent, he may wait and send the email—or set the email to go out—at a time that is less intrusive to the recipient.

Write Clearly, Succinctly, and with Purpose

As in all forms of writing, it is important to write emails clearly, concisely, and with determined focus and exacting precision. Because of the nature of email and the volume of messages that most of us send and receive, we tend to write emails quickly, often without the proper attention that this medium deserves. What follows are some elements that we should incorporate into our email practices: Send short messages; limit each email to one topic; introduce yourself if the recipient does not know you; use an appropriate subject line; summarize important points up front; and organize your message.

Send Short Emails—Emails, even more so than other forms of writing, should be concise; long emails will not be read. If you need to send a long email, make sure that it is as concise and structured as possible, and consider using headings, numbers, or other formatting tools to help the reader navigate the text. It might be a good idea also to send the message as an attachment to give the recipient the option of reading the content in a more traditional, more readable format.

Limit Content to One Topic—In most situations, unless the context calls for a different approach, it is best to limit your emails to one topic per message. This allows you to use an appropriate subject line and to keep the message as brief as possible. It may also facilitate the recipient's ability to file it appropriately or forward the message to others. If the circumstances warrant including multiple topics in a single email, be sure that each is clear and visible in the subject line and in the text.

Introduce Yourself if Appropriate—If the recipient may not know you, begin the email with a brief introduction. There is no need to state your name, which is indicated in the sender line and the closing, but indicate your position/role and the purpose of your email (e.g., "I am an associate at Smith & Jones and work with Robert Smith, who asked that I write to give you an update on the XYZ matter.")

Make Maximum Use of the Subject Line—Always use the subject line to indicate the topic of the email as well as the importance of the message and any action items. Be sure that you are not using a holdover subject line from a previous communication that is no longer suitable, and change the subject line as the discussion progresses, when appropriate. Avoid using the subject line as the entire message.

Summarize Important Points up Front—If your email is on the longer side, begin by summarizing the key points you make in the message. Highlight any action items and deadlines.

Organize the Message—Be sure that your email is well-structured and to the point. Follow the same habits of well-structured and organized writing that you would use in other forms of written communication.

Treat Email Writing as Formal Writing

Because email is a fast and efficient way to communicate, and perhaps because many of us use email to communicate with friends and family members, many view email as a method of communication that is less formal than other forms of writing. This is absolutely not the case in any professional setting, and when sending emails we should follow the same conventions as we would in other kinds of writing.

Here are some tips for maintaining the formality of emails: Use a professional user name; use formal salutations and closings; draft carefully and insert addressee(s) after you review your draft; watch your style and tone; limit time-sensitive and urgent messages; take care when copying and blind copying others; be careful with and format attachments appropriately; be cautious about forwarding emails.

Use a Professional Email User Name—Whenever possible, use the email address provided by your employer or educational institution. If for some reason you cannot (a job search while you are currently employed is an example that readily comes to mind), use a personal account that has an appropriate user name. If you have an old personal email address like CoolCarl@yahoo.com or SexySusan@hotmail.com, it is time for a new address. Using your full name is always a good choice; if not available, adding some numbers is acceptable. Avoid "esquire," "lawyer," "doctor," or other titles in your user name as they may come across as pretentious.

Use Formal Salutations and Closings—Begin your email with an appropriate salutation and closing. No matter how rushed you are, it is inappropriate to begin a message with anything other than "Dear" followed by the person's name.[13] How you address the recipient is a reflection of the relationship and prevailing industry norms, but it is always best to err on the side of formality and address the recipient by his or her title and family name(s). When in doubt, and especially when the email recipient is a stranger or in a senior position (supervising attorney, client, or more seasoned professional), continue to use the family name(s) unless and until invited to use the first name. Such an invitation generally should not be inferred. When a person signs an email using his first name, this generally is not such an invitation, and especially so when there is a significant difference in position or seniority.

When writing to someone you have not met who has a name of ambiguous gender, use Google to try to find a photo that can clarify whether the person is male or female. Women should be addressed as "Ms." unless a title such as "Dr." or "Professor" is appropriate, or unless she has indicated that she prefers "Mrs.," which these days is uncommonly used.

Even when you have a familiar relationship with someone, be sure to consider whether using her first name is appropriate when others are included on the mail. For example, although you may call your boss "Mary," if clients or other professional contacts are on the message, it may be appropriate to refer to her as "Ms. Smith." Again, context is important.

Your email also should contain a proper closing. Closings like "Sincerely," "Regards," and "Very truly yours," followed by your name, are fine choices. Following your name should be an address block containing your name, position/title, firm, address, email address, and phone number. If you wish to be extremely accessible (or if required by organizational policy), you might include your cell phone number in addition to your office number. Be sure that your closing has the same font as the body of your message, so it does not look like it is auto-generated.

Insert the Addressee(s) Last—Consider drafting your message before inserting the addressee(s). This prevents

---

[13] Context, however, is important. Some people make the judgment that they know all people on an email chain well enough to omit formalities. More junior members of a team are urged to err on the side of formality.

accidentally sending a message before you have completely finished drafting and reviewing it.

Draft the Email—Take care in drafting the email. I deliberately use the word *draft* because, like any other formal written communication, emails should be reviewed carefully and edited before being sent.

For emails that are more complicated or sensitive than others, draft the message in a Word document, which is easier to edit. Review and edit your messages carefully. This includes checking the addressee(s), any persons in copy (cc) or blind copy (bcc), and that any attachments are properly appended to the email.

Watch the Style and Tone—When writing email, use the same style of writing that you would use in other professional writing. Never use capital letters (which is tantamount to screaming) and be economic with exclamation points and contractions. Avoid slang, abbreviations (from traditional abbreviations such "ASAP" to those of more recent origin such as "LOL," except for established and recognized acronyms), and emoticons (which have no place in professional communications).

Always use language that is diplomatic, formal, respectful, and courteous, and pay attention to the tone. Thank the reader for her time and say that you look forward to a reply.

Limit Time-Sensitive and "Urgent" Messages—Be cautious about stating that your message is time-sensitive or urgent, and limit your use of those terms to when the situation really calls for it. Do not fall prey to "The Boy Who Cried Wolf" syndrome by overusing these terms; over time, they will lose effect and not be taken seriously. And when you use these terms unnecessarily, you likely inconvenience others who may believe that the matter is more urgent than it is.

When a message is truly time-sensitive, be sure to indicate that in the subject line and opening lines of the email. Follow up as appropriate and, if you do not receive an acknowledgement in a timely way in light of the urgency of the matter, follow up by phone or in person.

Finally, remember that a message does not become urgent because you have delayed dealing with something in a timely way. This notion is captured beautifully by the phrase "poor planning on your part does not necessitate an emergency on mine."[14] Be sure that you manage projects in a way that does not inconvenience others.[15]

Use CC and BCC Appropriately—Whenever sending an email, be thoughtful as to who if anyone should be in copy or blind copy. You want to be sure that those with an interest in the matter receive the message but that those who do not need or who would not benefit from the information contained in an email message are not burdened with receiving it.

When someone sends you an email with various parties copied, it is important to be thoughtful about whom to include in your response. Start from the proposition that the sender included everyone who was copied for a reason. Ask yourself whether that same reasoning applies to your reply. It can be very frustrating, for example, to include people on a message and to have to re-insert those people or forward the reply because the recipient did not "reply all" in response. If you pay attention to who was copied and think about why, you will usually reach the right result. Errors occur most often when we simply hit "reply" without due consideration.

Sometimes it may be appropriate to begin with a reply to all and move some of the recipients to bcc so that they will be removed from further communication that is not of interest to them. This is a very good way of dealing with introductions— when A introduces B to C, when B or C replies, he can indicate that he has moved A to blind copy so that A does not receive further messages between B and C.

A note of caution regarding blind copying (bcc): Blind copying people on an email is usually inappropriate unless it is a mass email. It can also be dangerous because if the recipient of the blind copy is not careful, she may reply to all in response,

---

[14] See https://www.goodreads.com/quotes/291995-poor-planning-on-your-part-does -not-necessitate-an-emergency.

[15] See Chapter 5.A.1., supra.

which will indicate to the initial sender that her message was blind copied, which appears surreptitious.

Take Care with Attachments—Emails often contain one or more attachments. Always reference attachments in the body of the email and explain their relevance. Be sure that any attachments are properly named (calling your resume "Resume" is fine for your own personal purposes but not helpful when you attach it to an email to someone else). Attachments themselves should have the same information that you would include on any other document, such as your name, a date, and subject as appropriate. Attachments may be printed and should be able to stand on their own.

Think about how best to format attachments. If the attachment is something that may be edited by the recipient, it is best to send the attachment in Word or another program that will allow the recipient to modify it. If the attachment is not one that would be edited, it is best to send it in PDF so that the formatting remains intact. If in doubt, send both a version that can be edited and a PDF file.

Finally, be certain that you have appended any attachments before hitting the "send" button. This is a common error that is easily corrected by taking a moment to check your email carefully before sending.

Take Care in Forwarding Emails—Forward emails with care and include the originator of the message so that he knows that his email has been forwarded to a third party. As a general rule, do not forward messages without the express or implied consent of the writer of the original email.

Acknowledge Receipt—Get into the habit of promptly acknowledging receipt of emails, even if you cannot provide a substantive reply. Acknowledging receipt puts the sender at ease that you have seen and read the message and that you are working on a more thorough response. If possible, you should also indicate when a more comprehensive answer will be forthcoming—and treat that as a deadline to which you have committed.

Occasionally we receive messages that are for informational purposes only and do not necessarily request (or even specifically disavow the need for) a response. Nonetheless, it is elegant to send a short email to acknowledge receipt and thank the sender for his thoughtfulness.

Announce Absences—It is common to use an auto-reply when we are out of the office for an extended period of time. Consider doing the same for other absences that are even just of several hours unless you have an assistant or someone else who regularly checks and responds to your messages.

Develop a Personal Email Management System

Managing email is an art unto itself, an art that must be handled with competence and efficiency given the volume of messages that most of us receive on a daily basis. There are any number of different systems that we may use in managing messages. What is important is that each of us has a system that works for us. Your personal email management system should have both a timing feature and a review and response system, and must become part of your daily routine.

Timing—Each of us needs to make decisions about how often to check email. How often you check your email may be a product of the nature of your work and personal style. Regardless, you should make a habit of checking email at regular intervals and be sure that the people who need to reach you most urgently—typically your supervising attorneys and possibly clients—know your system and know how to reach you more quickly if they need to. You may consider setting your phone to alert you when you receive a message from a sender to whom you would want to reply immediately.

Review and Response System—Each of us also needs to have in place a process for prioritizing messages so that you can triage those that are most important and time-sensitive. For instance, you may first look for messages from people to whom you would want to reply immediately, such as senior lawyers in your firm and clients. Alternatively, you may prefer to delete junk emails (personally, this is what I do first, to enable me to more quickly scan other messages) and then reply to those that merit a response, adjusting both for urgency and importance. You also need a system for deciding whether to reply to solicitations and other emails from people you do not know. I reply to almost every email that I receive, as long as it is from someone within my very broad circle (lawyers, law students, legal academics, etc.). This is one albeit modest way to develop a network and a reputation within the larger circle within which we all operate.

Finally, have a system for checking junk/spam folders on a regular basis to be sure that there is nothing there that merits a response. Adjust your spam filters as appropriate to be sure that you see legitimate messages in a timely fashion.

Emailing from Your Phone

When you send an email from your phone, follow the same rules as for other emails. A disclaimer such as "Sent from my iPhone; please excuse typos and other errors" does not give us license to be sloppy when using a mobile device.

3. Texting

Many younger professionals use texts (including WhatsApp and similar services) as a primary form of communication. While this is commonly accepted among close friends and relatives, it is generally not acceptable for workplace or other professional communication, unless you specifically have been invited to do so.

4. Using LinkedIn for Messages

People differ in the extent to which they use LinkedIn and are amenable to receiving messages through LinkedIn. Many of us of older generations (and possibly others) do not use LinkedIn as an everyday tool, and prefer to receive messages through email.

C. ORAL COMMUNICATION

"Practice your speaking at every opportunity. Your greatest enemy is anxiety, and each time you speak, you feel less anxious." Eric F. Grossman, Executive Vice President and Chief Legal Officer, Morgan Stanley[16]

---

[16] Email from Eric F. Grossman to the author (July 16, 2018), on file with the author.

1.   Oral Communication Generally

Others' perception of our competence is formed in large part by the way we speak and the effectiveness of our oral communication style. This in turn is influenced by the words we use to communicate as well as they tone, style, and body language we exhibit.

Much like writing, speaking clearly, succinctly, and with precision is an extremely important skill. Spoken communications can be somewhat less formal than written work (for example, contractions are generally acceptable in speaking) but in professional settings one should be mindful of the need for some formality in oral communication. For example, the ubiquitous phrase "no problem" should not be used as a response to "thank you." Similarly, watch your speech for fillers such as "like," "you know," and "umm," and work to eliminate them from your vernacular.

As indicated earlier, spoken communications, just like written communications, should be deliberate. Consider the audience and keep your goals at the forefront, so that the message can be shaped accordingly. Your words should be efficient and focused so that your message has the greatest likelihood of being received.

2.   The Special Case of Presentations

Presentations are sometimes easier than more spontaneous speaking opportunities because presentations can be planned in advance and rehearsed. These same features, however, may make presentations feel more formal and stressful. Depending on the context, it may be advisable to use visual aids, such as handouts or a slide deck. If you do plan to use a computer for a presentation, be sure that the necessary technology is set up in advance and have a back-up plan in case the technology should fail or ultimately be unavailable. I always carry a printed copy of my presentations, which has the dual benefits of giving me comfort in the event that technology services are not available and allowing me easily to make notes and review my presentation on the run.

Any questions addressed to you related to your comments should be viewed not as a confrontation but as an opportunity to provide further support for your position and to convince a listener who may not yet be completely persuaded. Questions should be taken seriously; never be dismissive about questions, even if you believe that the question is inappropriate or was already answered. Compliment the questioner and thank him for the question. Give a thoughtful and thorough response. If you are not prepared to answer fully, indicate that you will revert shortly with a response—and do it.

3.   The Special Case of Phone Conversations

The telephone is still very much in use, so it is important to understand basic phone etiquette for both making and receiving calls.

Making Calls

Announce Yourself Clearly and Courteously—When placing a phone call, be sure to state your name and affiliation clearly so that the person picking up the phone knows with whom he is speaking. Recall that the person picking up the phone may be the person you are trying to reach, or it may be that person's assistant or an operator. In all cases, you should be polite and gracious. If you need to leave a message with a person or on a machine, be sure to speak clearly and slowly and to repeat your name (and a spelling, if helpful) and number.

Make Sure a Call Is Convenient for the Other Party—Whenever possible, you should schedule a phone call in advance. This is sensible because it ensures that you will get through to the person you are wishing to speak with, which makes for a productive use of time for both parties. If a call is scheduled, make the call exactly at the time that the recipient expects it.

If the call is not scheduled in advance, it is thoughtful to ask the person you have called whether she has a few minutes to speak before proceeding. It is possible that you have caught her in the middle of a meeting or a time-sensitive project, or that she is about to leave for a meeting. Remember that it will *always* be the case that she is doing something else when the phone rings, so do not assume that your call comes at a convenient moment.

Be on Time for Scheduled Calls—When you do have a call scheduled, be on time. For conference calls, dial in at least a few minutes before the set time.

Announce Yourself—Never have your secretary announce you unless your goal is to be as off-putting as possible.

Get to the Point—Depending on the nature of the call, it may be appropriate to engage in some amount of small talk—catching up with someone you know, inquiring about the family, etc. Then get to the point and get there quickly. If there is background that the recipient of the call needs to know, that background is much better understood if she has the final goal in mind; this also gives her an opportunity to state at the outset that she lacks interest in speaking about the topic further. If the matter you have called to discuss is somewhat complex, prepare some talking points so that you have the issues organized in a manner that will be easy to communicate over the phone. Depending on the nature of the call, you may want to send some brief notes in advance so that the recipient of the call can be better prepared. Do not rattle on; this will detract from your goal and is disrespectful to the time constraints of your conversation partner.

Avoid Using a Speaker—Do not use a speakerphone unless necessitated by the presence of several people in the room. The sound is always compromised and, especially for junior people, the use of a speakerphone may appear arrogant.

Receiving Calls

Always answer the phone using a professional manner. Announce yourself in some way that makes you comfortable, whether it be "Hello, this is Toni Jaeger-Fine," or something to that effect. Speak clearly and slowly so that the caller knows whether he has reached the correct number. As is the case with making calls, always be polite, even if the subject of the call does not interest you. If you miss a call, return the call promptly.

4. Active Listening

"Listen more than you talk. Nobody learned anything by hearing themselves speak." Richard Branson[17]

Active listening can make you more effective at your job[18] and improve your relationships. Listening actively helps you learn, facilitates your understanding of a situation, and enables you to remember valuable information. Ultimately, listening is an act of humility because it appreciates that others may have information, experiences, or insights from which we can learn.[19]

It turns out that we do not listen as well as we would like to believe. In a watershed study in the 1950s, researchers at the University of Minnesota studied our ability to listen and recall conversations.[20] The average person is said to remember only about half of what he has heard, even if he was listening carefully, and tends to forget one-half to one-third of that within eight hours.[21] The reason for this remarkably low level of recall is that the pace of spoken language—what we hear—is far slower than the pace of our thoughts. Because we think much faster than we talk, "when we listen, we ask our brain to receive words at an extremely slow pace compared with its capabilities."[22] Slowing down the thought process is difficult for our brains, so our listening is interrupted with mental sidetracks that appropriate our attention.[23] There are mental activities we

---

[17] LinkedIn, Virgin Founder Richard Branson: Why you should listen more than you talk (February 3, 2015), http://fortune.com/2015/02/03/virgin-founder-richard-branson-why-you-should-listen-more-than-you-talk/.

[18] "A good lawyer will understand that it is the client's goals, values, needs, and wishes that will guide a successful representation." Mark A. Dubois, Mastering the Craft of Lawyering, in Essential Qualities of the Professional Lawyer 109 (2013). "A good listener will be able to develop an empathic relationship with his client, built on trust and respect." Id. at 110.

[19] See Chapter 4.C.4., supra. Listening attentively and respectfully is one of the top ten capabilities most important for starting lawyers based on the results of a study of 24,000 practicing attorneys around the country. See Institute for the Advancement of the American Legal System, Foundations for Practice: The Whole Lawyer Character Quotient 26 (July 2016), available at http://iaals.du.edu/sites/default/files/reports/foundations_for_practice_whole_lawyer_character_quotient.pdf.

[20] Ralph G. Nichols & Leonard A. Stevens, Listening to People, Harvard Business Review (September 1957), available at https://hbr.org/1957/09/listening-to-people.

[21] Id.

[22] Id.

[23] Id.

can undertake to help slow down our thoughts so that we can remain focused on what the speaker is communicating:[24]

- *Think Ahead of the Talker*—Think ahead by trying to anticipate what she might say next and what conclusions can be drawn from the words spoken.

- *Weigh the Evidence*—Consider the evidence presented by the speaker to support her position and mentally question whether the evidence is valid and complete.

- *Review and Summarize*—Periodically review and mentally summarize what you have heard.

- *Listen Between the Lines*—Continuously try to ascertain if there is a subtext to the spoken words. If so, think about why the speaker is avoiding saying certain things.

Here are some other things we can do to get the most out of our efforts to listen:

- *Remain Neutral*—Try to keep an open mind and avoid snap judgments. Enter conversations with objectivity and openness. Our ability to listen actively is undermined by emotional filters that each of us applies to the things that we hear. Often we plan a mental rebuttal that may not even be consistent with what the speaker is communicating. To avoid letting emotional filters compromise our listening we should attempt to withhold evaluation until the speaker has finished, and we should search for evidence that proves our emotional reaction untrue.

- *Be Patient*—Be tolerant of the speaker's pace so that she has the freedom to communicate in her own way, with ample room to make her points.

- *Give Appropriate Feedback*—There are numerous ways to give feedback to the speaker to let her know

---

[24] Id.

that you are listening and that you understand what she is communicating.

- *Non-Verbal Signs of Acknowledgement—* Slightly lean toward the speaker to demonstrate interest, maintain eye contact, and nod occasionally to signal attentiveness and compassion. You may also mirror the emotions expressed by the speaker as a way of demonstrating empathy.

- *Verbal Signs of Active Listening—*Verbal forms of acknowledgement include remembering and repeating the name of the speaker and some key things about him and what she has said; asking relevant and probing questions to build on or clarify what the speaker has said and to reinforce your interest; paraphrasing to show that you understand what the speaker has said; summarizing main points to demonstrate interest and comprehension; and minimal encouragers (such as "Umm-hmm," "Oh?" "Then?," "And?"). Do not interrupt the speaker to give such reinforcement.

- *Avoid Communication Blockers—*There are some responses which, rather than validating what someone says, instead are dismissive and may make the speaker defensive. These can be things like asking "why," preaching, interrupting, and dismissive or patronizing reassurances (for example, "Don't worry," "That happens to everyone," or "That isn't something to worry about"). Also avoid giving advice without being asked.

Feedback is an often-neglected element of communicating. As one colleague told me, "This is the secret sauce (and one I often forget in my haste). When I get effective reflection from people I'm trying to communicate with, it makes my heart sing."

5. Body Language

Broadly speaking, there are two motivations for understanding body language and its effect on how we communicate: First, understanding body language helps us to become aware of, monitor, and if necessary modify our own body language. Second, having the ability to read non-verbal cues expressed by others allows us to better understand what a conversation partner is communicating—intentionally or unintentionally—beyond the words and tone that he uses.

Studies suggest that most people make an initial assessment of someone within seconds of meeting her,[25] and the old adage holds true: First impressions are lasting, so you want your body language to communicate favorably.

A few general points bear mentioning in connection with body language:

First, there are cultural elements to body language that should be explored when possible before meeting with those from different backgrounds so that we can be better prepared to interpret their non-verbal cues and to avoid sending any inadvertent messages of our own.[26]

Second, some people are naturally awkward, and their body language may be nothing more than a reflection of their own self-consciousness. Do not read too much into body language if other things contradict what body language may suggest.

Finally, our own body language may need to be moderated depending on the style of our communication partner. This does not mean that we should become someone else, simply that we should be aware that a very forceful approach may seem too aggressive to someone who is shy and even-tempered, and that

---

[25] Estimates of how quickly initial impressions are made range from one-tenth of a second (see Janine Willis & Alexander Todorov, First Impressions: Making Up Your Mind After a 100-Ms Exposure to a Face, 17 Psychological Science 592 (July 1, 2006), available at http://journals.sagepub.com/doi/abs/10.1111/j.1467-9280.2006.01750.x) to seven seconds, see, e.g., Carol Kinsey Goman, Seven Seconds to Make a First Impression, Forbes (February 13, 2011), available at https://www.forbes.com/sites/carolkinseygoman/2011/02/13/seven-seconds-to-make-a-first-impression/#627285872722.

[26] See Chapter 7.B., supra.

a gentle approach may be interpreted as a lack of confidence by someone who is highly energetic.

Always be aware of your body language and the body language of a conversation partner or others with whom you come into contact as a way of better understanding and maximizing the value of our interactions.

D. QUESTIONS FOR REFLECTION

1. Do you consider your email communication to be efficient and effective? What do you do well? What could be improved? Can you give some examples of poor email communication that you have received? What made it ineffective?

2. Can you recall a situation where you were listening to someone and simultaneously thinking of something else? If so, how did that affect the interaction?

3. Recall a time where you heard a presentation that you did not enjoy or find useful. Name three reasons why that was the case.

CHAPTER 10

YOUR PUBLIC PROFESSIONAL PERSONA

Each of us should embrace a public legal professional persona. This chapter explores why we need to have a robust public professional persona; the importance of following ethical and organizational policies; and the importance of taking advantage of the numerous tools at our disposal—including but not limited to an online presence—to build and disseminate our brand.

A. WHY HAVE A PUBLIC PROFESSIONAL PERSONA?

A strong public presence can be a valuable tool as you develop your legal professional persona, allowing you to network; to showcase your expertise, knowledge, and professional attributes; and to learn about developments in fields of law that interest you. All told, such activities can lead to direct reputational benefits, career advancement, and business development opportunities.

B. FOLLOW ETHICAL AND ORGANIZATIONAL POLICIES

As you build a plan for enhancing your public professional persona, it is imperative that you know and understand any relevant ethical prescriptions that should guide your behavior as well as any policies established by your employer. Law firms and other organizations often have explicit policies regarding the use of social media and firm name, discussing clients and client matters, and certain substantive topics and issues that can be discussed that could impact client concerns. Everything that you do must remain comfortably within those boundaries.

Always remember that any equipment provided by your employer remains the employer's property. Comply with any restrictions the employer imposes on the use of its equipment, and beyond that, use common sense with regard to company-provided equipment. Remember that the employer retains the right and the ability to access material sent using its equipment (including emails) and to monitor the content you access on such devices. Limit the extent to which you use such equipment for personal purposes and be sure not to access any compromising Internet sites using company equipment.

C. DISSEMINATE YOUR BRAND

A great deal has been written about branding yourself in various ways, much of which I find superficial and ultimately lacking in utility. For those that find it useful, I leave the discussion of elevator pitches and similar gimmicks to others.

The kind of branding I refer to here is through deeds, not simply words. This can be done in any number of ways, the most useful of which are writing on topics within your areas of specialization (these may be short, practical pieces or more academic ones), speaking engagements/teaching, pro bono work, and joining committees and engagement in bar and other professional associations. None of this will happen by itself. As with other aspects of your professional persona, be intentional and proactive in engaging with the larger communities in which you work. These are, simply put, some of the best ways to get known within your field, and they are activities that many attorneys enjoy.

Law firms and many other organizations for which attorneys work brand and market themselves through websites and other material. Being featured in these materials can also help boost one's professional persona. Be proactive about this aspect of personal branding and think strategically about what you can do to merit your firm's attention on these platforms.

Another way in which we can disseminate our professional brand is through the Internet, discussed in Section E., below.

D. DRESSING THE PART

The way we dress should reflect the norms of whatever work environment we find ourselves in. This may differ depending on particular circumstances, such as whether we expect to have meetings with clients or prospective clients, co- or opposing counsel, judges, or others outside of our close circle of colleagues.

The issue of professional dress is fraught because it implicates questions of authenticity and core identity. For many, particularly those of older generations, a lawyer has a particular look, and that look may not translate into dress that is suitable to or comfortable for women, racial or ethnic minorities, gays, transgender individuals, and other minorities.[1] Members of these "outsider" groups often feel the need to conform or cover core identity elements in order to fit in and avoid the effects of implicit bias.[2]

The key here should be balance. Each person should dress in a way that makes her feel true to herself, but that respects the norms of the specific work environment, as long as those norms are not based—explicitly or implicitly—on insidious discrimination. When expectations regarding dress or appearance are not based on reasonable considerations, we should try to educate those who set those norms. At the end of the day, when people feel free to look and dress in a way that respects their core identity, they will perform better.[3]

As with other elements of our professional persona, when there is a disconnect between reasonable expectations in a particular work place and what makes us comfortable, it may be time to move on.

E. YOUR PROFESSIONAL E-PERSONA

The Internet, of course, is a powerful tool that can be used to promote and enhance your career goals. The Internet can alternatively impede and constrain your development as a professional. Your e-persona is an integral part of your legal professional persona. How the Internet serves—or hinders—your development is in your hands.

---

[1]   See generally Elizabeth B. Cooper, The Appearance of Professionalism, 70 Fla. L. Rev. ___ (forthcoming 2019), version available at https://papers.ssrn.com/sol3/papers.cfm?abstract_id=3171594.

[2]   See Chapter 7.B.5., supra.

[3]   Self-determination theory provides support for the notion that "by bolstering one's sense of autonomy, feelings of competence, and connectedness to others, individuals are more likely to find happiness and to succeed." Cooper, supra note 1, text accompanying note 24 (citation omitted).

1. Tools for Your Online Profile

LinkedIn and other online platforms offer the opportunity to connect with peers and build relationships with greater numbers of people than we are likely to come across in our "real world" activities. These connections offer prospects for referrals (for jobs and client matters) and in general allow us to engage broadly with a range of professionals, especially those outside of our immediate geographic area. (Caution should be taken, however; no one should rely on the Internet as a substitute for live networking opportunities that we all should vigorously pursue.)

Tools like websites, blogs, and discussion boards can give us a level of visibility that before the Internet age was reserved for just a few. Writing blogs, tweeting, hosting a website, issuing press releases or client advisories on new developments, joining and participating in discussion groups, and other similar activities are outstanding platforms that allow you to demonstrate your knowledge and expertise and through which you can establish your credibility as a professional. Posts need not be long academic pieces—brief updates on legal matters or developments can do the trick. Even sharing interesting items posted by others is a way to display your engagement and give you exposure.

All of your online interventions must convey the same level of care, integrity, and professionalism that you demonstrate in your "live" activities. Pay as much attention to the content, quality, accuracy, and style of online writing as you would with any other writing; if you do host a blog or website, it must be kept up-to-date, be well-maintained, and project a level of professionalism that will communicate something positive about you to colleagues, prospective employers and clients, and the public at large. I have been told by many attorneys with whom I work that prospective employers do thorough Internet searches as part of the hiring process. Do not let carelessness with online content stand in the way of a job.

LinkedIn

LinkedIn is a critical element of the lawyer's toolbox; every legal professional should have a LinkedIn account that can help him establish a public professional persona.

Your Profile—Your LinkedIn profile should be carefully crafted. Give some considered thought to what should be included; omit elements of your background that will not contribute meaningfully to a viewer's understanding of your achievements, skills, and goals. Anecdotally, we all know that users typically spend only a few moments viewing profiles, so it is important that the information you consider to be most important be prominent enough to be visible even to those who may view your profile for just a few seconds.

In crafting your profile, use an eye-catching headline that communicates what you want to project. Be particularly thoughtful about your summary, as the summary may determine whether others continue to read the rest of your profile and ultimately seek a connection. In drafting your summary use key industry terms that will be found by others when using LinkedIn's search functions. If you are actively looking for new opportunities, this is something you would want to highlight (unless, for example, your current employer does not know of your intentions). If you are looking to develop your network in specific substantive areas or geographic regions or with certain affinity groups, for instance, make those intentions clear.

As you draft your profile, look at the profiles of other legal professionals you admire—and whose profiles you think are effective—as a guide for developing your own. Do not exaggerate your accomplishments or skills on your LinkedIn profile; your online profile should stand up to and be fully consistent with the corresponding elements of your resume. Including your education and location in your profile reportedly gives you substantially greater visibility in searches.[4]

---

[4] See Kristen Bahler, What Your LinkedIn Profile Should Look Like in 2018, Money (January 17, 2018) available at http://time.com/money/5077954/linkedin-profile-tips-resume/, citing LinkedIn's Blair Decemberle.

Keep your profile up-to-date. Like your resume, your LinkedIn profile is a dynamic, fluid record that you should revisit on a regular basis.

Your Photograph—Your LinkedIn profile should include a photograph.[5] You do not need to pay for a professional headshot; you can find a blank wall and have a friend take a photo of you in front of it. Dress professionally, have a comfortable smile, and update your photograph from time to time so that it actually looks like you. Do not use a selfie and do not use a group photo that you have edited to reveal only yourself—it is usually obvious that you have done this.

Facebook

Facebook should not be used for professional connections, but the reality is that prospective employers, clients, and others in your professional network will find you on Facebook if you have an account.

Use the setting functions on Facebook to prevent people from viewing your profile and photograph and posting or adding tagged items to your page; and untag yourself from any photos with which you do not want to be associated.

The most prudent course as an overall strategy is to be careful about how you behave at all times, and especially when you are in the presence of anyone who is not a close friend or with whom you have a trusted relationship. As professionals, we simply cannot allow ourselves to be in compromising situations; the ubiquitous presence of cell phone cameras and the frequent use of Facebook by those in our broad professional circles make this an absolute necessity.

We need not think further than the photographs of Olympic medalist Michael Phelps using marijuana that surfaced shortly after his record-winning performance at the 2008 games. He later noted that when the photographs were taken, he was in a

---

[5] Profiles with photographs are said to get up to 21 times more views and up to 36 more messages. See Kristen Bahler, What Your LinkedIn Profile Should Look Like in 2018, Money (January 17, 2018) available at http://time.com/money/5077954/linkedin-profile-tips-resume/, citing LinkedIn's Blair Decemberle. See also Marcia Layton Turner, 8 Ways To Get More LinkedIn Profile Views, Forbes (February 28, 2017), available at https://www.forbes.com/sites/marciaturner/2017/02/28/8-ways-to-get-more-linkedin-profile-views/#6082c6e552cb.

house with 6 people, all but one of whom he knew well and trusted; it was this relative stranger that took the photographs of Phelps and sold them to a tabloid newspaper.[6] Inopportune photographs of most of us will not attract public interest, but Facebook makes us all vulnerable to images that may undermine our credibility as professionals.

Avvo

Every licensed attorney in the U.S. has an Avvo profile, but many do not claim it. There is a debate about whether it is better to claim or not to claim the account. The most powerful argument in favor of claiming your Avvo profile (which is very easy to do) is that simply by posting a photograph, contact information, and very basic biographical information and details about your practice area gives you an Avvo rating; those who have not claimed their profile will show up as raising "[n]o concern," or "[a]ttention" when public records indicate some disciplinary action.

Claiming your profile allows colleagues, clients, and others to post reviews. Those that are positive may drive additional business your way. If you receive a negative review, you can leave a comment in response; if the client is satisfied, she can update or delete the review. In more extreme cases in which the review did not come from a real client, a profile holder can ask Avvo to delete or edit the review.

Other Profiles and Accounts

Use the same care as you do for LinkedIn and Facebook for any other social media profiles you have, including Twitter, Pinterest, Instagram, etc. A good rule of thumb to live by is that if it is out there, others will find it.

---

[6]   Chris Chase, Michael Phelps explains why he didn't sue the guy who leaked the bong photo, ForTheWin (December 16, 2015), available at https://ftw.usatoday.com/2015/12/michael-phelps-bong-photo-why-didnt-he-sue-joe-buck-undeniable-illegal-suspension-olympics-gold-medals.

2. Protect Your Personal Data

Audit Your Settings

When using any social media platform, take steps to protect your personal information. For example, when you use Facebook to sign in to a third-party website or other application, those services may continue to use your data. To perform an audit, go to the Settings page and click on the Apps page to see what applications are connected to your account. This will allow you to revisit the permissions granted to each third-party and to see what information you are sharing. If there are applications you are no longer using, remove them.

These are just examples, and social media applications change their policies regularly, so user audits should be performed comprehensively and routinely.

Install a Tracker Blocker

Tracker blockers can be installed to prevent a tracker from collecting information from you. Applications often plant trackers in your web browser, which function—and may harvest your data—even after you have left that particular app. This is why once you are looking for a new sofa, pop up ads featuring sofas will appear even while you are searching for something else. It is prudent to clear your cookie and browsing history from time to time.

3. Making the Most of Your Professional Online Accounts

Your online presence should fully reflect your professionalism. You should read, comment, and share professional material on a regular basis to reap the maximum benefit from these tools, and always do so with care and formality.

Using LinkedIn

Use LinkedIn to make connections with those in whom you have a professional interest. Look for obvious affinities—universities attended, current and prior employers, similar positions held, memberships, and the like. Look at your connections' connections as a way of identifying others who may share common professional histories and interest. When you invite others to join your network, write a brief personalized, professional message, which is said to increase the chances that the recipient will accept your invitation. Join groups hosted by your universities, current and prior employers, bar and trade associations, and affinity groups.

Once you have created a community, use LinkedIn to broaden and deepen your contacts; congratulate your contacts on promotions, new positions, publications, and other accomplishments; send those in your network links to material that might be of interest to them; and introduce contacts that you think might be interested in knowing each other. Do not burden those within your LinkedIn circle by soliciting employment or seeking recommendations or endorsements. Use the LinkedIn Help Center to develop sophisticated ways of using this tool to maximize its value for you.

As discussed earlier,[7] not everyone with whom you are connected on LinkedIn will feel comfortable using this tool for ordinary communications, and you should consider each time you use LinkedIn to communicate whether an email or phone call would be more effective. Not all users check their LinkedIn accounts with the regularity that they check email. This is in part a generational issue, but LinkedIn does have some limitations that make it less than ideal for certain types of communications. For example, if you are trying to set up a meeting with someone, she may prefer email so that her assistant, who manages her calendar, can be copied. This is just one example of when LinkedIn might not be the best mode of communication.

Using Other Social Media Tools

There may be value to using other social media tools. With regard to any tools you use, take care in publishing content on the Internet. The immediacy of certain platforms like Twitter tends to diminish civility and reasoned analysis and reward a

---

[7]   See Chapter 7.B.2., supra.

lack of nuance[8]—which in turn can undermine our credibility as professionals.

4. Online Reputation Management: Avoiding and Dealing with Digital Dirt

Online reputation management is the process by which an Internet user monitors his reputation and addresses any potentially damaging content. Remember that what appears online is permanently archived and often difficult to remove.

Why Manage Your Online Reputation?

Monitoring your online content is critical because untrue, unflattering, or incorrect information can have devastating effects on your professional reputation.

Anecdotal evidence suggests that recruiters and those responsible for hiring in law firms and companies do look at online profiles and have disqualified candidates for inappropriate content (including photos and videos) or for speaking poorly of former employers. Employees represent their firms, and firms want to ensure that employees enhance rather than undermine their reputations, and this is especially pertinent in the field of law, where reputation and integrity are so important to building an ethical and reputable practice. Outside of the hiring context, of course, digital dirt threatens to ruin reputations, undermine credibility, and overall have a devastating impact on your professional persona.

The risks associated with online content are amplified given that content about you may be posted by others without your permission, and content that you post may be re-posted elsewhere. The risks are magnified by the fact that face-recognition technology allows users to match online images with names.

---

[8]   Carissa Byrne Hessick, Towards a Series of Academic Norms for #Lawprof Twitter, 101 Marq. L. Rev. (2018) (observing that "one rarely gains large numbers of followers or garners large numbers of retweets by offering sober, nuanced analysis. Pithy generalizations and partisan fodder are more likely to generate interest and followers."), available at http://scholarship.law.marquette.edu/cgi/viewcontent.cgi?article=5365&context=mulr.

How to Manage Your Online Reputation

Managing your online reputation involves educating yourself regarding effective and safe privacy settings for your online presence; monitoring your profile regularly; and demonstrating self-discipline when it comes to using online tools as a way of protecting and promoting your professional persona.

Monitor Your Settings and Content—Each of us should be vigilant about monitoring our online presence. As indicated above, be sure that you have appropriate privacy settings on any accounts that you use, and monitor them regularly to see that they are still in place and that they continue to offer the desired protection. This includes managing tags so that others are prevented from posting to or tagging your social media accounts.

Second, monitor any content associated with your name. This can be done in fairly simple ways, such as entering your name in the search box of various engines like Google, MetaCrawler, and Dogpile, to name a few. Get into the habit of checking multiple search engines as they may produce different results and in a different order. Some of these sites, such as Google and Twitter, allow you to set an alert that informs you when your name is mentioned. There are additional tools that allow users to track discussion boards, blogs, and other Internet content (e.g., Talkwaker.com, BoardReader.com, Minecraftforum.com, Omgili.com, and Mention.com).

Scrub or Bury Unfortunate Content—If you find inaccurate or unflattering content, try to get it removed by contacting the host. To the extent that you cannot get compromising content removed, you should at the very least try to get it buried.

How can you bury content on the Internet? Unfortunate content eventually can be pushed to a lower place on the results list by adding favorable content that will be more current. Due to Google's very complex algorithm (which takes into account more than 200 factors and is well beyond my comprehension), the placement of new material on the first page can take some time, so it is important to control content early and add to it regularly. Create a blog or launch a webpage that helps show you as the professional you have become and hopefully push other content to a lower position on the results list; doing so has other professional benefits as discussed above. In any case, if there is unflattering content about you on the Internet, you should expect that prospective employers and clients will ask you about it. Be prepared to give an explanation if it comes up.

F. QUESTIONS FOR REFLECTION

1. Do you feel that you have control over your online persona? If so, why? If not, why not? What can you do to better manage it?

2. Can you name all of the profiles you have online? Do an audit of your profiles and settings. Did you find anything that surprised you?

3. What could you do to better promote yourself as a legal professional in the real or online world?

4. Based on what you have read, describe your professional persona in one sentence.

PART IV

CONCLUSION

Chapter 11

SUMMARY AND PRACTICE TIPS

Developing a strong legal professional persona is not easy, and it cannot be done quickly. A robust professional persona embraces many elements which cover a lot of ground, as does this book. A one-time read may not be sufficient, so I encourage you to refer back to this book regularly and at different stages of your career. Keep it handy so that you can flip through it from time to time.

This concluding chapter is a summary of the major points addressed in this book.

Part I

Legal Professional Persona Fundamentals

Chapter 1

The Legal Professional Persona Revealed

- Your legal professional persona is unique, it is contextual, and it changes over time.

- Be deeply intentional about how you develop your legal professional persona.

- Your professional persona is an outgrowth of your personal persona. Authenticity demands that the latter inform and drive the former.

- Each of us has complete control over the development of our legal professional persona.

- Protect your professional persona as the valuable asset that it is.

Chapter 2

The Business of Law: The Changing Landscape of Legal Practice

- Back in the day, law firms treated associate training and mentoring as an investment in the firm's future.

- A lot has changed. Today:

  o There is far more mobility for lawyers. Lawyers today typically have a portfolio of positions over the course of a career.

  o Demand for traditional legal services is relatively flat.

  o Access to equity partnership is more elusive than ever.

  o New models of law firms have arisen offering new staffing and client service models.

  o Competency-based models of review have become prominent in law firms and other law-related jobs.

- External influences on the practice of law have greatly impacted the profession:

  o Clients are increasingly price-sensitive, demanding discounts and alternative fee arrangements.

  o Clients increasingly are moving much of their work in-house.

  o Corporate departments are consolidating the firms that they use for the work that they outsource.

  o Increased transparency and information sharing give clients more effective tools to evaluate counsel.

  o Technology and other changes to the profession further undermine law firms' status as unique providers of legal services but give young lawyers greater career options.

- What all this means for your legal professional persona:

  o Modern law practice demands a strong professional persona—more than ever before.

- o   Features of one's legal professional persona are major factors in decisions regarding compensation and advancement.

- o   Computers can never replicate the personal elements of lawyering, aspects at the heart of the legal professional persona.

Chapter 3

Legal Professional Persona Building Blocks

- • Questioning, reflection, observation, and coachability help us develop competence:

  - o   Our ability to develop through various stages of competence is undermined by various cognitive biases that make it difficult for us to objectively evaluate our own abilities and shortcomings.

  - o   Questioning and self-reflection must be undertaken with seriousness and commitment to try to overcome our cognitive biases.

  - o   Observation, imitation, and coachability help us better manage our cognitive biases and achieve unconscious competence.

- • Habits help us develop a strong professional persona:

  - o   Habits offer enormous benefits: Habits let us do things automatically, preserving mental energy and time for more important decisions.

  - o   Good habits lead to other good habits, and make us happier.

- • Lawyers need multiple forms of intelligence:

  - o   Forget about IQ. If you are smart enough to get through law school, you are smart enough to be an outstanding attorney.

  - o   Emotional and social intelligence are critically important. Develop yours by paying close attention to your feelings and the feelings of others.

- o Technology skills, practice management skills, and business/financial literacy are important for lawyers today.

- Leadership is a defining principle for lawyers:

  - o Leadership is not based on position or power. It is a general orientation toward life.

  - o Leaders are change agents and to promote change they must exhibit a range of personal and interpersonal skills that will motivate others to follow them.

  - o Leaders need strong, capable followers who will implement their vision. Most of us need to be both leaders and followers and understand when each role is appropriate.

Part II

Self-Management: Professionalism from the Inside

Chapter 4

Mindset and Dispositions

- Develop and maintain a positive mindset:

  - o A growth-based mindset reflects an achievement orientation, and gives each of us an incentive to improve ourselves.

  - o Dispositional and explanatory optimism arm us with tools to overcome challenges and setbacks, and confidence about the attainability of our goals.

  - o Enthusiasm and passion for our work makes us better at what we do and is appealing to those around us.

  - o Resilience and grit are important indicators of our motivation and ability to overcome adversity.

  - o Curiosity keeps us constantly engaged and allows us to build knowledge and to feel comfortable in new situations.

- Commit yourself to excellence:
  - Be resourceful: Use all the tools at your disposal, including colleagues, before reaching out to your supervisor or a client. Remember the Doctrine of Completed Staff Work.
  - Be diligent and dedicated: Work assiduously to get the job done, and take the initiative whenever you can.
  - Be disciplined and exercise willpower. Doing so will make you reliable and efficient in everything you do.
  - Be reliable and prepared. Once you develop a reputation for being reliable and prepared, people will come to depend on you.
  - Take pride in the *craft* of lawyering, even the mundane but important elements of the job.
  - Be adaptable and flexible so that you can respond to exigencies, which are common in our profession.
  - Be creative so that you can think of solutions to problems that may not be apparent to others.
- Develop a strong character:
  - Show gratitude anytime someone does you a good turn.
  - Be dignified at all times, in both professional and personal spheres.
  - Be discreet with confidential and sensitive information.
  - Treat others with respect and honor.
  - Be humble. Realize that you can learn things from others.
  - Be confident. No one wants a lawyer who does not exude confidence.

o Be authentic. Although we all must adjust to professional settings, we must be true to ourselves, our beliefs, and our core values.

o Act with integrity. Be honest and be driven by a strong moral compass.

o Have a sense of humor. Laugh when you can, but never at someone else's expense. Humor can diffuse difficult situations and put others at ease.

o Be elegant when the opportunity arises.

Chapter 5

Time Management and Organization

- Time is a precious and limited commodity:

  o Spend and invest it well.

  o Be on time and be timely, always.

  o Create a time budget:

    ▪ Start with a time audit to see how you spend your time and then decide how you want to spend your time differently.

    ▪ Schedule as many of the things you need to do as possible. We are more likely to get things done when they are scheduled.

    ▪ Give yourself some extra time, as we often underestimate the amount of time it will take us to complete tasks.

  o Make planning your day a ritual and evaluate the plan continuously.

  o Your goals should be specific and action-based.

  o Do not let the urgent hijack the important.

  o Avoid procrastination.

  o Limit multitasking.

- Each person should be organized in a way that allows her to be most efficient.

- o   Workplace and file organization:
    - ▪   Use tools that have served you well.
    - ▪   Clean or messy workspace? You decide.
    - ▪   Electronic files must be organized.
    - ▪   Remember that any organizational system must be transparent to others who may need to access materials or information under your control.
- o   Use a calendar and to do lists or have some other system to aid you in remembering appointments and deadlines.

Chapter 6

Wellbeing and Sustainability

Wellbeing:

- •   Wellbeing—physical and mental—is of crucial importance to us in both our personal and professional realms. Healthy and happy lawyers do their best work. Here are some ways to maximize wellbeing:
    - o   Eat well.
    - o   Get enough sleep.
    - o   Take other periods of rejuvenation, large and small.
    - o   Develop and commit to a fitness plan.
    - o   Learn how to manage the stress that is inevitable in the lives of most lawyers.
    - o   Avoid or eliminate unhealthy addictions.
    - o   Get help if you need it, and recognize that there is no shame in doing so.
    - o   Monitor your hours.
    - o   Seek intrinsic rather than external motivations and rewards.
    - o   Engage in mindfulness.

- o Develop and nurture outside interests.

- o Cultivate meaningful relationships.

- o Understand and continuously evaluate your personal agenda.

- Organizations should care about the wellbeing of their team members. This goes beyond the human case—there are significant business justifications for promoting wellbeing.

Sustainability:

- Each individual's approach to wellbeing should be one that is sustainable over time.

Part III

Relationships: Professionalism with the Outside

Chapter 7

Working with Others

- Foundations for working with others:
  - o Civility is essential to the practice of law and to getting along with others generally. Do not react in haste. Practice the 24-hour rule and cool off before responding when you are angry or upset.

  - o Be reliable, responsible, and accountable. If you are, you will develop a reputation as a person who can be trusted and relied upon.

  - o Collaborate well with others. Foster a space of psychological safety.

  - o Network to build genuine, sustainable relationships. Do not network with the objective of getting a job or something else in return.

- Each of us should develop intercultural fluency and sensitivity to enable us to work effectively with those who are different from us.

- o Race and gender have proven to be thorny issues that still plague the profession. Each of us should develop an awareness of and sensitivity to these issues.

- o Older generations of lawyers should learn to appreciate and understand the leaders of tomorrow; younger professionals should find a way to work effectively with and gain the respect of more senior professionals.

- o There are a range of different people we will come across in our daily lives as lawyers. Be attuned to these differences and approach them with a sense of openness, respect, and curiosity.

- o All of us should acknowledge that we have implicit biases, and try to recognize and control them.

- Within your organization:

   - o Learn how to be supervised gracefully and effectively by:

      - Preserving your supervisor's time and energy. Remember the Doctrine of Completed Staff Work.

      - Make your superior look good and never undermine her authority.

      - Understand your level of discretion.

      - Adapt your working style to that of your boss.

      - Follow up. It is your responsibility to make sure things get done.

      - Keep your supervisor aware of your availability.

      - Keep your supervisor informed of the status of pending projects.

      - Be compulsively responsive.

- Understand expectations. When in doubt, ask.

- Accept feedback as an opportunity to improve.

○ Mentors and sponsors are supremely important:

  - Mentors help guide us throughout our careers. They can come from within or outside our workplace. We should develop a range of mentors throughout our careers. We should also mentor others, even when very junior.

  - A sponsor is someone who helps you advance in concrete ways. She will enable opportunities for you and advocate on your behalf.

○ Learn to work effectively with a range of other constituencies:

  - Business development and client management are of crucial importance to success in the legal profession. Get out there and meet people and be the very best lawyer you can be. Treat the clients you have like the important assets they are.

  - Counterparties and collaborators are important members of our network and should be treated accordingly.

  - Judges have a singular role in the U.S. legal system and we must be vigilant about dealing appropriately with them and court staff.

  - Remember that common rules of courtesy and civility extend to adversaries as much as to everyone else.

  - As attorneys we have responsibilities to the public more broadly, and to behave always in a manner that promotes the dignity of the profession.

Chapter 8

Talent Management

- Talent management is of crucial importance in personal services organizations like law firms.

- Great supervisors:

  o Use a system of work assignments that gives every team member equivalent opportunities that play to their particular strengths.

  o Provide juniors opportunities to observe more senior attorneys in action.

  o Involve subordinates genuinely in the work of the organization.

  o Give juniors a sense of control and autonomy over their work and their career progression.

  o Model appropriate behavior.

  o Take responsibility for the mistakes of the team.

  o Be human, and in particular praise good work openly and often.

  o Encourage passion among the members of your team.

  o Embrace a culture of teamwork.

  o Have patience. Remember that the things you do well do not come naturally to everyone.

  o Be reasonable and clear about expectations.

  o Be accessible and communicate your accessibility.

  o Use power sparingly and only when necessary.

  o Make your own wellbeing and the wellbeing of the members of the team a priority.

- o Deal with conflicts fairly and directly. Do not let disagreements fester or taint organizational objectives.

- o Offer flexible work arrangements when possible.

- When working with support staff, always be kind. Support staff often do not have the same benefits and privileges as attorneys, but they are critical to our success.

Chapter 9

Effective Communication

- Communication skills in general:

- o Understanding your audience in any form of communication is of paramount importance. This should shape every aspect of your communication.

- o Professional communication should bear the hallmarks of formality.

- o Keep your objective(s) firmly in mind in order to best frame your communication.

- o Busy professionals want the answers they need. Less is more.

- o Write plainly and communicate without legalese.

- Written communication:

- o Write with formality and purpose.

- o Use exacting precision.

- o Remember the Five Cs: Writing should be clear, concise, convincing, complete, and candid.

- o Follow applicable protocols.

- o Produce an attractive document.

- o Use a logical, internally consistent structure.

- Edit and proofread with your eyes and your brain.

- Special rules for email:
  - Follow the same rules. The ease of email communication does not mean that you can become sloppy or informal.

  - Consider whether email is the right mode of communication.

  - Consider whether this is the right time to send an email.

  - Write clearly, succinctly, and with purpose. People do not read long emails.

  - Develop a personal email management system.

  - Use texting and LinkedIn for messages only when you know that the recipient is fine with accepting such messages.

- Oral communication:
  - Practice as much as you can. Your anxiety will lessen and you will get better with each effort.

  - Presentations require preparation.

  - Phone conversations can be an intrusion on the other person's time, so be respectful.

  - Be an active and engaged listener.

  - Use body language that communicates appropriately and endeavor to understand the subtext to what others say.

Chapter 10

Your Public Professional Persona

- Your public professional persona is important because it drives how others perceive us.

- Always follow any guidelines and policies established by your firm and any applicable bar authorities.

- Be proactive in disseminating your brand.

- Dress the part, consistent with reasonable expectations and in a way that is comfortable and affirming to yourself.

- Have a strong professional e-persona, and manage it closely:

  o Use the Internet to promote your brand.

  o Manage and maintain your reputation in the virtual world. Expect that others will find whatever is out there.

INDEX

References are to Pages